Love

AND

COACHING

Love
AND
COACHING

Understanding Men & Women in Life, Love and Business

FEATURING

John Gray Ph.D.

Author of the phenomenal #1 bestseller

Men are from Mars Women are from Venus

AND HIS CERTIFIED

MARS VENUS COACHES

First published in 2022 by Dean Publishing
PO Box 119
Mt. Macedon, Victoria, 3441
Australia
deanpublishing.com

DEAN PUBLISHING

Copyright © Mars Venus Coaching
5940 S Rainbow Blvd
Las Vegas, NV 89118
marsvenuscoaching.com

Cataloguing-in-Publication Data
National Library of Australia
Title: Love and Coaching—Understanding Men & Women in Life, Love and Business —
Revised edition
An earlier edition of this book was published by Dean Publishing, 6 March 2017
ISBN: 978-1-925452-54-9
Category: Relationships/Personal development/Business

The views and opinions expressed in this book are those of the author and do not necessarily reflect the official policy or position of any other agency, publisher, organization, employer or company. Assumptions made in the analysis are not reflective of the position of any entity other than the author(s) – and, these views are always subject to change, revision, and rethinking at any time.
The author, publisher or organizations are not to be held responsible for misuse, reuse, recycled and cited and/or uncited copies of content within this book by others.
This book is not intended as a substitute for the medical advice of physicians or psychologists. The reader should regularly consult a professional in matters relating to his/her health and or relationship issues that require professional help. The ideas within this book are only the opinion of the authors and are not intended to replace any medical advice or relationship advice. Always consult a professional for your health and wellbeing.

CONTRIBUTORS

John Gray

Rich Bernstein

Susan Dean

Adriane Hartigan-von Strauch

Asma Shaheen

Caterina Tornani

Chahira Taymour

Christian Braga

Clay Smith

Emily MacLeod

Eric Lanthier

Gabriella de Leeuw

Hilary DeCesare

Justine Baruch

Karen Leckie

Lena JO

Lesley Edwards

Liza Davis

Mahmoud Khater

Michele Festa

MK Mueller

Mohammad Al Huwaidi

Monique Sarup

Neelofar Qasmi

Nissara Chitwarakorn

Oksana Irwin

Rani Thanacoody

Reem Suwayd

Richard Wann

Samar Showail

Sophie Tan Li Koon

Tanweer Khan

Dr John Gray and his certified coaches share:

- Short films
- Audio downloads
- Podcast episodes
- Downloadable worksheets
- Tools for notes and bookmarking

. . . and more

The *Love and Coaching* interactive book is available via the Dean Library app, available on all devices.

deanpublishing.com/loveandcoaching

INTERACTIVE BOOK

CONTENTS

SAMAR SHOWAIL

"
MARS VENUS COACHING IS CHANGING THE WORLD . . . ONE RELATIONSHIP AT A TIME.

"

COUNSELING VS COACHING

— JOHN GRAY —

John Gray is the Brand Founder and the world's foremost authority on psychology, gender communication, and personal and professional growth. For over thirty years, John has taught his **Mars Venus** seminars around the world, entertaining, educating, and inspiring his audiences with practical insights on how to be more successful financially, emotionally, mentally, and spiritually. He is the author of sixteen best-selling books and has become one of the world's most sought-after media identities and celebrities.

INSPIRATION FOR A NEW WAY OF THINKING

In the late seventies, the movement—as far as the counseling goes—was to attempt to recognize men and women as the same, completely and 100 percent equal in the way they think, process emotions, handle stress, and work in relationships. As a counselor and a coach, I saw that this model and method simply was not working.

Men were trying to think like women; women were trying to think like men. Women were trying to make men feel like women, and vice versa. I realized that a man could say or do something and it would work for them. However, when a woman tried it, it wouldn't work. And the same for a man trying to say or do something that a woman would. I found through many of my clients that this new philosophy was doing more harm than good. We as a society needed—and still need—to respect the differences of the sexes in the name of equality. As I dug deeper into this, I discovered that in over ten years of coaching women every day for eight hours a day a woman's complaints about men were very different from a man's complaints about women. The place from which a person complains is where they need something the most.

From my work and everyday observations, I surmised that women needed more attention focused toward what they were feeling, thinking, wanting, and their desire for affection. These were not the same things that were of importance to men. These needs and desires had been overlooked and under supported by their spouses and partners because more and more women have entered the workforce, which has led to less time at home with the same amount of work. Because of this, women need more help but do not know how to ask for it without complaining or getting frustrated.

This is why working to understand our differences in a positive way so that both men and women may receive equal respect and equal appreciation in a relationship is so important. As my message evolved, I was able to discover the hormonal foundation of the distinctions between men and women. Certain behaviors stimulate estrogen and oxytocin. These are hormones necessary to lower stress levels and increase happiness in women. Estrogen and oxytocin are significant to men, but not nearly as significant as they are to women. Women require about ten times more of those hormones than men. Men, however, need ten times more of the masculine hormone—testosterone—in order to regulate stress and certain behaviors. Areas of communication will also increase testosterone levels in men. As the years passed, we were able to discover a biological foundation to the differences that I have observed. As I researched more and learned more, I realized that people *needed* to know this. We could fix so many problems in our society if more people knew and understood the differences in men and women. I went on to write a book and developed a coaching program to help other people share these ideas and improve relationships.

A NEW WAY OF COACHING

I've said before, "I'm only one guy with a great message." I knew I could only do so much by myself. I didn't set out to start a coaching program just to get this message out there. After the release of *Men Are from Mars, Women Are from Venus*, the response from readers was amazing!

People from all over wrote letters or came up to me on the street telling me how they had implemented what they learned into their own relationships and wanted to know how to share it in their families, their workplaces, and their communities. Many of the people I spoke with were counselors and coaches. I decided it was time to develop a coaching program. I am only one person; I can only do so much. If there were others out there—i.e., Mars and Venus Coaches—that could repurpose my seminars, workshops, and teachings locally and in other languages, helping clients experience my methodologies and apply them to their lives, then we could make the world a better place. That was my biggest motivator in creating the coaching program: teaching others to help make the world a happier place.

Becoming a therapist requires many, many years of training. To get benefit from therapy and see results, a lot of people will have to go for many years. Whereas, when it comes to understanding the differences between men and women, anyone can be taught how to work with those differences. Learning the Mars Venus method is like learning new software of communication. For so long we've operated in a particular way, thinking it was the right way only to see our efforts cause frustration and send us back to square one.

However, with the Mars Venus approach, our coaches help to educate people in new skills for understanding men and women and overcoming the challenges that we face in the modern world. As children, we watched our parents and saw the traditional ideas from their world. However, those strategies are no longer effective as the behaviors that our parents practiced will no longer provide success. Most people today will say that they have better communication skills than their parents, and yet divorce continues to rise; dissatisfaction in our relationships continues to increase, and stress in our personal lives is going up. This is because the world has changed dramatically. Relationships can be a powerful support system to help us cope with the stress of our lives. Stress is simply a challenge. If we have the right kind of loving support and communication in a relationship, supporting each other can come much more naturally. So instead of having stress tear us apart, it can actually bring us closer together. This is what we believe and what we teach through the Mars Venus methodology. By following these methods, even for a short amount of time, people can see tremendous results!

MARS VENUS VS. THERAPY

One of the limitations of therapy, as opposed to coaching, is that with therapy you try to go back and find forgiveness and heal. Therapy helps to change negative beliefs about yourself and others and have a new perspective on the world. Don't get me wrong, these aren't *bad* lessons to learn. However, therapy does not provide the tools and education to help you have a flourishing and rewarding relationship. When one leaves therapy, their thinking is typically, "I love myself more…but I don't have any practical instructions on what to do now." I believe that Mars Venus coaching is very beneficial to people who have done therapy and even for people who haven't. Why? Because simply learning the skills of having better relationships is a powerful way to build your self-esteem, decrease anxiety, and increase confidence and motivation in our lives.

True, one could learn the basic skills through reading any of the Mars Venus books. However, there is a difference between reading it in a book to learn what you can do in your own relationships and actually taking on the responsibility of teaching other people how to implement the Mars Venus approach in their lives to seek out emotional blockers.

An important part of coaching is the implementation of ideas that you may read in a book. You can read books all day long, but until you have a motivation and a desire to change, it will never happen. Coaching allows you to explore the personal challenges one might have in order to break down the barriers that have hindered sustainable changes in the past. Being able to share your challenges while implementing ideas is no simple task; trying to do it without a support system will ultimately lead to failure. We are often resistant to change and doing things differently, and it is through having a credible, reliable coach who can help us identify our emotional blockers that we find ways to overcome our obstacles, whether we struggle with resentment from the past, self-doubt, or a tendency to blame others. There are various types of blocks that people experience when trying to implement these ideas on their own. However, by following a system like Mars Venus, we help our clients overcome resistance, move through those blocks toward positive behaviors, and gain a new understanding and another way of looking at their situation.

Coaching in itself is beneficial. Mars Venus coaching includes the general tools that are helping clients explore their goals and recognize what is holding them back from achieving them. Mars Venus coaches *do* help people with that. We also, however, add additional insights and information on how men and women think and feel differently. Through the support of a Mars Venus coach, you will always receive something beyond what another type of coach would provide. Why? Because when it comes to challenges, both within ourselves and others, there is a reality of gender differences. How women best cope with stress is different from how men best cope with stress. How men find forgiveness for themselves and others is a different process than how women find the same thing. How men can achieve happiness, fulfillment, and motivation in their lives is different from how women find happiness and motivation in their lives.

COACHING FOR THE GENDERS

Mars Venus coaches are aware of gender differences. If you are not aware of the differences of men and women, your clients could suffer greatly. If I am a woman coaching a man, my instincts will tell him to follow the path that works for me as a woman. If I am a man coaching a woman, I instinctively suggest things to a woman that will work for a man. Mars Venus sees the limitations of coaching today. It doesn't take into consideration the gender difference because, biologically, what motivates us, what gives us the sense of fulfillment, what opens our hearts, what gives us self-confidence is always based on the set of hormones required by gender. Mars Venus coaching focuses on different types of strategies to support the evolution of our clients as a foundation of the well-being in our lives.

Without understanding, teaching, and nurturing the differences between the genders, you can't successfully coach. The astounding part is, many will choose a different type of coaching because they don't recognize the choices they have. There are limitations to coaching without gender intelligence. Without insights into why each gender behaves the way they do, there is less understanding, which creates more friction. Coaching is all about giving the client several points of view so they will have clarity of what they want and be able to implement their goals.

One of the reasons many people do not achieve what they want is they simply do not know what it looks like. Mars Venus coaches help the client see their options and choose what they want based on a clearer picture. I've seen it many times in my own practice. Someone will come to me and say, "I want a great relationship." So I ask them, "Wonderful! What does a great relationship look like to you?" Nine times out of ten they respond, "I don't know." That is the reason they can't have it; they don't know what it looks like! Then we discuss and create their great relationship so they can manifest it.

Mars Venus coaches are great at helping clients make realistic goals. Many come to coaching with grand notions about what an ideal relationship should be. However, a Mars Venus coach will give them a reality check on what is realistic and what is not. For example, a woman might have the notion that a man should always know what to do if he loves her and she shouldn't have to tell him; he should just know. A man may have the unrealistic expectation that if a woman loves him, she will always be happy and she will never be dissatisfied with the relationship. This is a very critical issue because we tend to have unrealistic expectations in relationships.

Adjusting our expectations to reality doesn't mean that we are settling for less; it gives us the opportunity to appreciate what is really real and experience lasting and passionate love, which is the goal for most people.

WHY CHOOSE MARS VENUS

Whether one chooses a Mars Venus coach or any other kind, it is imperative to interview the potential coach to make sure they have a clear awareness of how men and women have different perspectives, different needs, and different styles of communicating. If the coach doesn't have that perspective, their message to the client will be limited and, many times, unproductive. With a Mars Venus coach, you *know* you will gain insight and education into the differences of the genders, learn how to speak the other's "language," and understand how and why they do the things they do.

At Mars Venus, we aim to bring out the best in every one of our clients. We want to show them that happiness and success is achievable and sustainable. Our job as coaches is to help others see their potential and break through the chains that keep them tied down. Mars Venus coaches are committed and have the tools, training, and knowledge to support you in achieving your goals.

BUSINESS IS RELATIONSHIPS

— RICH BERNSTEIN —

Rich Bernstein is the President & CEO of **Mars Venus Coaching** and comes with a wealth of experience spanning over twenty-five years. He has owned and/or managed companies in varied industries, both private as well as publicly traded. Rich has been active in the coaching industry since 2003 and has functioned as a support manager as well as a global sales director internationally. His background in sales, support, marketing, and business management makes him uniquely qualified to help licensees and business owners learn important strategies for business successes. Rich has a full complement of skills and experience in marketing, sales processes, financial models, time management techniques, and team building.

EVERYTHING TO DO WITH BUSINESS

Before I became a coach, I owned my own business. I was working day in and day out. I couldn't get home for dinner; I missed my kids' recitals and football games; I was missing so many important events in my family's lives. I finally decided enough was enough. I sold the business. Through my experience as a business owner, I learned what not to do to become a success. I was continually thinking, "I have so much knowledge to share! I'd really like to help other business owners escape the perpetual work week." This is when I decided to become a business coach.

Until that point, I had never heard the words business and coach in the same sentence. The first time I heard it I thought, "Wow! That is a really good idea! I'd like to be a business coach." Because I was a business owner, I knew what it was like to not make payroll, not be able to cash your own check, not get home for dinner, and to work seventy hours a week. Trust me, it's no way to live.

After a few years of business coaching, I met John Gray. He recruited me to join his Mars Venus team as a business coach who utilized the practices of Mars Venus. When John Gray asked me to come to his team, the first question I had was, "What does Mars Venus have to do with business?"

John's response? "Everything!"

If you don't think business and relationships work in sync with one another, you're greatly mistaken. Your relationships with your clients, your customers, your employees, your vendors, and your suppliers—all these relationships are an integral part of the success of a business.

GENDER INTELLIGENCE

Realizing that relationships drive a business gave me a whole new perspective on business and success. When I first came to Mars Venus then, I started to learn about gender intelligence. Gender Intelligence describes how men and women think differently, process information in a different way, and the differences in the way they talk, shop, and relate. As I gained more knowledge on the subject, I started to wonder if since men and women *buy* differently, are salesmen *selling* to them differently?

With the supervision and input from John Gray, I created a sales training based on gender intelligence. In that training, I educated the students on John Gray's theories and added that because men and women are wired differently, men and women must buy differently. The purpose was to teach salespeople to sell differently. In addition to that, I also discussed how, if men and women process information differently, they probably guide others and are inspired in different ways.

Instructing and educating people is not a "one size fits all"; both genders react differently. Men do not want all the details; they prefer to be told what needs to be done. Women would rather have more information into the "why" of an assignment. Women have ten times more connective tissue between the two hemispheres of the brain than men; everything on one side of the brain is connected to everything else on the other side. So when you instruct women, you have to connect the instructions or end result with everything else in their life.

I have been doing gender intelligent business coaching now for almost ten years, and I can tell you that there is no way to grow your company without keeping these points at the forefront of your mind: men and women are different and need different things.

Before I came to Mars Venus, I mainly focused on coaching in sales and marketing. However, the problem with that was, if all that was taught was on sales and marketing, the minute I left, the business began to fall apart. When you focus only on sales and marketing, with no concentration on creating and continuing relationships with clients, business plummets. When I used John's methodologies, I would put sales and marketing on a *foundation* of relationships, and the results came faster and were more sustainable. John Gray taught me that you can teach business owners how to coach in relationships that will help their business grow. After all, sales and marketing are all about building a connection with your client. This is very important to a business's success.

John Gray's philosophy on the differences between men and women should be integrated into the business world. I have seen, firsthand, the achievements of a business when teaching leadership, sales, and customer service with the Mars Venus approach.

CONFERENCE ROOM CONFUSION

Because men and women process information differently, we also work differently. For example, say there is a meeting going on. There are five men and five women sitting around a conference table, and the leader is standing up, conducting the meeting. There is an unspoken understanding between the men; they feel if they have something to contribute, they will speak up and say it. They don't raise their hands; they don't wait to be called on; they just blurt it out. The leader knows this too. He doesn't call on them individually, "Hey, Bob, what do you think we should do?" because he knows that will embarrass Bob. After all, if Bob had something to say, he'd let it be known. Women, however, tend to feel that method is unprofessional.

Women are actually waiting to be called on, as they believe this is how an effective, professional environment should run. The men believe that if she had something to say, she'd say it! So why call on her if she's not speaking up? This miscommunication (or lack thereof) causes women to feel like they're not being heard. By the end of the meeting, the women leave, thinking, "I can't believe he didn't ask me anything! He doesn't acknowledge me; he doesn't value me as a member of this team!"

However, the man actually *does* value her, and that is why he didn't call on her. Isn't that interesting? There are so many similar situations happening in the corporate world today. If two men were standing by the water cooler discussing the game they watched over the weekend and a woman walks up, they stop talking. This leads her to feel left out or not included. However, the men feel as if they are doing her a service; the men assume she probably doesn't care about the game, so why keep talking about it? Before you know it, there's discord and conflict between the men and women in the company, and the business suffers.

This is why I find it so powerful to be able to teach leadership with a gender intelligent application. I was with John once at a speaking engagement in Las Vegas for the Anti-Aging Conference. We were backstage with a stagehand who was prepping the mic for John. He had a walkie-talkie and was speaking with a woman up in the sound booth.

The woman in the sound booth said to the stagehand, "Look, I want you to hook Pack A on his belt and put the little lapel mic on his collar. But, I also— and I want you to understand that the last time we did this, one of the batteries went out, and so we had to switch right in the middle of the guy's talk—so what I prefer to do is to have Pack B on the other side. Put *that* to his shirt so there are actually two of them. We'll need two mics. I might have one on and I am going to switch it over if something happens to the first line, and nobody will know the difference because you know this happened before . . ." She went on and on with a long explanation of what she needed to do.

And the stagehand looked at John and said, "I don't need to know all that. Just tell me to put the second mic on!"

John, being the authentic man he is, walked out on stage during his talk and told that story. "This is men and women," he explained. "She felt the need to explain *why* she wanted him to do something. However, the man just needed to know what needed to be done so he could do it. *That's* gender intelligence." The two genders need to be aware of the problems they cause one another by not communicating effectively and positively. Through Mars Venus coaching, men and women can change their way of communicating to one another in their "language." There needs to be recognition and embracing of these differences, and the ability to see the impact it has emotionally on the opposite gender.

And this is how I coach people in business. It's vital to understand that men and women will respond to your marketing practices differently. And men and women will respond to your sales process differently. When I approach a leader of a company about his or her business and I ask the same question: "Do you believe men and women buy differently?" Ninety percent say, "Of course they do."

Then I ask, "Knowing that, do you train your salespeople to *sell* differently?" Dead silence.

Then I ask, "What about your leadership styles? Do you lead men and women differently?"

Dead silence.

If a person truly believes and accepts that men and women are different—which they are—then how can they *not* use gender intelligence to help build their business? It isn't possible. But if you're aware of the differences and are sensitive to that, you can introduce this philosophy to create a flourishing company.

There have been many people who have said to me, "Rich, isn't that a little bit manipulative?" I always give the same example. When I was a little kid, I learned how to "talk" to horses from an old cowboy. He told me, "You know, horses are prey in the wild. We are the predators. Horses will be naturally skeptical of you and your intentions. If you walk up to the horse with your palms open and out, and walk toward them, they will run away. But if you close your hands in a fist and place them by your sides, they will run *toward* you."

Is that manipulation? No. It is just being a better communicator. Using gender intelligence to better guide the men and women on your team is being a better communicator. That's speaking their language.

YOU MANAGEMENT, NOT TIME MANAGEMENT

Mars Venus coaching is very special to me because I want to prevent business owners from uttering the words I found myself saying constantly, "Please record the kid's (insert extracurricular activity here) because I won't be there to see it." It killed me to have to say that. I don't want others to go through what I went through. I have been to countless companies and asked the owner how many hours he or she has been working, and they'll sigh and say, "Eighty? Maybe ninety?" That was me thirteen years ago. I know what it is like, and I really want to benefit those people.

One of the ways to get out of that cycle of perpetually missing out on life's events is effectively managing time. And, like everything else, men and women manage time very differently. Everyone gets twenty-four hours a day, whether you like it or not. So, technically speaking, you can't *manage* time. The only thing you can manage is *you*. What you do in this minute, what you do in this hour, those are choices that you make. Men and women do this very differently.

As a Mars Venus coach, I want to bring awareness to their lives that assists in their learning and understanding of how they can manage themselves around time in a more productive way.

Being aware of what you do and how you do it is the first step. Taking action is the next. Coaching is all about taking action, showing a client that they can flourish. Yes, it's about gaining new knowledge, but that's not all there is. Many people say, "Knowledge is power!" but I don't believe that knowledge is power. I believe that you have to *implement* it to make it powerful. It is kind of like the potential energy a rock has, sitting on top of a hill. It doesn't have any energy until it starts to roll down the hill.

ALL COACHING IS NOT CREATED EQUAL

When I first came to Mars Venus coaching, I felt like I had finally "seen the light," so to speak. My time as a business coach previously did not focus on leading, coaching, and interacting with clients using gender intelligence. Now I see that it is the only way. And this is not just true in the corporate world but in our everyday relationships as well.

The three parts of coaching are clarity, putting the plan together, and accountability. And each of these parts looks very different to men and women. For example, I've coached a couple before in which the woman stated she wanted to feel more supported by her husband. This was a cause of much conflict in their marriage.

I asked the wife, "What does support look like to you?"

She thought for a moment and said, "Well, I'd like him to find me in the house when he comes home and give me a hug, tell me that everything is going to be okay so I don't feel alone."

Then, I asked the husband, "Do you support your wife?" "Of course!" he said.

"What does support look like to you?"

"I go to work every day," he replied. "I pay the bills. I make sure she has a home, money for groceries, and a car. That's support."

Men and women see things very differently and have a very different perspective on the same word. The two had different definitions of clarity.

Understanding one another's perspective is the first step. Putting together a plan comes next. You can understand that your wife needs to feel supported, but if you keep doing what you've been doing, the relationship will not flourish; it will stagnate and brew resentment.

For example, if a wife has a problem and wants to feel supported, she may go to her husband and tell him what's going on. She goes into the conversation simply wanting to vent her frustration and hear encouraging words from her husband. However, nine times out of ten, the husband will start listing off ways to fix her problem. Why? Because by fixing what's wrong makes him feel like he is supporting her.

Except this is not the case. She needs to be heard. "Tell me more," he should say, or "That's awful! I'm sorry. That must feel terrible for you." Then she will feel heard, understood, and listened to. This is support from her perspective. The minute he tries to fix it she doesn't feel supported. But if he doesn't do anything about it, he doesn't feel he is supporting her. When a man solves a problem or has a solution, he builds testosterone. That is how he lowers his stress.

I used to take my wife's complaints about anything and everything personally. If we went to a nice restaurant and she said she didn't like the soup, I'd take it personally, as if she were insulting my ability to pick a nice place. It wasn't until I became a Mars Venus coach that I learned when she complains, she is not making a jab at me; she is just talking to me. She is bonding with me. I never looked at it that way before.

When we learn how to love in a more authentic way, to understand with more empathy, to work with one another better, the tools to love better, we embrace our differences. This helps the world become a better place. And that is John Gray's objective. And we as Mars Venus coaches are personally trained by John to go out into the world and teach others ways to relate within a couple or even within a business relationship because, as he has discovered, he can't do it alone; he is only one guy. But now, we have hundreds of coaches in thirty-some countries that are coaching on the basis of his philosophy.

YOU CAN MAKE IT WORK

If you believe that men and women are different and respond, react, interpret, and relate to the world and people around them differently, then there is no way you can effectively coach or be coached without the implementation of gender intelligence.

I'm an animal person. I've trained many different types of animals on my ranch. When training a dog, say you point to a tree, the dog will automatically look at the direction your finger is pointing. The dog understands that you are pointing to the tree. If you do that to a cat, however, the cat will look at the end of your finger. They don't make that connection past your finger; they just think that your finger is moving. This is clear evidence that their brains work differently. It's the same with men and women. So how can you coach a man the same way you coach a woman? You can't.

Gender intelligence is required to be a good coach. The methodologies of John Gray have changed my way of thinking. When I first started out, it never occurred to me that coaching should be gender-specific. Now, after seeing the positive, transformative effects that gender intelligence and the Mars Venus way of coaching has on people, I have become a more empathetic coach, husband, father, and friend.

THE POWER OF STORY AND COACHING

— SUSAN DEAN —

Susan Dean is a life and business coach, keynote speaker, workshop and training facilitator, publisher, and entrepreneur. She believes she was destined to help people flourish and prosper in all areas of their lives. Commencing her career as a youth officer and progressing into her own coaching business, she became the first female Mars Venus Coach in Australia back in 2003. John Gray and his teachings around gender differences were instrumental in helping Susan achieve so much in her own life and business. A master trainer in NLP, hypnosis, and Timeline Therapy®, she has completed trainings with many masters, including Anthony Robbins, John Gray, and other extraordinary mentors. Susan has conducted many Mars Venus workshops, including one- and two-day relationship workshops. She has witnessed the transformative power of coaching and is an advocate for educating others on gender intelligence.

Susan also pioneers the power of storytelling. She encourages people all over the world to share forward their life teachings, insights, and wisdom in order to help others make a shift in their lives. This storytelling movement, called "YSHIFT" (Your Share-It-Forward Teachings), was founded and created by Susan with the altruistic intention to benefit humanity with powerful and life-affirming messages.

Susan has been married for over thirty years with her childhood sweetheart Michael. They have two beautiful adult children Chloe and Monique who both work in the family publishing company and one beautiful granddaughter Zara and a grandson on the way.

HAPPY WIFE, HAPPY LIFE

This is the phrase I often tell my husband, "Happy wife, happy life," and luckily, he agrees. Throughout our twenty-eight years of marriage, I've discovered that when our core relationships work well, then so do we.

For me, a happy relationship is vitally important. I don't believe in leaving it to mere luck; it's something we can create and develop every day. This doesn't mean that the husband or man doesn't also need to be happy, but I find that when a woman has her needs met and is authentically happy, everything flows. Just like the queen bee that brings everyone together to coordinate and function as a whole, so too is the role of wife, mother, and caregiver.

When the energy in your primary relationship is positive and life-affirming, you can achieve anything, overcome any obstacle, and enrich each other's lives in the most wonderful way.

MAKE YOURSELF HAPPY FIRST

Before we discuss gender intelligence or how to create empowering relationships, we must put first things first.

Before you can be successful at any relationship you first must establish the most important relationship of your life—and that is the one you have with yourself!

The most important relationship firstly begins with you. You are the centerpiece. You are your primary relationship.

Learning to love yourself, know yourself, and heal yourself from any past hurts or limiting beliefs is the first foundation that must be built. If this isn't achieved, your interaction with others isn't built on solid ground. Often, people without the firm foundation of self-love continue to look outside themselves for the answer, waiting for someone else to love them in order to feel validated or recognized as "lovable," or "worthy." This is a common trap that many fall headfirst into.

"If he only loved me, *then* I'd be happy." That elusive "one day" where Prince Charming just rides into town and sweeps you off your feet; he makes your world magical and loves you with the passion of a Mills and Boon novel.

Internal mantras such as "If I were married (or engaged or had a partner) then I'd be happy," or "If he only loved me as much as I love him then everything would be OK," may not be voiced consciously; however, through coaching, I have found that many women in fact carry this secret limiting belief. Many believe it is the answer to their prayers, that "Mr. Magic" will somehow fix their aching heart and their longing to be loved.

Though the right compatible partner can and does in fact make a massive difference in our lives, if we expect them to be the savior to our limiting beliefs and the answer to healing our internal wounds, then we are sorely mistaken. Attempting to hand your own bag of self-deprecating beliefs, childhood wounds, and past regrets to another person is asking them to carry a burden that is not theirs to carry.

Sooner or later, relationships teach us that others can enhance your life, but it's *not* up to them to create or change it. Changing your life is up to you. Loving yourself is vital, whether you're in a relationship or not. Giving yourself regular, healthy doses of self-love and care means that you can be your best self, and when you are your best self, life works.

Life itself tests every human being, and you take yourself everywhere you go. When you authentically love yourself, you also authentically love others. No agendas or obligations attached. When you truly love yourself, you won't feel tempted to burden your loved one and dump them with your issues for them to "fix."

The first fundamental question about relationships is not "How do I get a partner?" or "How do I change my current partner?"; the foremost fundamental question is: "How do I become a better person today from the one I was yesterday?"

SELF-DEVELOPMENT IS THE KEY TO HAPPINESS

Self-development or coaching isn't just for people who aren't yet successful; it is really for people who are successful. We are all successful in some areas of our lives, but some people wish to grow and develop in other areas too, areas that may be untapped or unchartered thus far. Anyone that wants to improve themselves is already successful in my eyes; the desire to be a better version of themselves is all it takes to begin the exciting journey of self-discovery. You don't need to be in a relationship to learn about gender differences; the truth is it impacts your entire life whether you know it or not. Education and self-development are synonymous with success.

If you're not growing, you are dying. I have completed so many personal development courses that I'm sure some of my friends think there's something wrong with me, or that I'm searching for something. The truth is, it's not about finding one way or one thing; it is about continuous development of one's self.

Never stop learning; there is always more to learn about yourself and others. Some key areas that can be helpful in understanding ourselves better are:

- How the past may be still affecting you and therefore your future.
- How to release the past and identity negative conditioning.
- Understanding gender differences—the science behind how men and women have different needs or wants, and how the differing genders perceive and react differently to situations.
- Understanding our personality profile—what are your strengths and weaknesses?
- Understanding your unconscious and conscious mindset. How your inner beliefs are either moving you towards or away from success.

Some action exercises to help us create a better relationship with ourselves are:

- Be grateful for who you are and the strengths you do have.
- List what you have already achieved.
- List all the qualities you like about yourself.
- List all the things you love about your life.
- List all the wonderful things you bring to others.

This is a great beginning to being in the best relationship you can be in—the one with yourself. We don't know what we don't know; and sometimes we don't know enough about ourselves to see our "blind spots." A coach can help you see those blind spots and empower you to shift from ignorance to self-awareness. Self-awareness is the key to lasting change and empowerment.

CIRCLE OF INFLUENCE

When we tread the path of active self-awareness, we naturally increase our circle of influence. Firstly, we master ourselves. Secondly, we are then given the opportunity to help others become more self-aware too; coaches are in this category.

As we help others establish their own level of self-awareness and mastery, we can widen that circle of influence to include groups and communities. True education spreads like wildfire. As Victor Hugo said, "There's nothing more powerful than an idea whose time has come."

The circle of influence naturally expands from individuals to small groups, expanding to community groups and organizations, to global networks.

John Gray's circle of influence began with one person, and now it has expanded globally to change millions of lives. For this to happen, John needed a stable healthy relationship with himself first. Without a firm foundation of self-awareness and self-esteem, John's teachings may have stayed within his own counseling practice. Luckily for us and the millions of people he has educated and helped, John had the confidence and awareness to broaden his circle of influence, from one, to a global family.

SECONDARY RELATIONSHIPS

Once our relationship with ourselves is established, our secondary relationships have a better chance of flourishing.

How many people do you know that truly love and appreciate their partner?

How many others simply tolerate their spouse or just take them for granted?

How many people do you know that simply exist in their relationship rather than thrive?

Ask most people if they want a relationship of their dreams and they shout an affirmative "Yes!"

The world is full of people wanting a soul mate relationship; online dating makes millions of dollars solely around this universal dream. Billions of dollars are spent on personal grooming, clothing, gym memberships, hairstylists, and for some, even plastic surgery, all in the name of finding "the one."

We all dream and hope for the relationship of our dreams, but how many deliberately create it? Millions of dollars don't just fall at an entrepreneur's feet; they go out there and find a way to make it happen. If you want to build your dream home, you don't just conjure up the image and expect it to erect itself overnight. You make plans and initiate them step-by-step. You take action!

Why do we live with the erroneous belief that our ideal relationship should spontaneously happen? That it should be perfect without the least amount of effort? That it's something that we shouldn't need to work on?

We easily understand that we need to work on other things but somehow expect our soul mate to simply turn up and come pre-packaged with the "ideal" behavior, words, actions, and understanding.

If my near thirty-year marriage has taught me one thing, it is that amazing relationships aren't guaranteed—they are nurtured, built, grown, and developed. When your partner knows that you are always willing to work with them, rather than against them, the energy between you is synergized and optimistic. You both feel happier, more stable, and less stressed. When you work together and learn about each other in the effort to understand each other better, you soon become "a rock" for one another.

"Easier said than done" is often the case when emotions run high and your "ideal partner" is behaving less than ideal. However, with an attitude of continuous learning (yes, the same continuous learning I mention in your primary relationship too), we can all create and maintain the relationship of our dreams.

Never think that you're done or you already know everything there is to know about your partner, even after twenty plus years. There are always new things to discover. Be interested in those discoveries within each other. Consistently look for new ways to keep the relationship alive, exciting, and passionate.

When we focus on discovering new things about our partner, we don't take them for granted; we remain receptive to growing together.

Often the blessing of love and sharing gets forgotten about when the comfort and familiarity of a long-term relationship stabilizes. The attitude of gratitude and the excitement of discovery we have at the beginning of our relationships often fade if we don't continue to ignite them. Some people use the beautiful deepening of security and familiarity as a tool to emotionally manipulate. "If you truly loved me, then you'd move to Connecticut," or "buy me that house," or "agree with me." Using manipulation is not love.

Love isn't stagnant; it grows and changes and can get stronger with time.

Continuous learning and discovery in our secondary relationship is the key to maintaining passion, gratitude for each other, and growing together.

> *"You may wish to be loving — you may even try with all your might — but your love will never be pure unless you are free from resentment. When we are free from resentment, loving is effortless. When we have to try hard to love, this is generally a sign that we are repressing our resentments."*
>
> **John Gray Ph.D.**

WHAT IS TRUE SUCCESS?

Some people feel successful in their lives because they are married and have children; some may feel successful because they have a lucrative job or business venture; for others it could be their looks or reaching their ultimate body weight. Success is subjective to the individual. Only you can determine if you are successful or not. However, I believe success is not a point to meet or a number to achieve; it is about your definition of continuous success. If you're currently in a successful relationship, do you stop working on it? No, because there is no summit to reach or destination to arrive at.

If you eat healthy and exercise and become successful at your ideal weight, but don't keep working on it, do you think it will remain ideal? No!

Once again, success is about continuous tweaking, enhancing your definition of success as you go. Never fall into the mentality of "that's it, I'm done—pinnacle reached. Tick it off my list."

Sharing your ongoing learnings with a significant other brings you closer together. Regardless of other successful areas of your life, if you're not enjoying your intimate relationship, then you're not enjoying life to the full. Many people in a relationship still feel alone. They may have the status of "husband" or "wife," but the emptiness is gnawing in their heart. A 2013 study indicated that 62.5 percent of people who reported being lonely were married or living with a partner.

If we are candid and clear about what we're all *really* seeking, it's not just a partner. You can still feel alone even in a partnership. What we are truly seeking is: connection! Deep and meaningful connections. Deep-hearted connections with others, from our partners to our kids and even our business colleagues. True relationships aren't about how much time we spend with someone but the quality of exchange we have with them.

Are we truly listening and communicating? Are we truly present and attentive? Are we developing intimacy, trust, and connection in our relationships, or are we just expecting these qualities to spontaneously manifest themselves?

BUSINESS RELATIONSHIPS

We spend a third of our life at work. We don't want to waste that precious time in conflict with our work colleagues or clients.

All great businesses are built on great relationships. For example, famous entrepreneur Richard Branson builds his brands around the importance of relationships and personalities. He says, "When it comes to business success, it's all about people, people, people."

Building high-performance teams requires everyone to be focused on a shared vision. When a team is aligned to the same vision, positive growth and transformation are inevitable. The old adage "T.E.A.M = Together Everyone Achieves More" is timeless.

Running a multimedia platform in the publishing industry involves multiple roles and different personalities, and the Mars Venus Coaching tools I learned from John have been invaluable to my success, both in my personal relationships and business relationships. Gender differences reveal themselves in the workplace too, and knowing the way in which men and women respond differently to stress has given me the know-how to help others reach their own career goals and obtain their definition of personal success within a team environment.

STRESS IN THE MARS VENUS WORLD

Men's and women's bodies reduce stress differently. Specifically, the genders create very different hormones that reduce stress. Men create testosterone while women create oxytocin; men can learn how to create their own testosterone, just as women can learn how to create their own oxytocin. There are also many ways in which, if we understand ourselves better, we can naturally reduce our own stress. It is understanding these differences and then communicating them with the opposite sex that assists us in coping with difficult situations.

The way men and women react to stress in both life and business also dramatically affects the way they communicate. Under stress, men tend to focus more and want to retract and figure out how they are going to fix it. In a home setting, they may seem to disappear and end up in the garage or sitting in front of the TV just zoning out. In business, men may focus by closing themselves off in their office, focusing on one thing at a time.

Women under stress tend to expand more, and as a result need to share feelings when they feel overwhelmed. Women want to talk more about their problems as this is how they figure out solutions or reduce the stress by talking out loud. They need also to feel heard and understood, not interrupted or given solutions to fix the problem; they just want to talk it out, and then they feel better. Unfortunately, men can misinterpret this and see it as complaining.

Our differences are intensified by stress. When we are under stress, men and women become more different, not more similar. This then in turn causes more stress. Men under stress have an increase of blood flow to the left orbital frontal cortex; this is the part of the brain that gets activated when we're attacked, initiating the flight or fight response. In women, stress activates the limbic system, and this is associated with emotional responses, so women tend to become more emotional than normal when under a great degree of stress.

The part of the brain that produces the cross talk between the hemispheres is actually 25 percent smaller in men; so what that means is men tend to be more single-focused when under stress. That's why you may have heard that men can only do one thing at a time and that women are more multitaskers. Well, there is a scientific fact that makes this true.

When women are facing a problem, their whole brain lights up. In contrast, when men have a problem, their brain lights up in a sequential order: one part of the brain lights up; then it goes to another; then it goes to another. When women are under stress or facing a difficult situation, more parts of their brain are able to communicate with each other than is the case in men's brains. This allows a woman to not only multitask, but to figure out all the solutions at once. So, women are not only thinking about a solution to the problem, but also how it is going to affect the team, their partner, the community, etc. Through talking out loud, she is able to think and explore all the options to come up with the answers and solutions.

"A woman under stress is not immediately concerned with finding solutions to her problems, but rather seeks relief by expressing herself and being understood."
John Gray Ph.D.

INTIMATE RELATIONSHIPS IN GROUP ENVIRONMENTS

Whether it's families, teams, business groups, or large organizations, each individual still wants a sense of connection and belonging in their environment. Research has shown that people who feel a sense of belonging in their environment are healthier and happier than those who don't.

Whether you're a parent, coach, CEO, or boss, the culture that you build within the team and the sense of belonging you create within is paramount to building happy people and thriving environments. Those whose circle of influence is expanding rapidly need to ensure that the authentic sense of belonging doesn't get lost among the masses.

Our business culture with the YSHIFT movement is built on sharing: sharing ideas, sharing stories, sharing our knowledge and goals. Creating an environment where people can be themselves and share their creativity, ideas, and skills enhances profit and production. Working toward a common goal that involves everyone's strengths boosts morale and stirs passion and motivation.

One way to create this is to realize that you can't be "everything to everyone."

You can't be an expert in all areas—no one can. I don't attempt to be an expert in *all* areas of my company; instead, I hire and encourage others to use their passion and expertise in the areas I need. When someone is passionate about what they do, they live and breathe it; they love what they do so much that they learn as much as they can about the subject and keep up to date with new developments. This in turn benefits the entire team, and everyone feels a sense of belonging and contribution.

> *"Learn from the mistakes of others. You can't live*
> *long enough to make them all yourself."*
> **Eleanor Roosevelt**

BE OPEN AND SHARE YOUR STORIES

Coaching is an intimate process. The client needs to be able to trust you with their secrets and know you're the right person to support them. It can be a very vulnerable experience for someone to open up and share their personal thoughts and feelings. If you want your client to open up and share with you, you need to lead the way. Let them get to know you, who you are, what you stand for. Tell them honestly why you are the best person to help them shift to where they want to be. When you share about yourself, the client can choose you rather than feel a sense of obligation.

From an early age, I had a calling to help others. I became a youth worker in my twenties and found myself listening to other people's stories every day. Many were horrific accounts of personal hardship; others were inspirational and amazing. Many were both.

I was distressed to see so many of the teenagers diagnosed with attention-deficit/hyperactivity disorder (ADHD), suffering depression, mental illnesses, suicidal attempts, and drug and alcohol abuse. A lot of these teenagers were physically healthy, but they were mentally and emotionally unhealthy. Many were turning to illegal or prescription drugs in a desperate bid to cope. Most were lost and didn't know where to turn. Young lives being half-lived.

One client in particular springs to mind when reflecting. She was a sweet but troubled girl; her case file was two folders thick and bursting at the seams with notes. A gaunt figure with long brown hair and deep brown socket eyes, eyes that you could tell had seen too much for her age. They were innocent eyes that now had the look of distrust, fear, and suspicion.

We built rapport over time, and one evening we lay outside a community house on a rug just chatting. She was brought into this world by two people that never acted or behaved like parents, far from it. From a young baby, her life was filled with horrific details that no child should endure. I didn't know what to do, or say. What this young woman had known her entire life was far from what I had known.

Whilst laying there, wordless at first, I began to tell her of a true story I knew about a friend. My friend had also experienced some childhood issues and due to her mother's illness, she didn't sometimes have the life or relationship she wished for. I shared this story and how my friend came to make some changes. My friend's plan was the simplest one you have ever heard of, but I shared it anyway as I had nothing else to offer her.

My friend's plan consisted of two sentences:
1. Write down a list of what *I* truly want.
2. Make it happen myself.

Despite the fact she could have written a list called "bad things that have happened to me" and filled it more than two pages long, these mere two sentences became her focus and her newfound direction in life.

As we lay on the rug chatting, I told this girl about the changes my friend had made and the things she had accomplished since that small "note to self."

I felt a little embarrassed that I didn't have the answers to her unbearable past and only shared a story about my friend, a person that she didn't even know. But she immediately sat up and asked me excitedly, "Do you think that I could do that too?"

"Absolutely," I replied. *Why not?* I thought. It actually did work for my friend.

We began then and there to make a list. She included things she'd like to do, such as play the guitar, join a netball team, finish school, etc. The more she thought, the more she wrote; the more she wrote, the lighter she became. By the end of the list, her eyes had changed. No longer did they look fearful and suspicious; instead, they danced and appeared full of hope.

From this day, I realized the power of stories. True stories of humanity and hope. Ancients have long used storytelling as a way to teach the next generation and embed knowledge within them. They used stories wisely and powerfully. I think stories still hold this power.

True stories aren't simple fables or imaginative fantasies; they are immersed in a depth that offers an invitation to ignite our own spirit. Nelson Mandela, Gandhi, Rosa Parks, or Helen Keller didn't set out to deliberately inspire others; they simply chose the path that felt right to them. No one likes being told what to do or how to do it. Sharing stories inspires people to find solutions for themselves, within themselves. Change only happens when one decides to change; however, seeing the possibilities that exist within dire circumstances lights the darkness and offers hope to those who need it.

Sharing stories creates bonds in our relationships and helps us understand each other more deeply. That's why I love coaching and books, whether it's listening to someone's story or reading an inspirational autobiography—true stories help educate, motivate, and nourish and enrich my soul. So, producing and publishing people's real-life amazing stories is more than just a day job to me; it's a passion-driven vision that thrills me and my team every day. Inspirational stories connect us globally.

STORIES AND RELATIONSHIPS

Whether you are aware of it or not, we all live in many different stories. We have:

Our individual story: My name is Susan Dean; I am a mother, coach, and publisher, etc.

Our partner story: Michael and I are childhood sweethearts and have been together for twenty-eight years.

Our family story: The Deans are a close-knit family of four; we have two amazing grown-up daughters and a property full of amazing Australian wildlife.

Our community story: The Deans belong to a country community and are active citizens that support our local businesses and farmers, etc.

Our national story: We are Australian with a family heritage from Scotland and England.

Our global story: We are human beings, citizens of the earth.

We live and breathe within these stories, often fluxing from one to another when the environment or social setting requires it.

In every single story, there is YOU. In every story, relationships exist; in fact, they are inescapable. Learning about them is perhaps one of the smartest things you can do, as it affects every part of your life. The more your circle of influence expands, the more relationships you are involved in.

Look at all the stories you belong to and ask yourself this question for each category: "How can I be a better version of myself within this story than I was yesterday?"

OUR GLOBAL STORY

Just like the young girl I chatted to as a youth worker, our story is truly what we make it.

Our global story is what we make it too. I believe that once we have cemented great relationships with our partners, children, friends, work colleagues, and community, we must still be "continual learners." We must expand our circle and include our relationship to the world itself.

I believe it is our right to give back in this world, and everyone has something that they can offer. We are all unique individuals who have experienced different lessons in life. Some people are experienced through their expertise in education, others from life experience. Whether by heroism or hardship, we all found a way to grow and learn. Ancients used storytelling as a way to pass wisdom on to the next generation. I believe that genuine wisdom is needed in today's world more than ever before, and we need to share forward our teachings. I am so truly grateful that John Gray has done just this.

THE BEST INVESTMENT YOU'LL EVER MAKE

— DR. RANI THANACOODY —

Dr. Rani Thanacoody is an energetic, dedicated and experienced educator, who enjoys sharing her knowledge and research on work-life balance and wellbeing with her students from various social and cultural backgrounds.

Her international career in academia includes working in Australia, Mauritius and China, and she has published academic papers on work-family research in reputable international journals. In 2020, she was named Griffith Business School's 2020 Outstanding International Alumnus. One of her fondest memories involves acting as a recruitment officer for the Sydney Olympic Games in her first human resources position.

In addition to working in academia, Dr. Thanacoody is a certified rapid transformational therapy (RTT) hypnotherapist, Mars Venus life and relationship coach, breathwork coach, compassion practitioner, energy healer, tarot reader and astrologer. She supports her clients using various modalities to overcome their traumas and live purposeful, meaningful lives.

COMPASSION IS THE KEY

I began my academic career in 2004. After I completed my PhD at La Trobe University in Melbourne, Australia, I moved from one institution to the next, teaching and conducting research. As I traveled the world and progressed my career, I noticed that a common problem seemed to follow me wherever I went: bullying. No matter where I ended up, the same patterns repeated, and similar bullies emerged. The world of academia is very competitive. It's a place where egos clash, and others try to bring you down. After moving three or four times, the bullying only got worse. Where was it all coming from? What was the problem? Why were the same patterns repeating? I longed to understand the situation better, so, in 2014, I began my search for answers.

At first, my journey took me to psychology courses, which were helpful but didn't provide the solutions I sought. Finally, I found hypnotherapy. I'd later go on to become a practicing hypnotherapist myself, helping clients overcome their own unresolved issues. Before that, however, my focus was solely on seeking my own answers and trying to heal. When I used hypnotherapy to dig to the root cause of my issue, I realized that the problem stemmed from my childhood, where my needs for love and safety as a child were not met. The people who brought us up weren't perfect. They made their own mistakes. They had their own problems to deal with. They did the best they could with what they knew, and I am very grateful for that. They have been my greatest teachers.

As the famous poet and philosopher Kahlil Gibran said, "We come through our parents and not from them." As an adult now, I am responsible for shaping my life.

When I was young, I never felt good enough and always felt empty within myself. I was always trying to achieve but never felt appreciated. Through hypnotherapy, I realized that these past traumas had created a mindset that made me an attractive target for bullies. You should always seek the root cause of any issue because that's where true understanding lies. Once you understand something, you can let go, move on, and live a more fulfilling life. Gabor Maté said, "Knowing oneself comes from attending with compassionate curiosity to what is happening within." Only by looking inward can we come to know and understand our true selves.

I learned to accept myself and the people around me because everyone is on their own journey, and no one is perfect. We all have issues we're battling with and trying to overcome. In truth, we all make mistakes. Marisa Peer says, "We are flawed people in flawed relationships." I grew to view my bullies from a different perspective. Now, I feel sorry for them, knowing that they have their own unresolved issues to address. When a bully perceives any easy target, they see an outlet for their own inner turmoil, as the bully themself usually has some unmet childhood need. Understanding this helped me build the confidence needed to stand up for myself. Once our bullies realize that we're not such soft targets after all, they direct their hurt elsewhere. They prefer the path of least resistance. When it comes to dealing with people who've hurt you, the key is compassion and understanding why people behave in a certain way.

The Mars Venus feeling letter is a great tool for reaching a place of forgiveness, self-compassion and love. When you use this method, you write a letter, one that you'll never actually send, to someone who hurt you. You explain everything they did and everything their actions made you feel. Then, you write another letter in the place of that person, speaking as if you were them reacting to your words. Finally, you respond with forgiveness, thanking them for what you've learned from the experience and offering them your love. The feeling letter brings everything together. It's all about acceptance, forgiveness, and love for yourself and others. The feeling letter really is an amazing technique, and the mindset it helps create is similar to the one I cultivated during my own healing journey, when I learned to accept, forgive and love those who'd hurt me.

LOOKING BACK AND CONNECTING THE DOTS

In academia, I was constantly searching for a mentor, someone to help and guide me on my journey. I did have some temporary mentors along the way, but they were never supportive and were only in it for themselves. If they didn't have anything to gain, helping me wasn't worth the effort. After my success with hypnotherapy, I continued to search for a committed mentor. My research focuses on workplace social support, so I know that having a supportive supervisor helps people perform better. Unfortunately, no one seemed willing to be that person, so I looked outside of academia.

At my current job, I joined a mentoring program set up by the organization. The program aimed to help find willing mentors for young academics. However, my application was rejected. Instead, they suggested that a coach might be a better fit. That's when I embarked on a new and beautiful journey. As Steve Jobs said, "You can't connect the dots looking forward; you can only connect them looking backwards."

Over a nine-month period, my university-assigned coach helped me gain clarity and learn to focus on what I wanted to achieve. He also held me accountable and assisted me in seeing the bigger picture when I couldn't see it clearly myself. Following my coach's advice, I took a course called "Stepping into Leadership," and part of the program focused on coaching. The more I learned, the more I knew that I had to go deeper.

Hypnotherapy is great for helping people eject past issues and traumas, as most of us repress our feelings during our childhood and adult lives. As we grow up, we carry those unexpressed feelings with us. As a therapist, I have seen many clients who have held onto feelings of anger, fear, guilt, shame, resentment and anxiety that they have not expressed in several years. Holding on unconsciously to those unresolved emotions can lead to illnesses such as cancer, insomnia, depression, phobias, kidney, liver and autoimmune diseases, weight issues and other ailments. A great quote from Marisa Peer is, "The feeling that cannot find its expression in tears may cause other organs to weep." In order to be happy, one must feel those feelings and let them go. Peer says that you must, "Feel your feelings until they are no longer required to be felt." Hypnotherapy is a powerful practice. However, to help clients truly move forward, coaching is the ideal complementary tool.

Since I began this new and exciting journey, I've had several different coaches, including those for love, motivation, mindset and money, and each one has been invaluable in certain areas of my life. Eventually, I got a life and relationship coach, who helped me see the bigger picture and create a greater vision. Even though I'm now a coach myself, I still meet with mine regularly. Through coaching, I've been able to develop my creativity and focus on what I really want in life. From this point on, I plan to always have a coach: someone who's not judgmental, who'll listen, who can keep me on track to my goals.

Discovering coaching was truly a life changing experience, but we're always a work in progress. We're not perfect. We have flaws, but we can grow. We're here to discover our authentic selves and cultivate more love and compassion for ourselves and others. When I look back and connect the dots, I'm eager to see what the future holds.

EQUIPPING THE RIGHT TOOLS

A woman once contacted me asking for help with her sister. The catch was that the sister didn't want—or think she needed—any assistance whatsoever. However, after the first hypnotherapy session on dealing with the anxiety, her attitude began to change. In short, my client lacked confidence and self-esteem and was easily influenced by other people. If someone told her she couldn't or shouldn't do something, she'd listen to them and give up on herself. Her lack of confidence and self-esteem and the accompanying anxiety made following her dreams and achieving her goals very difficult.

Although hypnotherapy improved her situation, she still experienced other issues in her marriage and life in general. I couldn't just leave her like that, so I offered extra support through coaching. I suggested that she write a feeling letter to reconcile with whoever had hurt her in the past. To my surprise, she wrote the letter to herself. I hadn't told her to do that. The experience was incredibly powerful and taught her how to love herself again. She still writes to me on special occasions. I thought she would've moved on and forgotten me by now, but perhaps she'll always remember the profound impact those sessions had on her life. As a coach, having multiple tools at your disposal is important.

Hypnotherapy involves getting to the root cause of an issue. We're like onions in a way and must keep peeling off the layers until we find the true answer at the center of ourselves. Hypnotherapy helps remove those layers, those blocks that prevent us from reaching the core, and coaching assists in removing them for good. With hypnotherapy, we address the past. With coaching, we look into the future. We can't live in the past, and we can't let it determine how we exist in the present. The key is to always look forward. When using hypnotherapy, I realized that identifying clients' blocks wasn't enough. They needed coaching to avoid returning to their old ways and repeating the patterns of the past.

Coaching and hypnotherapy are both powerful tools of transformation, and the two techniques complement each other nicely.

Once I understood that different clients require different approaches, I invested time and energy in learning multiple modalities. As well as offering hypnotherapy and coaching, I use tapping, eye movement desensitization and reprocessing (EMDR), the compassion key technique, and chakra healing. All of these methods are about going within yourself, and each one is useful in certain situations. Some clients are so deep in trauma that they freeze and can't remember anything, so I learned the techniques that could help them. People respond to each tool differently, which is why having a comprehensive toolbox is important.

When my clients' lives change before my eyes, it brings me great joy. To see people really living, doing the things they want to do and learning to love themselves is very rewarding. Being able to facilitate positive change in those I coach is a privilege that I treasure greatly.

Learning to love yourself is one of the most important steps to happiness and fulfillment.

Oscar Wild said, "To love oneself is the beginning of a lifelong romance." When you love yourself, you see others differently, and a new world opens up before you. Everything comes from within, and you must look inside in order to change your life and your relationships. When you have self-love, you create more abundance, and life becomes a dream. To hire a coach is to invest in yourself, and investing in you is the best investment you'll ever make. We only have one life, and it won't last forever, so the time for living is now.

LIFE IS FULL OF
*Re*LAUNCHES
— HILARY DECESARE —

Hilary DeCesare has a unique understanding of and a 360-degree perspective on the successful evolution of life's critical pathways and choices. After a ten-year career at Oracle Corporation garnering numerous sales and managerial awards, including Top Account Manager Worldwide, she shifted her focus to helping C-suite executives and women looking to reLaunch in the spectrum of life, business, and relationships to reach their goals and align to optimize their future possibilities.

As well as being a mother and stepmother to five kids and wife to a loving husband, Hilary is a self-confessed adrenaline junkie. She has jumped from planes, dived in some of the rarest waters, and is up for anything that resembles a challenge or growth opportunity. When she's not coaching or spending time with family, she devotes time to writing and enjoys exploring exotic or unique locations and cultures that bring a new perspective to both hers and her clients' lives.

UNDERSTANDING 3HQ™ (HEART, HEAD, AND HIGHER SELF)

My coaching deals with the realities of *re*Launches, which can be personal or professional and sometimes both at the same time. Stress is inherent in transition and a signal that we're seeking solutions that seem out of reach. After hundreds of experiences with clients in *re*Launches, I realized the answer is that there is no "solution." There is no "balance." Instead, there is a process of alignment via what I call the 3HQ™. Each of us possesses a great gift: an inner navigation system that can guide us through the challenges of confronting who we are, what we do, and what we need in order to be our authentic, optimum-functioning selves. The 3HQ™ is a partnership of the heart, the head, and the higher self, working as a powerhouse team, not unlike separate departments in an organization. This time, it's Organization You.

In the sixties, seventies, and eighties, IQ (Intelligence Quotient) focused on how smart people were, how much they could comprehend, and how well they solved problems. By the nineties, EQ (Emotional Quotient, or Emotional Intelligence) had moved into the spotlight. EQ related to how connected people and their actions were to their emotions and those of others. I believe that things have now evolved to the next level. While people have always been at this stage, awareness of the possibilities has heightened as science and previously unimaginable technology has revealed and measured more about our bodies and brains and their chemistries.

The 3HQ™ involves mastering a conscious control of the unconscious. Getting out of your heart's instinctiveness and into your head's consciousness. Mastering your choices rather than having them master you. The journey between the heart, the head, and the higher self occurs in an infinite loop. Nobody scores 100 percent on any single aspect of the 3HQ™ because there is no test, no right, no wrong. Reality doesn't allow it. Life constantly—even minutely—throws curve balls and forces new transitions upon us—what I call *re*Launches.

When referring to the heart, we're talking about an emotional connection—inner strength. In the case of the head, we really mean knowledge, which is power. And the higher self is our connection to intuition, to our unfathomable wisdom. Some seek to circumnavigate their intuition, saying things like, "I trusted it once, and it wasn't right." They think that because it wasn't accurate one time, they should ignore it later. But, more than likely, their intuition wasn't faulty; their interpretation of it was.

Personal *re*Launches, such as relationship breakups, divorces, and moments of rapid growth, can cause people to question their purpose in life. When your expectations of where you should be don't match reality, you can start to feel like a failure, like you're not good enough, like you're not worthy. Perhaps what you envisioned for yourself previously isn't mapping to whom you see when you look in the mirror today.

Whether your focus is personal or professional, you can apply the 3HQ™ method and its guided approach to reveal your authentic self and the obstacles that may be holding you back. This allows you to get to the "why" in your heart and understand and deconstruct your inner limitations, knowing that you have an emotional presence you're trying to create. Through this process, you can identify the core essence and purpose of who you want to be in the future.

To remove lingering obstructions—the ones that whisper in your ear, "I can't do it" or "That's not me"—I have created a protocol that I call Belief Blasters. The pathway I've crafted obliterates self-doubt, self-sabotage, and repressed barriers born of limiting beliefs. Belief Blasters aims to remove limiting beliefs that often relate to lack of success, failure in relationships, poor work environments, an absence of self-respect, and early-life trauma. How many times did I hear from a client that something as simple as a comment from a first-grade teacher can cause lasting impact? How humbling it can be to realize that the trauma spectrum has such unique and deep cultural ramifications. No one can tell anyone what their limiting beliefs are, or judge them.

The discovery process and arriving at a conclusion on their own are critical. It's a lifelong cascade. Due to the way our brains are wired, one discovery can fire off sparks to something else, a new way of thinking, and amazing things happen from there. Once we remove our limiting beliefs, we can replace them with more empowering ideas. When you have your heart working with your head, you can truly tap into your intuition to accelerate your sense of clarity.

Often, we hear gurus saying things like, "Love your life. Love your job. Love your partner. Love, love, love, love, love." But so many of us are caught up in self-sabotage, which stems from the heart level, that we can't even consider crossing the vast chasm between the place of not liking ourselves and loving ourselves completely. When I coach people away from self-sabotage to a place of loving themselves, they can then take 3HQ and apply it to business and other aspects of their lives. As you can see, it's all connected.

BUSINESS, SILICON VALLEY, AND THE THIRD SEX

When I discovered John Gray, my business partner suggested that we look into Mars Venus Coaching. As soon as my coach introduced me to the world of gender intelligence, a light went off in my head. The concept intrigued me. While I had a psychology degree and had already been coaching and dealing with relationships for some time, I hadn't really looked beyond basic rapport building. But when I heard John Gray discuss the different ways to communicate with men and women, I was fascinated by the concept of gender intelligence. As I dove deeper and studied more, I realized there were so many ways to apply gender intelligence to business. In fact, I suddenly saw myself in the crosshairs.

My direct and indirect work in Silicon Valley had brought in nearly one quarter of a billion dollars in revenues. It had also turned me into something that, before John Gray, I had never really understood: another person, a member of the third sex. I speak of this from the perspective of gender intelligence and emotional identification. In the corporate environment that I worked in—and many that exist today—there are three gender-attributed avatars: the man, the woman, and the woman who's trying to be the man. During my time in Silicon Valley, I was the third, the hybrid avatar. I wanted so badly to be a part of the so-called boys club that I put on a totally new persona. My colleagues would say to me, "You're such a pit bull," but that wasn't the real me, the me inside. This created a huge disconnect.

My wake-up call happened at home in my kitchen when my mom, who was babysitting because I'd put in another fifteen-hour day, called me out on it. She wanted to know where "her Hilary" had gone. When I finally took John's course and learned more about gender intelligence, I realized what I'd been doing.

When I was trying to scale Mount Everest in Silicon Valley, I didn't want to believe there was a difference between myself and a man. I couldn't acknowledge the fact because doing so would separate me from who I wanted to be. But once I stopped trying to be the third sex, new doors opened up and more success came my way. I now understood the power of our masculine and feminine sides, and I could finally be the real me. The most successful leaders know how to leverage both aspects of themselves. They don't try to push one part away to solely become the other. We all must learn the slow dance of working with both our masculine and feminine sides and form a symbiotic relationship between them, because doing so is crucial to success.

This continuous calibration is the essence of the 3HQ™. We expect to function on autopilot, yet so many women have sacrificed themselves to stress by "leaning in" to the altar of success, creating this dysfunction I recognized in my clients and, in retrospect, myself.

ADDING MARS VENUS TO THE COACHING TOOLBOX

While I'd already been coaching for many years before I discovered John Gray's work, adding his techniques and knowledge to my toolbox was a revelation. Gender intelligence was a bell that, once rung, frequently occupied my thoughts. While I obviously knew that women and men were different, I'd never actually applied that knowledge to my personal lifestyle or business principles, such as sales, marketing, leadership, communication, values, and culture.

Women in tech were scarce, and those who succeeded were immersed in technology or corporate finance. There were very few female managers or executives to whom I could look up to as role models. Generally, when I was making my mark at Oracle, women just had to get in there and act like a rabid pit bull if they ever hoped to climb the corporate ladder. Women like me really were the third sex, zipping on the persona to succeed. I just never put two and two together at the time. The rationale and any potential solutions eluded me. Sure, I was successful—but at what price?

John's work allows us to view people and relationships differently. For instance, when you use the Mars Venus approach, there's a calibration that takes place. Working with men, the process can be more linear and straight forward: statistics and facts with the extraneous details removed. Women can be more emotionally open, calling for a more open-ended, qualitative approach. This isn't about wrapping up coaching in a pink or blue ribbon with a bow. It's about reaching the messy essence-without-borders of who an individual is. It's a chaotic, finger-painted rainbow. Once I learned more about gender intelligence, I realized just how important understanding these critical differences was.

The Mars Venus tools and techniques perfectly complement the 3HQ™approach, as well as others I've honed over the years. My heart has always been in transformational, versus transactional, coaching. We really want the person to change and not just learn how to run a business. I often say that you must first become invisible in order to be visible. Society today is all about being seen on social media, stages, and anywhere else you can get your brand noticed, but that's the wrong way to go about implementing 3HQ™.

The 3HQ™ lifestyle—and workstyle—involves priming yourself for transformation. It's about first tapping into your deeper, invisible self. If an element of your life isn't ultimately doing what you want it to do, it creates discord. Therefore, before you can go visible, you must look internally, get to that invisible space within yourself, and recognize what's going on inside that's directly impacting the outside. Only then is visible transformation an option.

After decades of emphasizing the bottom line, we're starting to hear business leaders say they're leading from the heart. Values are moving from "the soft stuff" to center stage of the business platform. Forrester research has long established that the key common factor in companies with sustained high performance is a base of values that's strong enough to provide employees with a common bond, a purpose beyond profit.[1]A growing body of research shows that there is a strong link between values-driven organizations and financial performance. Meanwhile, recent world and social events have caused 50 percent of consumers to re-evaluate their own values. Clearly, we as coaches are at a tipping—if not crisis—point for *re*Launches.

When a crossover between personal and professional occurs, transformation becomes holistic. The *re*Launch Co. approach focuses on this idea, especially regarding women who seek to launch or *re*Launch their businesses or corporate positions. As they undertake the journey, the rest of their lives also experience positive change. Why? Because their businesses are a direct reflection of them. We're able to show our clients how to better achieve alignment and, therefore, less stress in their lives. I propose that this alignment and not the ubiquitous, unsolvable work/life balance theory is the key to finding solutions for the mass dissonance that has an ongoing, disruptive impact on women in the workplace. Until this dissonance is addressed, women and their employers will grapple with an unsettled culture.

FROM LAWYER TO SUCCESSFUL NOVELIST

Award-winning author Liani Kotcher leaped off the hamster wheel of college, law school, and working at a top law firm to follow her passion and become a writer. But the road to literary success was far from smooth. Growing up, Liani's parents frequently told her that writing wasn't a viable career path, yet she always longed to be a storyteller. While working as a lawyer, she bridged the gap between passion and practicality by taking writing classes on the side. Even so, she struggled to summon the courage to truly commit to her dream.

I first met Liani when she moved to California. At the time, she said she felt that her inner purpose was to tell stories, but she didn't know how to take the leap. In fact, she had a deep fear of being an impostor. How could she ever call herself a writer? She just couldn't imagine it. When we decided to work together, our goal was to adjust her mindset and remove the limiting belief instilled in her by her parents, the belief that she'd never make it as a writer.

So much of Liani's identity was tied up in being a lawyer, and it took a long time for her to truly own that feeling of being a writer. In order to move forward, she required coaching that would hold her accountable and keep her on track. During her transition from lawyer to writer, I used my twenty years of coaching experience to help guide her on her journey. Today, Liani is not only the award-winning author of a successful, critically-appraised young adult series but also a literary blogger, influencer, and coach. In addition, her book is now being made into a movie—her ultimate goal.

During Liani's reLaunch, we focused on moving her past the core limiting belief that had held her back for so long. We achieved this via a workshop that removed that roadblock from her mindset. One step of this Belief Blaster process ties in with John's "Feeling Letter." I call it the Release Letter, and it allowed Liani to tap into her innermost feelings, the emotions she'd walled off for years. She was then able to trust in the authenticity of her higher power truth. Her work has, in turn, taken her beyond writing to connecting with others and helping them live their own passions.

Liani found fulfillment by moving forward one step at a time—she didn't rush the process. Gradually, she built an undeniable skill set and finally learned to believe in herself. Once she embraced her inner truth and sense of purpose, Liani had the foundation to not only become a writer but to handle future *re*Launches as well.

CHOOSING TO TAKE CONTROL OF YOUR OWN THOUGHTS

When you understand 3HQ™—the heart, head, and higher self—you can accelerate the goal attainment process. When all three aspects work in alignment, success will come much more easily and at a faster pace.

In coaching, you should aim to help your clients build a strong, powerful core. A good coach doesn't give answers. Instead, she should walk the path with her clients, holding the light, showing perspective, and allowing them to make their own decisions. A lifestyle of success looks different to each person. There's no one answer that applies to every situation, and each client requires a customized approach. One size doesn't fit all.

For some, a breakthrough may require only a few weeks of coaching. Whereas others, during difficult periods, can take a little longer. Life always happens, and you can't avoid reality. Some people discuss choices as if you don't have any—but you do. You can choose which thoughts occupy your mind. It's the one thing you can control. If you view a situation in a negative way, negativity is what you'll get in return, and you'll remain at a lower vibrational level. If you don't believe you can choose to change your thoughts, you're literally forfeiting that choice. You're practically saying, "I'm willing to keep my vibration at a very low level and accept the victim mentality—and that's where I want to stay." But when you instead announce, "I'm not going to think like that anymore," you start to climb the vibrational scale, which means you begin to attract the things you really want in life. Isn't that worth the effort?

RELAUNCH! SPARK YOUR HEART TO IGNITE YOUR LIFE

When I was writing my book, *RELAUNCH! Spark Your Heart to Ignite Your Life*, I based a lot of the content around stories of life, clients, and business. I weave these tales around key concepts that allow you to effortlessly step into the 3HQ™ lifestyle. I'm a storyteller, you see. I also learn better when I hear stories, and I know that others do too.

Hearing someone else's story often makes us realize that it's okay to be where we are now. You know that if they can make it through a difficult situation, you can too. If they can beat adversity and attain a lifestyle of success, so can you. If they can turn a story of despair into one with a happy ending, you most certainly can too.

I took that journey myself in writing my book. Within its pages, I relive some of my own most significant stories and *re*Launches. I even included one chapter that I wasn't even sure I should publish. To this day, I'm embarrassed by some of the mistakes I made, and sharing such monumental failure with my readers and showcasing such a clear lack of judgment wasn't easy. But I wouldn't be where I am right now if I hadn't done so.

In the end, I tried to make each of those experiences work for me in a positive, proactive way, defining myself as a person, and realizing that a job or even a gender is not a cookie-cutter value. Your 3HQ™, heart, head, and higher self, synergize to create your own definition of value. As women, both clients and coaches must ask, "Who am I as a person? What are my inner values? What's stopping me from being all I can be? What steps can I take to close that 'stress gap' between intent and reality?" The *re*Launch platform can help answer these questions. It's about opening a doorway to transformation and helping others step through it.

FAMILY, LIFE, AND BUSINESS

— MAHMOUD KHATER —

As an avid problem solver and people developer, **Mahmoud Khater** is passionate about making a better world, one word at a time. He enjoys coaching, speaking, training, consulting, writing, and change management.

He is an expert in leadership and applying its tactics into leading yourself, your family, your career, your team, your company, your customers, your audience, and your society to transform, grow, and shine. He cofounded Flourishing Academy after working for more than sixteen years in the corporate world. He is an associate certified coach, a certified professional coach, a Marshall Goldsmith Stakeholder Centered coach, a Mars Venus success coach, an NLP practitioner, EFT practitioner, and a certified Ex-DISC. He holds an MBA from Manchester Business School with a background in computer engineering and accreditation in project management and risk management as well.

He has been trained by John Gray, Dr. Marshall Goldsmith, Tony Robbins, Jack Canfield, Sue Knight, Brene Brown, Dr. Barbara De Angelis, and Dr. Shirzad Chamine, and is a member of International Coaching

Federation, International Positive Psychology Association, and Canadian Positive Psychology Association. He's also a father for Judie and Omar, likes traveling, scuba diving, and having a wise legacy.

COACHING FOR ALL AGES

In my journey, I have always given support to everyone, including adults *and* children. When I work with children, I also work closely with their parents. After all, many times coaching a child can only be successful if the parents are also on board and willing to do the work necessary to bring about change in their child's life.

I have worked with children that are as young as seven years old. Each child has different needs. Sometimes the need is working on developing their public speaking skills, helping them build self-esteem and self-confidence, reducing their anger episodes, building resilience and emotional intelligence, or becoming calmer and gaining more control of their emotions. I help the child think about what they want out of life and how they can start selecting their specializations for high school. I might also ask the parent(s) to have a talk with the kid's teachers or other influential adults from the family's social circle, especially if the child is a teen or involved in extracurricular activities.

With adults, they usually seek my support in one of two areas: relationships (family and parenting) or business (leadership and career success). I believe coaching is about having an everlasting effect on one's behavior and growing in all important areas in one's life. I am confident that with the different coaching methodologies, I can help people manage their behavior and lead themselves, their families, their partners, their companies, or their new businesses to achieve success in any setting they find themselves in.

MY THREE GOALS

No matter who I coach or what problem they need help with, I always have three goals to meet with each client. I want to *inspire* my client to desire change; I want to *motivate* them to change, and I want them to get the *value* of achieving their desired change faster with the coaching support.

When I first meet with a new client, I appeal to their desire to get better and give them hope that they do not have to stay in a state of frustration, loneliness, or despair. There is a lot of value in reading books and blogs or watching videos. However, simply reading something will not change one's life. It's only by taking action that one can change their future. By motivating my clients to take action, they can see that achieving success is absolutely possible.

Many people that come to me feel as if they have no hope. They need support to know that whatever problems they are experiencing, they can see improvement in the management of these difficulties. Those feelings of loss, fears of the future, fears of rejection, or the fear of not being good enough can be handled in a more constructive way. I want to inspire others so they can live a more fulfilling life.

After one has been inspired to change, they need to be shown that it takes action to make things happen. This is where people start to get scared. They *want* to exchange their problem with a solution but either don't know how *or* they see success so far in the distance, it seems impossible to get there. But, by breaking down that journey into small, manageable steps, they can get there. Remember, a marathon begins with a first step.

Many believe that, "If I could just *talk* about what's bothering me, I'll feel better." But what have you done to make progress after you've talked about your difficulties? True, talking about one's problems gives clarity about a situation, but action is what helps you get the results you want. Coaching is not only about *feeling* better but also about using these new positive feelings to fuel your journey to success. It is about realizing you *can* have what you want and making plans to achieve those goals.

INSPIRE

If one is not developing or maturing, they are simply standing still. If you're not growing, then what is the alternative? Many people fear change because it can be scary. It requires bravery. Bravery means you know the fear is there, and you can feel it, but you do not let it control you. You put together a plan and tackle it anyway.

Coaching is about working with people to get a sustainable change for their future. You can tell people *what* to do, but it won't be self-sustained change. It's like when you tell a child, "Don't touch the oven. It's hot." The minute you turn your back, what would the child do? Touch the oven! Mars Venus coaches do not tell people what to do; they support them in defining the plan and then putting it into action. After all, I am not the expert in their life; I'm the expert in innovation.

For example, if a client came to me and said, "I want to start a business, but I don't think I can," there is typically one of two things stopping him: (1) he still needs to be wholly definite about what he wants, or (2) he needs to be certain about the value of his product/service.

People often believe that there is no way they can get what they want. But they can learn! We live in an age in which information is literally at our fingertips. We have Google, the internet, instructional videos on YouTube, books on how to build/learn things; the possibilities are endless! So why would a client come to me, a coach, to learn how to open a business? Well, he's not. He's coming to me because he needs to break through the barriers—fear, worry—create a plan, execute it, and measure its success and determine how to readjust the plan. He needs to be fulfilled. Many people can open a business and achieve the success they thought they wanted. Yet, when they get there, they feel hollow and unfulfilled.

My goal is to help the client focus. His focus should be on creating a more specific plan of what he wants to do and achieve. It's much like the water gun game you see at the circus. People sit down in chairs and try to shoot water into the bull's eye to win a prize. If you don't pay attention and have no control over what you're doing, water will go everywhere. But if you focus on the bull's-eye—the center of what you want—you can hit the mark and win the prize!

This is why being specific about what you want is a must. For the client wanting to open a business, I would ask a couple of questions: What business are you looking for? What value do you want to give to the client? Once they answer these questions, we can dig deeper. Such as, if your product, your value, is meeting your client's needs, then they will be addicted to your business. This will then start a chain reaction of word-of-mouth advertising and referrals, leading to success.

I worked as a project manager for many years. In my opinion, a good project manager delivers what the sponsor wants, but a great project manager delivers what the sponsor needs. This is true of coaching as well. Often in my coaching practice I'll ask clients what they want. They typically respond with, "Uh, I don't know . . ." They don't know what they want because they cannot see it. As a coach, you have to help your client visualize their goals.

Worst of all, they also don't know what the prospective client will pay for! They have their own, untested assumptions. I help new businesses—and even existing ones—based on my knowledge of project management and my consulting experience. We use tools like the Business Model Canvas for determining their operating model and to be able to see their business in action with more specifics. One challenge is that they don't know what they don't know! They don't know how to run a business, how to find clients and add value.

MOTIVATION

For the client coming to me who wants to open his own business, I first inspire him to let go of his fears so he can see that his dreams are attainable. After that, he needs to be motivated to start working on it. I ask my clients, "Where is the fuel to move your plan into action? Where is your plan to get this idea moved into a reality?" If the client is not committed, he or she will find justification for their actions.

You have no idea how many people come to me and do not know what they want. Then, the people that do know what they want don't know *why* they want what they want. These are the people who will not be motivated to move forward; they will have no fuel and have no purpose. They will have no energy or drive to get it done. You've got to be hungry for what you want. If you don't have the hunger within you, you cannot get what you want. Without this desire, you will not be able to overcome any obstacles. You will rename them as "excuses" instead of making them into strategies to get you through difficulties.

Thomas Edison, the inventor of the lightbulb, tried—and failed—one thousand times to make the lightbulb. He could've given up, but instead he used those failures to drive him to continue. He is famously quoted as saying, "I didn't fail. I just found one thousand ways not to make a lightbulb."

This is how Mars Venus coaching helps to motivate others. One of the mantras I coach my clients is, "If someone else did it, I can do it!" Mars Venus coaching helps one to come to their own conclusions and their own truths. We teach that there is a solution to every problem. Even if that solution seems buried deep, we just have to keep looking and digging for it.

Like Edison, I believe that people never fail. After every time Edison didn't create the lightbulb, he learned something new. This is why failure is never really *failing*. If someone tries doing something and it doesn't turn out like they wanted it to, they still *learned* something from the experience. When assessing results, you either get the outcome you want and get success, *or* you learn from your mistakes.

Learning is a success! Teaching oneself and others to look at disappointments in a more positive way will empower one to keep going. It is an amazing way to look at life; imagine the self-esteem of someone who believes they never fail, as compared to those who attach their self-worth to their results! What lesson can you learn from this situation that can help you in the future? Ultimately, setbacks are in your life as a lesson to learn.

My coaching style focuses on how to help my client make results more attainable. We as humans learn by taking small steps. When you break down the steps into small skills, you'll become better, and soon, those skills will be automatic.

I tell my clients, "You know you have obtained automatic skills when you do these things without thinking about them, when they become involuntary decisions and actions." That is when one is driven by the purpose and faith in their value and abilities, when the skills and decision to keep moving forward are automatic. When you want to learn and you have curiosity to drive you to learn, nothing can hold you back. After much practice, I focus on the small skills. These skills become a habit when they become automatic. Repetition is the key to gaining these skills. The old saying, "Practice makes perfect," is a damaging statement. Nothing and no one are perfect. However, practice does make permanent. Practicing skills over and over makes them habitual and makes them last.

This is where a coach comes into play. Coaches assist the client in assessing their progress. It is difficult to look at ourselves objectively when we work on behavioral changes. We have to rely on the people around us to tell us if they can see a difference. This, however, can be misleading because people will give their *perception* of the truth. A coach gives a more realistic, unbiased perception.

At the end of the day, you are the planner and the doer of your life. If you make plans but never follow through, your dreams will always be out of reach. A doer has to stick to the plan. When a person is driven by the purpose and the plan, they are more motivated to keep going. Focus on the happiness you will feel when you achieve your goal. Instead of thinking, "I'm going to fail!" change your thinking and put it in the positive—"I have value to share!"

Bill's Business Dreams

A client of mine, Bill, had been working as a graphic designer for a company but ultimately wanted to open his own business rather than just be a part of the staff. He was already branching out and doing some freelancing, but he wasn't taking it to its full potential. He had a vision of opening a large design firm but was not making any changes or taking the necessary steps to achieve this goal.

Bill and I first met at an event at which I was talking about using LinkedIn to promote your personal brand. After my talk, he approached me, and we spoke about his dream of building his own business. We began working together as coach and client. We started by discussing what he wanted specifically and what was stopping him from getting there. We started visualizing what his goal was with more details and put more specificity to it. Then I supported Bill in getting to his goals, and we began working formally on his plan.

We used SMART goals (specific, measurable, attainable, realistic, and timely) and timeline visualization. I asked him what his five-year vision was. As he told me his vision for the next five years, I had him add in specific and frequent milestones, especially during the first and second year. Then we looked into what Bill's purpose was in opening a business, which led to finding his voice, putting more clarity into his message, and discovering what value he had to offer. We defined his purpose, his "why," the fuel driving his behavior, his strength against setbacks.

I worked with Bill during our initial sessions by reframing his understanding of success and failure, as well as building his self-esteem and self-confidence.

Then we went into the vision and goals. We started working more into the "how" of building his business, diving into more specific actions that he could take to achieve his goal.

First, we identified Bill's target audience and determined where they would be getting their information from. Then we ascertained what the client would need. Because he had experience in freelancing, he had some awareness of what people were looking for. It helped Bill to get in touch with those clients and ask them what they needed. What did they value the most?

Next, he designed his business, focusing on the main needs of his target clients. After he started to see that his operating model was working well, we went into how to expand his market, how he could reach other clients, and how to direct leads from the market into his sales process. And, more importantly, when we were deciding on his operating model and sales process, we were also designing the measures that could be used to evaluate his plans and get feedback of their effectiveness and efficiency to confirm that they were working as expected or to determine where more work was needed. As he started growing his clientele, his market and his business became bigger. He's now executing his plan and getting more leads and clients!

One thing people should understand about launching a new business is that instead of focusing on how much happier they will be by being their own boss, they need to add value to the client's business and life. They must offer a positive change for the client. It is imperative they market and articulate their value to the client. It's important also to overdeliver.

Parenting Style MV

As I stated above, I coach a variety of people. One of my passions is helping parents and their children to thrive. The Mars Venus method of coaching has a positive parenting style that states love alone is not enough. You can love your child to the moon and back, but it is essential to understand the child's needs and be able to fulfill those needs in the way they expect, not in the way that we as parents prefer to do it.

The very basic foundation of the Mars Venus Positive Parenting Style is to use *love*-based parenting rather than *fear*-based parenting. It's a scientific fact that every behavior is driven by an immediate pain or a desire to please; this is referred to as the "pain/pleasure principle." Many parents use fear, threats, or punishment to build a painful area for their child so they can drive their behavior toward the way the parents desire.

In Mars Venus, however, we believe that this is very unhealthy for the child's physiological, mental, and emotional health and that the parent creates an environment of high stress for both of them. When using love-based parenting—using the skills below—the results bring a much calmer parent and a much happier child.

The five messages and beliefs of a Mars Venus parent:

1. **It's okay to be different.** Through this, the child can understand that he is unique and different from everyone else—his siblings, his peers, etc.—and rather than trying to conform, he should yearn to build on his uniqueness and discover his talents.

2. **It's okay to make mistakes.** This can be translated to: when we make mistakes, we learn from them. And, accordingly, he can start to believe that we can learn even if we don't get the results we want. This helps the child to recover from setbacks.

3. **It's okay to express negative emotions.** This belief by itself is one of the most challenging for parents and young boys. Culturally, men are told to not show emotion, whether positive or negative. If a man is crying, many would say, "Man up!" This causes them to suppress their anger, their fear, and their sadness rather than handle it. That is a very unhealthy attitude in the long run. Once boys start to suppress these emotions, it begins to have negative effects on their behavior. With girls, if they suppress their emotions, it hurts them too; though it's more culturally acceptable to allow a girl to cry than a boy. We have to teach our children how to manage their emotions and learn to control them. I teach the kids I coach to *name* their emotions and increase their vocabulary around how to describe them. I encourage them to say, "I feel _____ when you do _____" rather than saying, "You make me feel _____." When someone says, "You make me feel mad!" This implies *you* control their emotions. Once a child can learn that *they* are the only one in charge of their emotions and that they can take control of them, they feel better.

4. **It's okay to want more.** The problem with this message is that parents always assume that if their kid wants more, then he is not satisfied with what he has. This hurts the parents—the mother especially—as she is typically a giver and sacrifices for her kids. This in turn starts the fear within the mother that her efforts are not good enough because her children are not satisfied since they want more. At this point, I help to break the cycle by letting the child know it's okay to want more and also by explaining to the parent that wanting more does not mean dissatisfaction with the current situation.

5. **It's okay to say "no," but Mom and Dad are the bosses.** This goes both ways. The children need to realize that Mom and Dad are the bosses. But, the parents also must come to terms with the belief that it is okay for the child to say "no" as well. This is a very big challenge for the parent because they think if they allow the child to say "no" one time it will become a pattern. Parents need to nurture the will power of the child, not break it.

The child should be allowed to say "no" and is allowed to express freely, debate, and discuss. Through Mars Venus coaching, we teach parents to use the different skills of asking rather than ordering, nurturing rather than fixing, rewarding rather than punishing, commanding rather than demanding, and giving time-outs rather than spanking. This helps to build cooperative children rather than *obedient* children. That is the main component of the parent leader. The very definition of a leader is one who, rather than *ordering* his followers to obey his will, has his followers *wanting, cooperating,* and *willing* to follow. He manages to help them keep their will working for them as well as for him by gaining their trust and respect and aligning the goals that he has assigned.

Suzanne's Child Challenges

Suzanne, a single mother, was referred to me by a friend. She had two sons; one was nine years old, and the other was five. Her nine-year old, Jason, was having difficulty controlling his temper in school, and it was negatively affecting his academic performance. Suzanne was worried Jason may also be bullied and was unsure of how to handle the situation. She had her own fears and concerns but was not sure if they were true or not.

We started with the initial session. Now, when I work with parents and children, I ask that the parent sit with me frequently so I can give them guidance on strategies they can use with their kids. I can work with the children only an hour or hour and a half a week, while the parent can keep working with the child using the Mars Venus techniques and parenting strategies daily.

A challenging point usually for this age is earning the child's trust and respect so they can allow the adult to take control. In order for me to earn Jason's trust, I had to start building my "relationship bank account"; i.e., I had to start "scoring points" with him. I shared some personal stories of myself. This helps to build trust because when I share a personal story of mine, he can feel that I trust *him*. Then, in response, he can trust me as well. And, of course, I assure them that the sessions are completely confidential and I will not be sharing any content to the parents.

Earning a child's respect starts with gaining points by giving the child the gift of time and sharing in his preferred hobbies. This helps the child to relax and communicate. Once you earn the trust and respect, you can start going into deeper communications with him by understanding how his current situation limits him from reaching his full potential and by starting to instill the belief of excellence: for example, the belief that there is no failure, only feedback, or the belief that he has worth, regardless of the results.

I applied the five messages and beliefs of an MV Parent with Jason and later shared them with Suzanne. I explained to her that there are four types of kids, each with a different temperament (this is from John Gray's *Children Are from Heaven*).

The four temperaments and their specific needs are listed below:

	Temperament Type	Needs
1	Sensitive	Listening and Understanding
2	Active	Preparation and Structure
3	Responsive	Distraction and Direction
4	Receptive	Ritual and Rhythm

I worked with Suzanne to determine which temperament types Jason displayed the most. Then I worked with a custom temperament-appropriate plan alongside Jason to explore more details about the problems he was facing, as well as his long-term goals and vision. What did he want to be when he grew up? Did he want to play sports? Etc.

I also worked with him on building self-esteem and resilience using Mars Venus tools. Luckily, Suzanne was not only using these skills with Jason but also on her younger son! She was receiving very positive feedback on how her children were responding to problems in much more agreeable and constructive ways after she implemented those techniques. Jason showed much improvement by the third or fourth session, especially on his emotional resilience. As soon as I let him know that expressing negative emotions was okay and showed his mother how to deal with those emotions, it was very effective. It helped Jason cope in a better way, and his performance at school went up 12 percent and continues to climb!

VALUE OF MARS VENUS COACHING

The first questions people usually ask me when they learn what I do are, "What is coaching? What are you going to do for me?" I explain to them that coaching is not about me giving you a solution to your problem; you are the expert for your problem. Coaching is about supporting the client to get to his or her goals. It's not about giving behavioral solutions. As a coach, I support the client in changing behaviors to achieve their desired goals. People come to be coached about relationships, parenting, their career, etc. All of this is manageable and coachable.

John Gray speaks specifically about this in *How to Get What You Want and Want What You Have*. He discusses how to achieve your goals and how to attain inner and outer success. This includes maintaining stable relationships and helping them flourish as well as dealing with broken relationships, loss, grief, etc. This means that the client usually knows a lot about his or her problem and the solution. In other words, they know what they need; they just don't realize it. The client needs a push, motivation, and support to help him get what he wants and needs.

Most people who say, "I don't know what I want" are really saying, "I don't know how to get what I want" or "I don't think I can get to what I want." Because many people do not know *how* to be happy, they settle for "I don't know what I want." This is a protective measure on their part. If they don't know what they want, then they can't go after it. If they never try to go after it, then they will never fail. It's a crippling cycle that produces more and more stagnation, causing one to stop growing, learning, and realizing their value.

To them, not knowing is better than knowing and failing. Many times, it is because we have been cultured and conditioned to not believe in ourselves. I believe I am helping people to become self-confident leaders, in their families, in their peer groups, in their businesses, and ultimately in their societies.

SELF LOVE
— CATERINA TORNANI —

As a psychologist and life coach, **Caterina Tornani** has had the honor of working with people from all stages and walks of life: children, adolescents, adults, couples, families, athletes, and corporations. The range of people she has worked with has allowed her to be a collaborative part of healing a multitude of relationship and life challenges that her clients have faced.

Through this work, she has learned that nothing in the world can succeed in creating harmony between people more than collaboration, but it needs a very important ingredient: loving feelings. And for Caterina, this is where John Gray's teachings come into her practice.

GRADUATING WITH A BANG

A few months before my graduation, I had an insight that, at the time, seemed and felt incomprehensible: I "knew" a lot—but I "was not." For me, it was all too clear that in a short time I'd be out of the comfortable reality of being a student and immersing myself in the world of work, but I didn't feel I had the tools to do what I'd trained for: support people in actualizing their human potential. I felt erudite in theory but not effective in practice. My studies fueled the idea of psychological therapy, but nothing I learned actually worked. In my opinion, for all I had learned in all my studies, I didn't have useful, true, workable solutions for the people I wanted to work with. I knew in my heart of hearts that I was missing something, something decisive, something that could make my work more effective for both my clients and myself—and I had no idea what that something was.

I felt directionless and, worse, questioned myself at my deepest levels. What had I done? Had I wasted years of my life? What was I going to do? That's when I found John Gray's books.

MARS VENUS IN MY LIFE AND CAREER

While I was a student at the University of Psychology, I read all of John Gray's books. A professor told our class to read *Men Are from Mars, Women Are from Venus* if we wanted to learn smart strategies to understand men's and women's minds.

While I read, I realized that understanding the differences between a man's and woman's way of thinking wasn't as difficult as I thought. There are features inherent in men and in women. If you learn these recurrent features, and you are also able to consider the singular case, you can understand most men and most women, and, consequentially, you can make them feel better.

My objective is to make the life of my clients more fulfilling and to enhance their personal resources. Johns Gray's teachings are very easily approachable, understandable, and useful—even for people who do not have a psychological or medical background.

Once I was introduced to the Mars Venus methods and teachings, I attended several seminars given by John Gray. From there, I decided to become a Mars Venus coach in addition to a licensed clinical psychologist. I appreciated John's methodologies so much that I decided to help others using his techniques. He uses plain language in coaching and in workshops, emotional closeness with clients, and personal anecdotes about life to make people feel more comfortable and willing to share.

I felt that the Mars Venus approach was based on the principles of positivity, change, hope, and a desire to succeed. The Mars Venus principles allow people to focus on goals in a realistic, achievable way because the motivation comes from love toward us and love toward other people. The Mars Venus approach is based on the reality of our *differences*, on doing and observing, but also on feeling. I was drawn to Mars Venus coaching as a method, especially for its accessibility, positivity, and practicality, and I saw real results in my practice. Once I took on the role of a coach, my clients became more efficient at taking tangible and lasting benefits from their work with me. In my work as a Mars Venus coach, I find that my clients and I can more easily focus on the solution rather than fossilize the problem.

THE STORY OF MICHAEL, AN ATHLETE

After some persuasion from his friends, Michael came to me to be coached. He was shy, had extremely low self-esteem, was insecure, and had a complete lack of self-confidence. These issues were so debilitating that they were preventing him from reaching his full potential in his favorite sport: swimming. Michael was already a fantastic athlete, but his deep emotional problems were impeding his progress and growth, and stopping him from reaching his very attainable goals.

When I met Michael, he was twenty-seven years old. He appeared to be very self-deprecating; he felt that he was not good enough. As Michael's story unfolded, I discovered that his father was very overbearing; he had wanted him to become a champion swimmer, so he forced him to swim every day from the age of three. Michael, on the other hand, did not even want to swim; he would have far rather played football, but his father refused to allow him to play. Instead, Michael was forced to focus solely on swimming.

The result of his father's overbearing attitude was that Michael became an excellent swimmer and won many competitions, but he also became increasingly lonely and unhappy, to the point where he thought that his life was not worth living. Michael's real desires were to meet the right woman, to find a good job, and to eventually start a family, but he felt that these goals were unattainable due to his father's tyrannical hold over him.

One day Michael decided that he could not take it anymore and stopped swimming. His father was so angry that he stopped talking to him completely, and they ceased to have any kind of relationship. Michael gave up swimming competitively and began working at a swimming pool, teaching children to swim. It was at this point that he contacted me. Michael was happy with his decision to pass on his knowledge, yet he felt that he needed to conquer his feelings before he could find true happiness and contentment. He had three desires: to overcome his deep-rooted insecurity in order for him to know what his true goals in life were, to work toward these goals, and to feel satisfied with his life.

It was clear to me that Michael was suffering from a lack of self-esteem because as he was growing up, he had not received the love that a child should receive in order to feel self-worth, and if you do not receive love, you do not know how to give it—to yourself, or to anyone else. My strategy with Michael was to help him to reconnect with himself: his mind with his body, and his soul. I had to coach him in how to love himself deeply and sincerely, from the heart. I used the techniques of John Gray and taught Michael to focus on love and self-esteem while taking a balanced approach to life.

For example, in the book *What You Feel You Can Heal*, John Gray—through his experience in working with others to heal their pain—has found patterns and messages that many of us received while growing up. These messages can keep us from loving ourselves and from loving and receiving love from others. We all receive messages throughout our childhood that become ingrained in us. These include all of the teachings, mindsets, and beliefs that our parents in particular convey toward us. Whatever our parents teach us during childhood, they believe to be good and proper, and we agree with those teachings because we think with a child's mind. However, when we become adults, it is possible for us to change our ideas about those beliefs.

By exploring how these messages became ingrained in us while we were young and how we are using them in relationships today, we can change old patterns and thoughts about ourselves and others as well as create long-lasting, fulfilling relationships. John Gray tells us that, "Loving yourself in the presence of others means being able to express your inner gifts and talents without fear. When you don't love yourself and mask your real self, the cycle works in the opposite direction, decreasing love and true self expression."

It was of the greatest importance for me to help Michael to rebuild the relationship that he had with himself and to change this relationship from one of self-loathing to one of self-love. It was also important to build the necessary confidence in his own ability to dictate his future and to set his own personal goals, not those of his father. We had to start from his basic beliefs, rebuilding his self-esteem, his identity, and his personality. Once this was achieved, and Michael was surer of himself, he could be coached on achieving the goals that he set for himself.

As I worked with Michael, he learned to connect with himself with acceptance and, finally, with true love. He then began to talk about his true goals in life: what he desired for himself and the life that would help him achieve happiness. As the process took place, Michael allowed his true desires to have expression. He spoke about the fact that he wanted to continue his work at swimming pools, not as a swimmer, but as a coach, training adolescents. He realized that, as well as continuing to do this, his real life dream was to become the manager of his own swimming pool. Prior to our work together, he had not even allowed himself to entertain this thought due to his emotional crises.

I have been coaching Michael with great success and with much personal satisfaction because he was really motivated and focused on his life goals; he also had a real desire to change his life. Self motivation really is the number one element on which I begin coaching. If a person is not motivated, no matter how much anyone tries to help him/her, they will fail. The person has to truly want to change. Other people can help, but at the end of the day, it is up to you.

Michael is now a thirty-year-old man working as a sport coach in a very famous swimming pool, as well as striving toward his new project of managing his own swimming center.

THE STORY OF GEORGE, AN ADOLESCENT

George was an eighteen-year-old young man referred to me by his family members; every part of his life was a problem. From school to family, to friends, to relationships with girls; every part of his life was a mess. He was very unhappy with his life. He didn't enjoy spending time with friends or other people in general. He preferred to spend all his free time using computers, playing video games, or shopping online. He didn't like sports and had never had a girlfriend. Sometimes at home with his parents, he manifested problematic behaviors of anger. His family was overwhelmed with all his problems, and they did not know what else to do. Nothing was working, and they felt that they had failed him. When I first met George, it was obvious to me that he was living his life in ignorance of his situation: he was unhappy, yet he did not know what or how to change, or even that he needed to change. He was shy and insecure and had no sense of perspective.

George hated everything about himself; his body and his personality were, in his opinion, ugly and stupid. He believed he would never be worthy, interesting, or charismatic.

In my first meeting with George, I discovered that although his family provided him with many material things he wanted, they had never provided him with the *emotional* things he needed. The whole family suffered from frozen emotions; they were unable to love unconditionally, and they used money to fill this void. No one can survive on money alone, no matter how much they have. A child has to be taught how to love himself and others through the love shown to him as a child. If this love is not demonstrated, then the child will grow up without being able to show or feel deep true love for himself or anyone else and, at worst, live an unfulfilled and unhappy life.

As George's story unfolded, I learned that he had grown up in a world of privilege: his father was a very famous and wealthy businessman and his mother, as the wife of a wealthy man, had never needed to work, and so she lived a life of luxurious leisure. Both of George's parents believed that money was "all important" and that money could solve each and every problem in the whole world. As George had been brought up in this unhealthy household, he was like a spoiled child in the body of an eighteen-year-old man.

At first, George proved to be very resistant to working with me. Although he was deeply unhappy, he was, in a way, comfortable in his reassuring childish personality and did not understand why he needed to change. He believed that it was the job of others to make him happy; he did not think that he should have to work at anything because, in the past, he never had to. I had to make George realize that it was up to him to modify his reality, but in order to do so, I had to make him see a new road for his life that was congruous with his objectives, which, together, created a concrete plan of action for his future. I had to show George that he was wasting his life by thrashing about in anger and frustration at other people and continuing to act in a way that was not working for him.

George finally understood that his strategy for dealing with life was not working; therefore, he had to change it. At first, George's realization made him feel overwhelmed, so much so that he did not know how to proceed. At this point, George decided to put his trust in me and my ability to show him that he could lead a happy and fulfilling life. During our coaching sessions, talking about his life and his feelings without judgments, we discovered that George did indeed want to "be a man": to support himself, to be independent financially and emotionally, to travel, have meaningful relationships, and eventually to start his own family. The first step was the hardest one: changing the life that he had been leading for the last eighteen years. George moved out of the family home and found himself employment as a waiter in a good restaurant in Florence. Although George did not make great money at his job, he made enough to pay the rent for his new apartment.

The main methodology used by John Gray, which I used when coaching George, was creating a safe space of empathic listening where George could express his deepest feelings, those things he had never said aloud. Learning to listen to our needs and feelings is the first way to make ourselves free to choose things that can make us happy in life.

George was not used to sharing what he was feeling deep inside. Instead, he pushed those feelings down and used television or the Internet to make him feel better. By getting George to talk about himself, he discovered his feelings and his needs, which helped him create a fulfilling life. Finally, he discovered his power to listen to his needs and make them come true. Also, he discovered how to grow his hormone of wellness (testosterone) by learning the differences between men and women and their needs.

Having moved out of his parents' house, George realized that he did not need to be rich to feel fulfilled; he felt happy and free, actually enjoying his simple existence. The fact that he was supporting himself gave him his sense of self-worth; he no longer felt hopeless and unhappy. Coaching gave George the skills necessary to succeed in life and, more importantly, to live happily, without a lot of money. How did he do this? By respecting, loving, and believing in himself and in his personal resources. He was no longer hoping or trying to find external soothers; he was finally accepting of his limits and his capacities and therefore was able to recognize what could make him fulfilled in life and catch it.

THE STORY OF MR. AND MRS. Z, A COUPLE

Mr. and Mrs. Z came to me with their marriage in a state of crisis, which had been growing progressively worse. They were very busy at work, stressed out, and overwhelmed. They spent their days at work in a big company, and in the evening, when they returned home, they usually continued to read emails or work on projects.

Year after year, their ability to communicate became poorer and poorer. They were able to manage everything else in their lives, except their relationship. They were growing apart, and they had not been communicating effectively for some time, had stopped having sex, and were at the stage where they were no longer even talking to each other. This seemed to be an extremely difficult, if not impossible, case to solve; however, they had one redeeming factor: they were both motivated to change, if they could.

Mrs. Z explained to me that her husband did not seem to understand her or hear her needs, let alone meet them. Instead, he refused to help her manage the household; he was rude to her and showed her no warmth, love, affection, or appreciation. There was a complete lack of respect. As Mrs. Z was also a housewife, her primary job was to manage the house; however, she also needed to be viewed and appreciated as a woman, beautiful and worthy of her husband's care and affection. She felt very alone and isolated due to her position—not having a life outside the house—unlike her husband, who was employed outside of the home. Mrs. Z related that her husband spent more time outside the home with his colleagues, going out to dinner and staying out drinking, instead of spending quality time with her.

When I spoke to Mr. Z, he told me that he stayed out all the time rather than coming home because his wife was angry with him all the time. He could not understand why she was so rude and disrespectful to him; after all, he was working very hard to support them, to pay the bills and all their family expenses. He told me that he had never been unfaithful; he came home every night without fail and had done so ever since the first day of their marriage. What woman could want more than this? When he couldn't understand her anger at him, he reciprocated with his own.

The situation with this couple was as clear as day to me, and yet they couldn't see it. John Gray states that there are fundamental differences between men and women, in particular: "When men and women are able to respect and accept their differences then love has a chance to blossom."

The biggest problem with Mr. And Mrs. Z was, in fact, that the two partners were no longer able to express love to each other. They felt love deep inside, but they were not used to expressing it clearly. As John Gray says, love grows up when it receives love from the partner. You are able and happy to express love when you receive love. Love makes you become a better partner and a better person. In this couple, the two of them were no longer giving love, even if they actually loved each other.

I explained to them that men produce testosterone, which is the masculine hormone of happiness, when they feel needed, appreciated, and indispensable. Especially important for men is the physical manifestation of love: they need to connect physically in order to demonstrate the depth of their love. I also gave them "homework" to verify and train themselves on actualizing their potential. Conversely, women produce a different hormone of happiness, which is oxytocin; this hormone works well when women feel heard, understood, and cherished. Women feel loved and in love when their partners are emotionally present and caring. So, when this balance is out of sync, it is completely understandable that sexual relations and attraction cease.

Everything that we feel originates from our minds. If we are in balance within ourselves and satisfied with our lives, we love to be intimate with our partners because we are able to let love flow toward ourselves and them. According to their "mental structures" and culture, I suggest various activities or homework for couples, such as massaging each other, dancing (from tango to belly dancing), or conversation schemes (expression without judgment, etc.). On the other hand, if we are in a state of imbalance, we are not emotionally fulfilled, and we do not feel loved. As a result, we close our hearts to the world and become angry without understanding or knowing why.

Love is the motor of life: if it flows, everything is wonderful; if it doesn't flow, everything is painful. We need to learn to give love and receive love as well if we desire to be in balance with ourselves. As John Gray says, "Love brings up our unresolved feelings. One day we are feeling loved, and the next day we are suddenly afraid to trust love. The painful memories of being rejected begin to surface when we are faced with trusting and accepting our partner's love."

Gradually, day by day, we lose the most important relationship that we have in our lives. As John Gray teaches us, men realize their love for their partner when they connect with her physically, and women connect with their partner when they feel understood and heard. If we understand these simple principles, relationships are simple; everything becomes natural and not exhausting. Knowing these principles and working with them makes us unselfish, open-minded, and mentally flexible. We are able to lead a more fulfilled life because we not only understand ourselves better; we also understand the opposite sex.

I first coached Mr. and Mrs. Z to see how the differences in the way men and women think and feel were connected with anger, misunderstanding, and resentment. Neither one was communicating to the other in the right way or by using the right words. They had to learn the importance of words and how to use them effectively. They needed to realize and to stop living their lives in silence, absence, and anger, and instead spend more time together—physically and emotionally. After that, they had to stop working at home and spending their free time in front of a PC. They also had to rediscover their emotional and physical intimacy, their time together, their hobbies together.

By coaching them, with these principles to guide them, by teaching them to talk, to listen to each other, and to be generous with their partner, they became more flexible, open-minded, and no longer judgmental toward the opposite sex. I coached Mr. and Mrs. Z for six months, and in that time they exceeded all my expectations.

WINNER STRATEGIES

John Gray's Mars Venus methodologies are winner strategies; they are so simple and clear to understand. I think that sometimes the right choices and the right strategies are the simpler ones. In today's world, everything is about appearance and superficiality. Because of this, people are desperately looking for humanity, emotions, and truth. I think I have realized that my main mission, as a coach, is to inspire my clients in having these kinds of objectives.

Being a Mars Venus coach makes you more capable of understanding true love for others and, consequently, more capable of helping people love themselves, their partners, their family, and their jobs. If you are inspired by true love for yourself and for life, you will be a winner in anything you do, because you are capable of using your resources in the best way, achieving your goals, and, at the same time, being humble.

If we understand and respect gender differences, we will increase in our clients the possibility of developing more harmonious relationships with their partners. The key, the secret to living a rewarding life, is to accept, respect, and appreciate our partners' natural differences. In doing so, we stop trying to change other people, and we grow to love our differences because we aren't looking at them as "defects" but as precious and miraculous features.

WE CAN SHINE FROM WITHIN

— NISSARA CHITWARAKORN —

In 2020, **Dr. Nissara Chitwarakorn** became the first Thai coach to be certified under the Mars Venus program. As a practicing dermatologist, she is accustomed to using her medical knowledge to treat patients' ailments. But as a coach, she appreciates using powerful questions and inspiring words to challenge clients' awareness and beliefs.

She discovered coaching in 2015 after attending an event in Thailand. Since then, her life has never been the same. After completing several programs, she began her coaching career and has since helped countless people change their lives for the better. With each client and coaching moment, Nissara's own life grows, and she strives to remind everyone she meets that "We can shine from within."

ONE RELATIONSHIP AT A TIME

I grew up in a very warm family. My father was a doctor, and my mother was a pharmacist. Of course, they expected me to study hard so I'd have good opportunities in life. My parents and other family members always supported and inspired me to do my best. One of my aunts was especially influential. She always offered unconditional love to the people around her and never hesitated to tell me that I'm special. Her compliments made me feel confident. I admired her very much.

Due to my supportive upbringing, I always believed that I could do whatever I put my mind to. I bring the same style of support to my coaching, empowering clients with compliments and helping them realize their own value and self-worth. When you focus on sharing whatever you can to make the world a better place, you suddenly notice big positive changes in your life. Coaching often impacts me as much—if not more—than it does my clients.

In my view, sickness is one of the most painful parts of life, which is why I decided to study medicine. My goal has always been to help humankind by improving the quality of people's lives in any way I can. After I completed a postgraduate program in dermatology, I worked at a public hospital during the week and attended seminars on weekends. Some of these events, particularly the coaching programs, took me on new journeys and transformed my life. When I first began working at the hospital, I said to myself, "I'll always do my best to help my patients." Even though skin diseases aren't usually life-threatening, they can impact a person's quality of life. During my eight years as a dermatologist, I've served many patients and helped them live better lives.

Dr. John Gray's book, *Men Are from Mars, Women Are from Venus*, is famous in Thailand, and I read it many years ago. When I started running my own coaching workshops, a friend recommended another book to me: *Mars and Venus on a Date*. I'd never come across the book before, but I soon realized how important the material was for anyone in the dating world. As I continued to explore John Gray's work, I discovered the Mars Venus Coaching program online, and the company motto instantly caught my attention: "Mars Venus Coaching is changing the world . . . one relationship at a time."

Sometimes, someone or something comes into your life, and you know it's meant to be. That's how I feel about coaching. I consider the quality of relationships to be the most important part of our lives, so learning the Mars Venus motto sent a bell ringing in my head. But how can coaching change the world?

I received my answer after I completed training and began working with clients. When I assist people with the deeper aspects of their relationships, they become happier, and our beautiful world becomes filled with happy people. If you consider someone to be a role model, that person has likely brought great value to your life. That's how I feel about Mars Venus Coaching—it's my role model. I truly believe that I've found my calling, the thing I'll do until my last day, and I fully intend to change the world, one relationship at a time.

CREATING RIPPLES THROUGH COACHING

One of my clients, a 37-year-old single woman, decided she was ready for a long-term relationship. She understood the value of coaching and wanted some guidance before taking such a major step in her life. After our first session, she invited me to be her personal coach and help her find her dream partner.

So, we got to work.

During the following sessions, we focused on improving her self-confidence, and she quickly learned how to build herself up. Soon, she attracted a new guy, and they began a relationship together. Even though they broke up later, my client learned a lot from the experience and grew more confident when it came to navigating the dating world.

In our last session, she said that she was in a great new relationship with an amazing guy. Curiously, she'd met her new partner in a coaching class I'd recommended. I still remember how happy she was, and her smile is always in my mind. Every time I think about how much I love coaching, I recall this experience, and I consider the big impact a coach can have in someone's life. Recently, I had another conversation with my former client, and she informed me that the relationship was still going great and she was now on a journey to becoming a coach herself—amazing! The impact of coaching often creates a ripple effect that expands indefinitely and touches everyone in its path.

LET YOUR HAPPINESS SHINE

I've had some tough experiences with love, which is why I wanted to be a dating coach.

After my first love relationship ended, I had a difficult time bringing my best self back. Luckily, this was around the time I first discovered coaching. I began practicing the techniques I'd learned and focused on self-empowerment, which produced a noticeable change in my life. However, growth doesn't come quickly or without effort.

I was young at the time—in my twenties—and I still had a lot to learn about life and relationships. After the relationship ended, I realized the importance of self-love. When you rush into a relationship and don't love yourself enough, you create a difficult situation. At that time, I was always trying to impress other people, but I never gave myself the attention I needed. Although the experience was difficult, the lessons learned during that time have been invaluable.

Some people who've had experiences like mine refuse to fall in love again, but I don't feel that way. I'm much more optimistic than that. The dating world is an exciting place, and I'm hopeful for the future. Coaching is a key component of the positivity I feel.

I believe that everyone needs a coach, and the benefits I've gained from both coaching and being coached strengthen my desire to help others who might be struggling. Additionally, through my own personal experiences, I'm able to better understand the plights of others as they attempt to navigate life and relationships. As a dermatologist, a lot of people come to me because they want to be more good-looking. I always say, "When you're happy on the inside, your happiness will shine out for everyone to see." True outer beauty begins within. I frequently tell my clients, "You should be proud of yourself. You don't need to compare yourself to others—just be the best version of *you*."

BEFORE THE JOURNEY BEGINS, KNOW YOUR DESTINATION

I'm here to help others find and fall in love. That's my mission. That's my purpose in life. In every relationship, if you take care of others in the same way you would yourself, you'll face very few problems. I base my principles on self-esteem and self-acceptance, and I believe that everyone is special in their own way. When I help bring clients into their best self state, they attain ideal outcomes in both relationships and life.

Cultivating a positive mindset takes work. When my clients struggle with negative thoughts, I encourage them to acknowledge those ideas, write them down, and replace them with something better. I also suggest that they use positive words or phrases for self-affirmation each morning. Starting your day on a good note is important and will positively affect everything that happens after.

My philosophy on coaching and life is:
- Everyone deserves a great love.
- Having a good relationship isn't difficult when you know the right principles.
- Do everything for others in the way that your best friend would for you.
- Know how to ask powerful questions.
- As your inner world changes, the world around you will also change.
- Love relationships are one of the most important factors in the wheel of life.

I firmly believe that the quality of our relationships affects our quality of life, which is why I pour so much passion into helping my clients find and fall in love. I guide them to realize that they already have everything they need to achieve their dreams. The greatest enemy you'll ever face on your quest for success is yourself. If you don't believe in and love yourself, your mindset can negatively affect your life and relationships. My job as a coach is to offer accountability and support to my clients and to help them manage their thoughts. If we can fine-tune their beliefs in positive ways, everything else gets easier.

When I help clients who are ready to seek fulfilling relationships, we must first build a strong foundation for love. The process consists of three steps that harness the principles of self-esteem and self-acceptance:
1. When people are willingly single, it often relates to the principles described. Helping clients realize this is the first step to progress.
2. Next, they must decide the partner identity that will best suit them, their personality, and their needs.
3. Finally, for lifelong happiness, they must learn how to keep their relationship in flow.

As a dating coach, facilitating these steps is my core responsibility. I believe in the principles mentioned, and I integrate the same ideas into my own life. Growth is a lifelong process, and I'm committed to practicing the techniques I teach so I can better relate them to my clients.

Through my coaching, I hope to make the world a better place, one relationship at a time. The secret to being a great—and not just a good— dating coach is to build positive attitudes around dating and help clients create momentum from the very first moment they meet a potential partner. In other words, a coach should help people keep their relationships fresh, fun, and filled with desire. When couples are able to maintain momentum, lasting relationships are possible.

As well as coaching clients around dating, I'm committed to doing my best in my own love life. I wish to give myself what I deliver to others and develop exceptional, long-lasting relationships that leave me happy and fulfilled. With enough work, everyone can have the life experience they deserve. The path to any lofty goal holds countless pitfalls and challenges. Journeys of great discovery and growth were never meant to be easy. If they were, the rewards would be much less precious and pronounced.

When you want to go somewhere, you must first make a firm decision about your destination. If you can't decide exactly where you're going, you'll never get anywhere. Next, you must focus on how to get to that place and consider all of the avenues available. Only after you've made your plans and mapped your journey can you start moving towards your destination. You should, of course, frequently review your progress and make any necessary adjustments along the way. Sometimes you may need to repeat some steps or change the process altogether. However, if you take the right steps, you'll eventually arrive exactly where you want to be.

Lastly, as I always remind everyone, "We can shine from within." It means I believe that each of us can take part in shaping the world in the way we're meant to. Personally, I'd love to shape the world with my coaching and create wonderful couples and lasting relationships. In other words, I'll use true love to make the world a better place.

THE GREATEST GIFT YOU CAN GIVE YOURSELF

— ERIC LANTHIER —

Eric Lanthier is a chaplain and Mars Venus coach. Previously, he discussed current events on social networks and various written and spoken platforms. He has also hosted shows on multiple radio stations and writes articles for the French pages of the Prince Arthur Herald, HuffPost Quebec, and Quebec Nouvelles. Now, he's sharing gender intelligence principles on three radio stations and on social media.

Over the years, Eric has supported several causes, founded non-profit organizations, and gotten involved in politics. He holds degrees in education, school administration, writing, social communications, and pastoral theology. He's reachable via several avenues, including his website.

AN ARTIST WITH A BLANK CANVAS

Growing up, I was always the artist in the family. I played bass, performed in theaters, and was even part of an improv group. As a teenager, I wrote poems. Often, I'd sit at the bar writing on paper napkins, and my friends would laugh at me. But I loved to write. At the turn of the century, I took a writing class, and a coach helped me improve my craft.

As I journeyed through life, I thought I was on the right path until a dramatic, realityshattering event changed everything. My wife had been in a deep depression for many months. The problem began in November 2012 and on April 6, 2013, she took her life. Losing my wife was the greatest tragedy I'd ever experienced. After her suicide, I knew I had to establish an identity outside of her. We'd been married for twenty-five years, and now I had to find myself while facing a very challenging situation. At that point, losing anything else— my house, my possessions, my reputation—would've meant nothing because I'd already lost what I valued most in life: my wife.

She'd always been a good listener and was adept at getting people to talk. But when it came to us, she found our relationship difficult because I wasn't connected to my emotions. Following her death, I went to therapy, changed the vision I held of myself and reality, and begun to connect more with my emotions. Due to this adjustment, I was also able to connect more with the emotions of others and ask better questions. Instead of saying, "What do you think about that?" I'd ask, "How do you feel about that?" I tried to express more emotional rather than rational speech, and this change in communication allowed me to create more of an impact. As I developed a deeper understanding, I realized that the true challenges we face are more emotional than rational. Energy is always fueled by emotion and when someone feels overwhelmed, they struggle to perform and make the changes needed to succeed. It's why I always encourage my clients to discuss their emotions. When they do, they leave with a smile. They feel reenergized. They have renewed hope. Such achievements are very precious to me and if I'm able to help someone attain a better quality of life, I've done my duty as a coach.

Following my wife's death, I realized that I was alone and that my life was now a blank canvas. I was as free as a bird and could go anywhere and do anything I wanted. Freedom is fun, but it can also be scary. Having too many options overwhelms us and prevents us from moving forward. But I didn't let fear of the future paralyze me. Instead, I went back to school and got a certificate in communications so I could start a career in radio. I also began writing a book, which I've almost completed, about my wife's battle with anxiety and depression. When it's finished, I'll write a second book about life after death that discusses how I dealt with the challenge of losing someone so close to me. I'll also discuss the gratitude I have for being able to start life over again. I'm now remarried, and I've recently become a grandfather. My purpose when writing these books is to give hope to people who've lost someone to suicide because, as a survivor of that tragedy, we have an experience to share.

WHEN COACHING COMES NATURALLY

Before discovering Mars Venus, I'd already been coaching for over thirty years, helping teachers, church leaders, and entrepreneurs. Coaching, however, wasn't my primary focus. Even so, after every session, I returned to the office with a zest for life. Coaching felt natural to me, and, eventually, I decided that's what I wanted to do for a living. I knew I was missing the tools I needed to be more efficient, refined, and insightful. I was already a good listener, but I was sure I could do more, so I began exploring relevant resources to enhance my skills. Initially, I failed to find exactly what I was looking for, but a conversation with one of my radio colleagues quickly changed that.

Strangely enough, I was on her show explaining the differences between men and women in the workplace. She had her own coaching business, which was blossoming, and I wanted to dive into a similar venture. The questions she proceeded to ask brought instant clarity to my mind: "What is your niche? Who would you like to reach? What makes you different from other coaches?" From that moment on, the answer was clear. I wanted to reach singles, couples, and families. At that point, I knew that I needed a coaching school that specialized in gender intelligence. Without hesitation, I consulted the Mars Venus website to learn more about what the organization could offer. Eventually, I contacted the Mars Venus Coaching office to gather additional information about the program, how to enroll, and what opportunities would be available once I graduated. After talking to Richard Bernstein, the CEO of the company, I knew I'd found my place. I understood immediately that Mars Venus was an organization that had a genuine desire to see couples walk hand in hand to happiness and success. How did I know this? Because Rich wanted to talk to my wife to see if I had what it took to be a coach and to ensure that she was one-hundred-percent behind me on this new venture.

I did, of course, have what it takes, and my wife, thankfully, completely backed my decision. Once I'd been accepted into the program, I completed life and business coaching training with Rich, who gave me the exact tools I needed to work more efficiently with my clients. Before, I'd have to listen to someone for several hours to find that crucial connection needed to help them. Now, I have the sharpest tools available, know how to ask the right questions, and can discover critical information much quicker. With the help of the Mars Venus methods, I've been able to fast-track the coaching process, which means I can help more clients in a shorter amount of time.

The techniques I learned are simple to understand, easy to explain, effortless to use, and, above all, very powerful. The Mars Venus tools help to clarify a client's state of mind, identify blockages, and understand fundamental needs. Thanks to the principles of gender intelligence, we're able to adapt our vocabulary and approach each challenge according to the client, their gender, and their gender energy. The beauty of these tools is that they're not static. Each person's journey is different, and the Mars Venus methods allow us to identify which approach is relevant at any given time. I try to discern which technique will most effectively move the client forward and which will bring clarity. Having the right tools and knowing when to use them makes all the difference.

In truth, a coach's greatest asset is his own coach. Even when I'm away on holiday, I never miss my weekly sessions with Rich. His wisdom is invaluable and helps save a lot of precious time. Before my wife died, I thought that being accountable to a coach and therapy were punishments, something you underwent when you'd done something wrong. But now I believe in coaching wholeheartedly. It's a gift I give to myself. It's a chance for me to grow, to become a better person, and to live a better life. Many of us enjoy a massage because it feels great. But coaching is a massage for the heart, and the benefits are undeniable.

REVIVING CONNECTIONS, RELIGHTING FIRES

My first Mars Venus client discovered me on my radio show when I was using John Gray's material to discuss relationships, parenthood, and business. One day, a woman called, wanting to hire me as a coach. She was seventy years old and planned to divorce her husband after forty years of marriage. The retired couple had fallen out of love, seemed to be living separate lives, and life itself had become stagnant and boring.

I agreed to coach her, and we created a ninety-day plan together—but she didn't need that long. After just two months, she'd fallen back in love with her husband, and he felt the same renewed feelings of affection for her. During our time together, I coached her on how to show him that he occupied a great place in her heart. I also showed her how to make him feel valuable and how to express her feelings with more than words. Before, the husband would work alone in his garage all day, but he began stopping at around 10am to have a coffee with his wife, to talk, and to listen to what she had to say. They'd completely revived their connection and their relationship. That was a proud moment for me because she was my first client, and, with the help of the Mars Venus methods, I became the instrument that reconnected them and relit their fire. Love returned for the couple in a deep way, and to begin my coaching career with such a significant victory was incredible.

My approach to coaching focuses on listening and intuition. During a session, I try to get the client to talk a lot so I can discern their real needs. People hire coaches because they want to change something and develop a better state of mind, stronger relationships, or advance their careers. The change they seek—and the one they truly need—always relates to who they are, and listening is the only way to discover a true connection. Hearing isn't enough; you must listen carefully and connect the dots. When I discern an important connection, I ask questions, let the client talk, and keep listening until we unearth a deeper truth.

When I coach, my clients know that I'm concerned and aware. They often tell me I'm a good sounding board and when we uncover critical information, they say things like, "Wow, how did you figure that out?"

My response is always the same: "You gave me the answer. I simply listened." I'm very patient with people, and clients often feel like they can tell me anything. I always take notes so I can use their own wording to clarify a point or return to an idea. While I might understand something in my terms, being able to use their words helps with clarity.

Since my initial coaching success, I've helped many more clients using the Mars Venus methods. With each encounter, we experience an indescribable emotional connection. I've witnessed how truth frees us from the lies and false beliefs that prevent us from growing. The testimony of one person stands, as it touched me deeply. A client of mine felt bad about inviting people to get involved in her business. Her main concern was that the enterprise wasn't as successful as she wanted it to be, so I asked her, "Why are you involved in this business if the income isn't what you expect?"

She said, "It's because on a personal, relational, and emotional level, I'm enriched. Working in this company contributes to my enrichment."

"There's your message!" I said. By listening, I'd discerned the solution to her problem. I could see that she needed a little more meat around the bone, so I added, "Why don't you go out and recruit people who're looking for a work environment that contributes to their personal, relational, and emotional development? If that's how they can be enriched, why not invest in that avenue?" Her eyes sparkled like never before. The key was there all along; she just needed someone to offer a new perspective. The beauty of coaching is that it activates hindsight more quickly. In one conversation, we can save days, weeks, months, and sometimes years of reflection, because we often lack perspective. Discussing a problem reconfigures the elements that comprise the present and directs us to a more fruitful future.

THE GIFT OF COACHING

John Gray's material is powerful because it touches on the reality of life and relationships. Although he wrote his first book decades ago, the material is still relevant, down to earth, and life-changing. The Mars Venus methods have helped me become a great coach, and I'm thankful for John's dedication to the concept of gender intelligence. Do you know why I believe in the principles so strongly? Because when I applied them to my own marriage, they worked, and I continue to see them work for my clients.

A good coach is swift to hear but slow to speak. The more I listen, the more I'm able to detect red flags, contradictions, and those all-important golden nuggets. My philosophy is one of consistency and nonjudgment. When my clients feel that I'm not judging their beliefs or values, they're open to sharing what they're experiencing with great authenticity. I firmly believe that a nonjudgmental environment allows us to express what exists deep inside. The truth sets us free and for it to be expressed, the client must feel safe. I've had people confess things that are deeply intimate because they don't feel judged. I never try to put people in boxes. I'm there to guide them to an awareness of what they require to move forward and grow. I don't do anything magical. I listen carefully, ask questions, take notes, and keep silent at the right times. Coaching is like art. In both cases, to achieve a harmonious result, we need inspiration, intuition, and the tools to support this work.

As strange as it may sound, a coach's purpose isn't to offer miracle solutions. He's there to help clarify the present. The more someone becomes aware of the real challenges they face, the better they can understand where they are, how they got there, and where they're going. When they feel that they're heading in the right direction, nothing can stop them. Coaching is a source of vitality for me because it facilitates a connection with the truest parts of people. This connection is what gives me so much depth in my media communications, and, if you're interested, most of my interventions are available on my website.

I believe that everyone should hire a coach at least every five years. Sometimes, routine can cripple us, cause stagnation, and stunt our growth. In order to live significant lives, we must change habits, seek truths, and alter reality. But doing these things takes courage, and coaching grants us the strength and energy needed to accept the challenges we must. A coaching session is one of the greatest gifts you can give to yourself, and it's a gift that everyone deserves.

The French version of this chapter is available at:
https://ericlanthier.net/le-plus-beaucadeau-que-
vous-puissiez-vous-offrir

INFORMATION LEADS TO TRANSFORMATION

— MK MUELLER —

Mars Venus relationships coach and award-winning author **MK Mueller** is a TEDx speaker and internationally respected authority on communication and attitude transformation. She has written several books for adults based on her 8-step process, including *8 to Great: The Powerful Process for Positive Change* and *Taking Care of Me: The Habits of Happiness*. She has also created one of the top programs in the country for middle school and high school students entitled: 8 to Great for Your Best Life Adventure: The Road to Respect, Responsibility and Resilience.

Today her 8 to Great® process for greater happiness and success is taught world-wide by over 3000 life coaches, business leaders, and educators. A big believer in giving back, she was named a Heartland Hero for her service to at-risk families while living in the Midwest. Now she continues to give keynotes and work with schools and businesses to certify coaches in her *8 to Great*® program from her headquarters in Southwest Florida.

A LONG AND WINDING ROAD TO MARS VENUS

Looking back, my journey to coaching began at age thirty-four when I entered a women's shelter for victims of domestic violence. I had gotten married at twenty-seven years old, and everyone told me that marriage would be hard, so I wasn't surprised when problems arose. I know now that my situation was unusually difficult, but, at the time, I kept telling myself, "I have to make a go of it."

Although I had dated some wonderful guys in my twenties, my low self-esteem led me to choose a spouse who was suffering from his own low self-esteem issues. During our marriage, I received little if any affirmation or acknowledgement. I remember living in fear of criticism, anger, and rage. At the time, I was a successful teacher, speech coach, and song leader at my church, and on the outside my life looked happy. When the verbal abuse turned physical, I left home with our three-year-old daughter to seek refuge at a women's shelter.

I learned a lot from the counselors there, and I grew to understand that I needed to change myself if I wanted to avoid attracting the same situation in the future. One of my favorite quotes from John's Mars Venus books is, "You cannot, nor should you ever try to, change your partner. That is his or her job. Your job is to change the ways you react and respond to your partner."

The women at that shelter helped me see that I had never learned to take care of myself as well as I had others. I saw that in order to show up for others, you have to invest in yourself. I gained the confidence to say, "No, I won't be doing that, but thank you for asking." I also changed my self-talk from "I should" to "I could" and "I can't" to "I haven't yet." During my time at the shelter, I came up with a theory that I've now taught for forty years: although I was flawed, we are all **half-jerk and half-jewel.** I saw that for every weakness in a person, there is also a strength, and vice versa.

For example, my weaknesses in organization, which I regularly berated myself for, were connected to my gift of being a right-brained creative. I was the type of person who was better at coming up with new ideas and starting things rather than being the left-brained analyst or finisher. I saw that creativity was as important a gift as being linear and logical.

Growing awareness of concepts like these allowed my self-esteem to rise to a healthier level. Unfortunately, the shelter did not teach me how to stop "giving" all the time. I had been giving and doing more, thinking that would "make" him happy. Now, thanks to John's teachings, I realize that I had not yet learned to be a grateful receiver. While I am not condoning verbal or physical violence in a relationship in any form, and now spend my life working to help people communicate in a peaceful and loving manner, I can see that both of us were missing key skills that healthy relationships require.

After I left the shelter and filed for divorce, I started reading everything I could get my hands on to understand more about the balance between self-care and care for others. I started a support group with six neighbors I called "Taking Care of Me," which soon grew to twenty women gathered in my home each week. To accommodate the expanding group, I held classes in church basements and libraries, and soon I was receiving invitations to speak at businesses and women's conferences. The result was that within three years, I became a sought-after national and then international seminar presenter and keynote speaker.

Unfortunately, I continued to overgive to my job, to my kids as a single mom, and to my dating relationships. I longed to receive all the love and attention I was giving to whatever man I was dating, but found that instead of getting more as I gave more, he would eventually walk away, only to come back months or years later saying he had made the worst mistake of his life. By then, I had always moved on.

When I took the Mars Venus course, I'd already been coaching for thirty years, yet I wanted John's specific set of skills, not only for my personal growth, but for couples who came to me for help. Sometimes they had been together for twenty years or more and were desperate for my coaching. I would always let them know I was not married, but most had read my books and wanted me to coach them anyway. Now, after becoming accredited with Mars Venus, I'm more comfortable and confident, and so are the couples I help.

I believe John's teachings are crucial for all couples and should be reread every decade for a refresher. You think you get it the first time; however, as life evolves, this material becomes newly vital and applicable. Today I'm passionate about helping people understand how men, who are stronger in testosterone, and women, who are stronger in estrogen, think and act differently. Meanwhile, this understanding has greatly enhanced my own relationships.

I recall an evening when my gentleman friend got very quiet after I shared something emotional. In the past, this reaction might have upset me, but now I know that he was just taking time to process what I'd said. Two minutes later, when he started to change the subject, I gently invited him to first reply to my previous statement, with no judgment on my part.

"What did you think about what I said?" I asked. We ended up having a great conversation, and I explained that it would mean a lot to me if he would share his reaction out loud when I share something that personal, and not just stay in his head. He agreed, and the problem hasn't repeated. It's a basic Mars Venus concept, but asking without judgment is such a powerful tool. My partner didn't fail to respond to my emotional statement because he was being rude; high testosterone men just process things differently. Understanding concepts like these can save a lot of frustration in our relationships.

RECOGNIZING PATTERNS

As a life coach of thirty years, I've learned a great deal about how relationships work. By observing both unhappy and happy individuals along with couples, year after year, I began to recognize the common factors in both groups. When I started John's course, there were patterns in my own dating relationships that I couldn't explain, like the one I mentioned about how loving men would leave abruptly for seemingly no reason.

In the beginning of my relationships, my partners would have an all-in attitude. They would even buy a new car they thought I'd like better, or a new home, or plan a trip to Paris for us. However, down the road—and usually out of the blue—they'd suddenly decide they were out. I'd be stunned and confused, wondering what had happened. After leaving without warning or even giving me a reason, one man tried desperately to rekindle our relationship for weeks, and ended up banging on my door at five in the morning. He was a good dad and a successful businessman, and I couldn't understand his inappropriate behavior. I let him know I'd have to call the police if he continued. He never came back, but the incident shook me, and I didn't date again for years.

When I did finally begin another relationship, the same pattern emerged. The next man I dated was a kind, healthy, successful guy with good friends and happy kids, but he pulled the same sudden vanishing act. Shortly thereafter, right on cue, I received a fifteen-paragraph text begging me to take him back. At the time, I felt I couldn't trust someone who walked away at the first sign of a challenge, and we went our separate ways.

Once I noticed this pattern in my own life, I began to see it in the lives of others. One day I found myself sitting beside a woman on a plane, and she shared that she'd been happily married for ten years. I replied, "May I ask you a question?" She nodded. "I'm just curious if while you two were dating, did he ever leave or break up with you without warning?"

"Oh, yeah," she replied. "Let me tell you all about it . . ." As it turned out, it wasn't just me. A lot of women had a similar story. I had to find out why the phenomenon occurred.

During my research, I looked over my vast library of relationship books and realized the one I was the least familiar with was John Gray's original, *Men Are from Mars, Women Are from Venus*. I brushed off two decades of dust and sat down with the book again, only to feel like I'd never read it at all. I'm so grateful for John's timeless insights, which have helped me and my clients see the opposite sex with new eyes. Thanks to his material, I can now see those patterns that plagued me for what they are: a normal part of a relationship.

In addition, I can now help women recognize the "rubber band" chain of events that many men exhibit during the dating cycle. I coach women to see that while we all have both testosterone and estrogen hormones, we function best as women when we are higher in estrogen, and men function best when they are significantly higher in testosterone. The challenge happens when men get romantically involved. Due to their increased feelings of tenderness and closeness, their estrogen can soar, resulting in lower testosterone levels. Unfortunately, these givers may believe that their resulting decreased energy and lack of sexual interest are about *her* rather than about their own need to step back and rebuild their testosterone.

This concept helps my female/receiver clients realize that a giver's distancing isn't a personal rejection but simply a need for time apart from romance to revive their testosterone and start missing her again. Then, as John taught me, when the man returns, he usually exhibits all the love and devotion she was hoping for, as long as she doesn't punish him for taking time away. This concept has been a game changer for women like me who have been caught off-guard in the past.

SUPPLEMENTING WITH MARS VENUS

After writing five books and certifying thousands of life coaches in my eight-step process, the Mars Venus concepts continue to add new pieces to the puzzle and help me see the bigger picture. I have integrated John's communication insights and skills into every aspect of my work, even adding a section to my **8 to Great**® high school curriculum. I realized that understanding how our emotions and behaviors can both impact and be impacted by our hormones was information that could be taught as soon as dating begins.

> *"In a romantic relationship we are primarily either the Giver (higher testosterone) or the Receiver (higher estrogen). People, like magnets, are sexually attracted when they're facing the opposite direction. When we get out of balance hormonally with our truest selves, it can result in low energy, low libido, and even depression."*
> **Mars Venus**

Since rereading John's books, I've loved celebrating the receiver in me. For most of my adult life, I was a leader, in charge of my growing business, countless committees, and our little family. In other words, my days were full of high testosterone activities. I loved my life, but I didn't realize that it was impacting my relationships when I didn't allow my estrogen to rebuild with softer, sweeter, and more self-nurturing behaviors.

I also felt that I needed to give back to men as much as they gave to me in order to let them know that I appreciated them. Now I realize that givers want to know that their gift has been gratefully appreciated, and that always giving something back in return can dampen their enthusiasm and lower their testosterone. What a difference this simple concept has made for me!

MY MOTHER-SON RELATIONSHIP SHIFT

"Men are single-focused. Women are multi-focused."
Mars Venus

One of my favorite examples of John's impact on my life involves my son. He came to live with me for a short time during Covid, and I was so grateful for his company and the lessons he taught me. I recall one day when he entered the kitchen from his office area in my home, carrying an empty glass.

When he opened the dishwasher, he saw that the dishes were clean. I was working nearby, so he remarked, "Oh, these are clean?"

"Yes," I replied. "I haven't gotten around to unloading them yet."

"Okay," he said, as he placed the dirty glass on the counter and closed the dishwasher door. At first, I was ready to judge and interrogate him. Instead, I used my new insights and realized he was still in "work mode." I also remembered to use "Would you" rather than "Could you" and asked if he *would* have time to unload the dishes.

"Oh, sure," he replied. Three minutes later he was finished and had put the dirty glass on the dishwasher rack.

"I really appreciate that," I said when he let me know it was completed. He just nodded and went back to work. That one insight saved us from conflict then and many more unnecessary future confrontations, growing my appreciation for my son and for these skills.

"Always assume love."
Mars Venus

Julie, one of my coaching clients, shared how this powerful concept of "assume love" caused her to do a 180 in a situation that could've threatened her budding relationship.

"I had been dating my boyfriend for about a month when he decided to have an afternoon lawn party. He lives on a cul-de-sac and invited his neighbors to bring their lawn chairs and listen to his friends' jazz quartet perform on his driveway.

"It was perfect weather, and he and I had spent the morning setting everything up. A few hours before the party was to begin, we went for a walk. I remember feeling so comfortable and happy just being around him. From that romantic high, I broached a subject that was very important to me. I said, 'Since I'll be meeting lots of folks today, when people ask me how I know you, what should I say?'"

"Oh, pickleball partners, of course," he quickly replied. "Doesn't that make sense?"

At that moment, Julie said she felt her heart shut down. She immediately jumped to the conclusion that he didn't see them as a long-term relationship. But after they walked in silence for a few minutes, she remembered me coaching her to "Assume love." She took a deep breath and decided to ask one more question.

"I can understand that you're not ready to let your neighbors know we're dating so—"

"What?" he interrupted. "Of course I want them to know we're dating. I'm anxious for them all to meet you!"

At this point, she explained to him how his first response had sounded. He apologized profusely for being "Clueless" and, that afternoon, introduced her to all the guests as "My girlfriend." After everyone had left, he showed her a letter of acceptance from a major university for a master's degree program out-of-state.

"I'm not going to do it now because I don't want to be away from you for twelve weeks," he shared. "I'm crazy about you."

Julie is so grateful for the lessons of Mars Venus that helped her keep her heart open to love.

COUPLES WHO PLAY TOGETHER . . .

After getting certified in Mars Venus gender intelligence, I couldn't wait to share the information I'd learned, so I created an online class, "A Course in Loving." Throughout the program, I watched as John's simple yet powerful concepts made a significant difference for couples who were struggling, and enhanced relationships that were thriving.

After the third group had completed the class, I recognized a pattern. Couples were following the best practices for communication, and finding life-changing benefits, but they were often forgetting the FUN Factor. Since being playful is essential to romance, overall mental health, and hormonal balance, I added a section to the course entitled, "Couples Who Play Together: 101 Ways to Improve Your Love Laugh." It was a huge hit, and I look forward to publishing it as a couples' resource soon. Here are fifteen of the 101 ways:

PHASE 1: Getting to Know You

1. Play pool or ping pong or darts indoors.
2. Play bocce or corn hole or frisbee golf outdoors.
3. Attend a paint-and-sip class or a cooking class or a lecture together.
4. Sing karaoke or drive go-karts or go line dancing.
5. Visit a botanical garden or a zoo or an aquarium.

PHASE 2: Upping the Risks and Rewards

1. Fly in a hot air balloon or go parasailing or go skydiving indoors with iFLY.
2. Play rock-paper-scissors, arm wrestle, or thumb war to make a decision.
3. Share some of your most embarrassing moments with each other.
4. Test drive a Tesla or a Corvette or rent a convertible for the day.
5. Go on a murder mystery train, to an escape room, or create a fun scavenger hunt and invite other couples to join you.

PHASE 3: Intimacy Games for the Fun and Frisky

1. Get a couples' massage or go to a sauna or enjoy a hot tub.
2. Go to a Bed and Breakfast and make the host believe it's your first date or meet each other in a bar assuming new identities and try to pick each other up.
3. Go on a dinner date without wearing underwear and exploit that fact.
4. Clean house together naked or just wearing one article of clothing chosen by your partner.

5. Have a YES ONLY rule to her/his requests for half an hour each of your date.

I'm offering my **"Couples Who Play Together: 101 Ways to Improve Your Love Laugh"** list to couples who want to bring some extra fun into their relationships. For your copy, email me at info@8togreat.com. I'll send it your way and add you to our mailing list for even more fun ideas.

BECOMING HAPPY AND THEN HAPPIER

One of my favorite teachings from John is that a romantic relationship can't make you happy, only happier. He is clear that we are the ones responsible for our own happiness. I believe that is why my books and his are great complements for each other. Mine are about the process anyone can use to move from a general unhappiness to happiness and from despair to hope. His are about how to be happier through a loving relationship.

As I mentioned in my TEDx talk, in every moment we have something we could complain about, but we also have something for which we could be grateful. Which of those we choose to focus on most often will decide our level of happiness and success in life. I'm so grateful not only for getting to use this 8-step process myself, but for being able to share it with my clients and audiences year after year, watching the powerful transformations that result.

I have seen shifts occur in the lives of CEOs on cruise ships and in young adults behind bars. Every so often one of my readers or former audience members will stop me in the street. "You probably don't remember me," they'll say, "but you changed my life." I love to remind them that when the student is ready, the teacher will appear—and they were ready.

I titled this chapter "Information Leads to Transformation," but perhaps better wording would be: information *can* lead to transformation when the receiver has an open heart and mind. When we are ready and willing to surrender to coaching, then the information, like a seed planted in dark soil, can take root and help us grow into the light.

John's books and training have been transformative for me, and my hope is that the information I've shared will be helpful for you. Feel free to reach out with questions, connect with me on Facebook or LinkedIn, or sign up for my monthly Highlights by texting **22828** to **8togreat**.

Meanwhile, three of my books are available on Amazon:

- *8 to Great: The Powerful Process for Positive Change*
- *Taking Care of Me: The Habits of Happiness*
- *8 to Your Ideal Weight: Release Your Weight and Restore Your Power in 8 Weeks*

For more information on our **8 to Great Life Coach Certification Program**, email me at info@8togreat.com or reach out through our website, www.8togreat.com.

I wish you all the best on your journey!

– *MK*

FINDING
TRUE LOVE
— LIZA DAVIS —

Liza Davis is a certified dating, relationship, life, career, and executive coach and trainer. She joined Mars Venus Coaching in 2010 and has coached and trained professionals in the US, Europe, Latin America, and Asia. She coaches clients to transform both their personal and professional lives and helps people to fulfill their dreams and find love. Liza has worked with top multinational businesses, and her clients include IBM, Samsung, and Wells Fargo.

Liza was trained in world famed peak-performance transformation tools and has worked with the finest coaching organizations in the nation. She has also shared her talent by working as an executive coach with a global talent management consulting firm. Garnering a master's degree in foreign languages, she speaks five: English, Spanish, Russian, French, and Italian. She also facilitates training and coaching in English, Spanish, and Russian. In addition, Liza speaks Venusian, and many believe she has advanced skills in Martian, so that actually makes it seven.

CREATING MY LIST

Date: December 2, 2010
Goal: Get married to my ideal match by December 31, 2011

My Ideal Future Husband

1. Great at expressing his love to me
2. Treats me like a goddess
3. I see that he is going to be a great dad to our children
4. I look up to him and admire him, who he is and what he has achieved
5. Adores me
6. Happy
7. Positive energy
8. Great sense of humour
9. Adventurous
10. Likes to try new things
11. Spends plenty of time with me and our children
12. Likes active lifestyle
13. Doer
14. Great at making decisions
15. Secure
16. Faithful
17. Confident

. . .

109. Thinks and knows that I am the best thing that ever happened to him.

This or something better!

It was a beautiful and warm December day. I had made myself comfortable at a cozy downtown LA Starbucks and took my time to carefully create the list for my ideal future husband. I knew that writing my heart's desire was the first step to manifest this perfect guy for me. I had read so many books about it; I attended so many seminars, and I was ready to plunge in and find my destiny. I already had my coaching business, and I had just started my journey to getting my Mars Venus coaching certification. I remember thinking, "Being trained by John Gray, the best relationship expert in the world, you can't get better than that!" It was finally time to put it all into practice and find the man of my dreams; then I could help my future clients to do the same thing.

I grabbed my computer and a cup of hot passion tea and spent a couple of hours at that Starbucks. OK, it was more like the whole day and lots of cups of passion tea! By the end of that day, my dream man and everything I ever wanted to find in a husband was right there in front of my eyes. He was looking right at me and staring at me from my computer screen. The love of my life was neatly organized in 109 characteristics of musts, wants, and nice-to-haves. This man was simply amazing: we were completely in love with each other, and there was nothing he wanted more than to marry me and have two beautiful children together. Plus, of course, he was very successful and good looking and had all my common interests, and all that other great stuff.

My coach taught me that 109 was a magic number, and that's how long I made that list. Some rosaries have 109 beads, and somehow that number really worked for people. So there I was writing away and really enjoying this process. The interesting part was that when I finished and looked at what I had created, I really felt that I was in love with this man already. I was in love with him before I ever met him.

MAKE IT YOUR OWN JOURNEY

How about you? Would you like to find your true love? Coaching is not just about listening to someone else's story. It's about creating your own story. It's about asking and answering powerful questions that challenge you and help you to open yourself up to new and exciting possibilities. It's about taking action . . . even when it seems scary. It's about creating a new story, not just complaining about how it hasn't been working for you. It's about taking what seems to be impossible in your mind and making it possible, one step at a time.

I invite you to join me at Starbucks and explore how you could create the relationship of your dreams. Grab your favorite drink and maybe a nice dessert or whatever you like! I am having banana bread today. I will ask you some deeply revealing questions, and I will give you some exercises to awaken the love inside your heart. Take the time to answer honestly— remember this is for you. Trust me, the time you put into it may be the best investment you make towards your happiness, fulfillment, and lifelong desire for love to come true!

PUTTING IT INTO PRACTICE

Now back to my creative writing day at Starbucks . . . When I finished writing that dream man list, I didn't stop there. That day I also jotted down all my reasons *why* I wanted to meet this wonderful man and created a powerful action plan of *how* I was going to meet him. Part of my plan was doing online dating. I was very skeptical about it at first, but I still decided to give it a shot, and I was blown away. I was reading profiles and communicating with more men than I could possibly remember. I was going on dates several times a week. Sometimes I had two dates on Saturdays and Sundays. That's a lot of new people to meet and a lot of free meals, new interesting places to see, and great—or sometimes not as great—conversations. That's a lot of dating experience I didn't really have before.

I took "dating" on as a science and an art! I was experimenting with it and really enjoying the process. It was fun and I was obsessed. My friend told me, "Liza, if you spent half as much time developing your business as you have been on dating, you'd be a millionaire already!" I was on a mission!

FIRST DATE BY THE BEACH

One day I went out on a date to meet with Paul. We met at the beautiful beach in Palos Verdes, California, a pristine spot and an enchanted place along the coast. He greeted me with a lovely red rose and a magnetic smile. We took a pleasant walk along the shore and then had a delightful lunch right by the ocean's edge. I considered two dishes, and he ordered them both for us to share.

I loved the way he looked at me and the way he really listened. I loved the way he talked, the way he walked, the way he looked, the way he later would take my hand, greeting the sunset, and the quiet confidence he exuded.

His whole presence made me feel at bliss.

Ironically, the beach where I met Paul was the exact same beach where I had made an inspired decision just three months before to move to California. Back then I lived in NY, and I flew in for the "Date with Destiny" event with Tony Robbins and to visit a dear friend living in the Los Angeles area. My friend brought me to this very same beach, and I was sitting on those same rocks, walking on that same sand, and looking at that same ocean. This beach was magnetizing me with its beauty and calling me to move to the West Coast. I remember an overpowering feeling that it was the right thing to do. A month later I packed up my world in New York and followed my dreams by moving to LA.

As Paul and I sat on that same beach, enjoying each other's company over a wonderful lunch, I experienced that same overpowering feeling of rightness and bliss. Could it really be that the universe pulled me to this beach all the way from NY to meet *my* Date with Destiny?

CREATE YOUR OWN LIST

The first step in finding and developing a happy and lasting relationship is to know what you want. This is one of the major coaching principles. It's hard to get what you want if you are not completely sure what it is that you want, or if all you do know is what you don't want. The great way to start this process is with writing a list to envision the ideal man or woman for you.

Take your time to write out your list. You may say, "I'll know when I see him (her), I don't need to write anything down." It's best to have a plan in place. It really helps to have a list of qualities that you are looking for. What do you want? Write it down so you have a guide to finding the right person for you, for your dream life.

Think of what you want him/her to be like: personality, interests, physical qualities, habits, hobbies, as well as asking yourself the deeper questions. These can include: How will your perfect person treat you? How will he/she feel about you? How will you feel about him/her? What do you want to do together? Think about what you want this person to want in life, his/her values, priorities, etc.

It's important here in this moment to stop being realistic—or what you think is "realistic"—and unleash your imagination. You can always get "more real" later. First, think about what you *really want*. If you had a magic wand and could produce the man or woman of your dreams, what would that person be like? The idea is to write something you feel that you want and be open to something close to that or maybe very different and even better than what you first envisioned. It's a start.

Writing this list may be easy and fun for some and quite challenging for others. This process may bring up some doubts about whether this person really exists, or whether you deserve him/her. It may bring up painful memories of what you didn't get in the past and uncertainty about whether you could actually get what you want. You may think, "109 items, are you crazy? I can't even think of 20!" It doesn't need to be perfect: just write what comes up for you. You can always adjust your list later as you get more clarity and practice. The list will take shape as you give it more thought, meet new people, or even get inspiration, input, and ideas from others around you.

Exercise 1: *Create a list for your ideal man/woman. Aim for 109 qualities and just make it as detailed as you can.*

STATE IT IN THE POSITIVE

It's important to be positive when describing what you want. As you are writing your list, turn a statement like, "I don't want someone jealous" into, "I want someone secure." The rule of coaching is that you want to focus on what you *do* want (positively phrased), not on what you *don't* want (negatively phrased). Otherwise, by law of attraction—that doesn't understand negatives—you will actually be attracting to yourself that which you *don't* want. Here are some examples of how you could rephrase it:

No Way	Better Way
Doesn't drink/smoke	In great health, leads a healthy lifestyle
No commitment issues	Wants to and ready to marry me and spend our lives together; we get happily married
Not jealous	Secure
Not angry	Balanced, treats me with love and respect, treats me like a goddess
Not in debt	Financially successful

If your list looks like the "no way" column above, you would actually be attracting to yourself an abusive jealous person with lots of addictions who is broke and has no plans of committing to you whatsoever. Is that what you are looking for? I didn't think so. Be sure to review your list and turn everything into the positive. It could take imagination sometimes. If you are not sure how to phrase it, ask someone to help you come up with ideas.

Exercise 2: *Review your list and turn everything into positive. Make sure you use powerful wording to ask for what you really want.*

FORGET ABOUT YOUR LIST

Now that you've put all your heart and soul into your list, here is what John Gray says about it:

"Have your list, but then . . . forget about your list."

"What do you mean, forget about your list?" you may be thinking. When you write it down, you set your intention of manifesting this person for yourself. Yet not all people have crystal clarity of what they want and need from the start, and sometimes they don't really know what's truly best for them.

At the bottom of your list, write: "This or something better". Often, we have many preconceived notions about perfectly good people and close doors on possibilities of our future. John Gray recommends that we should be open when we're going on dates. He/she doesn't have to meet all your 109 characteristics and desires to go on a date with you or even to marry you! You're out to have fun; you're out to meet someone new; you're out to practice opening your heart and sharing the unique you with someone. As a matter of fact, John Gray suggested to me that I should try dating "against type." I followed his advice and went out with people who weren't exactly my type in terms of looks, occupations, hobbies, etc. just to be open-minded and get practice dating. You may be thinking, "How is that going to get me true love?" You never know; one of those practice dates may turn out to be the love of your life!

ARE YOUR BELIEFS LIMITING YOU?

Now that you have your vision, it's time to look at your beliefs about dating and relationships. Here is one of the first questions I ask when guiding someone to find love:

On a 1–10 scale (10 being the highest), where is your belief that you will find your ideal match and be in a happy relationship?

Is that a resounding 10, an 8–9, or maybe a 5 or a 6 or a 7? Even lower? If you said 10, is it really a 10? Be honest with yourself. Why did you pick that number? If it's anything less than a 10 (a real 10!), you may have some unsupportive beliefs around relationships, love, or having a family.

COULD I BE WRONG? TRANSFORMING MY BELIEFS

My limiting beliefs were around creating a family. For a very long time I felt that I was not ready to have children. I *wanted* to have children! Yet, I felt that I was not ready because I didn't have the right person in my life to be their dad; I didn't have enough money, and I could still do more with my career. And here I was in my mid-thirties, still waiting until everything fell into place and all circumstances aligned themselves just right for me to be ready.

At the time, I went to a very powerful self-development seminar that had me look honestly at my beliefs. Using transformational self-discovery exercises, I realized that I was actually *attracting* the people who were not right for me *because of* my "not ready" belief. That belief was the actual *reason why* I didn't have children and, I can tell you, it was not giving me great results! I decided it was time to let it go.

I changed it to "*I am ready, bring it on!*" Short, powerful, and sweet!

I was thinking to myself, "Listen, some women have five or more kids by this age, and they have absolutely nothing. They have no money, no career whatsoever; they may not be in the greatest relationships—if they actually have relationships—yet *they do* have children. And here I am, with everything that I have going for myself, still waiting because 'I am not ready.'"

I had to question my beliefs: Yes, it was true that I wasn't in the right relationship for having a family. Yes, I wanted to do more with my career. Yes, I could have more money. Yet, I had to get to the deeper truth . . . And I realized that at the deepest level, being happily married and having children was what I wanted most in my life. The truth was that *right there and then* was the best time to do it and as long as I believed that I was not ready, I would still somehow attract situations and relationships to myself that wouldn't be ideal.

I actually convinced myself that I was ready—bring it on! I convinced myself that if I really believed it, then the right person would come into my life; the right person would appear and make it real. I repeated it to myself again and again and again until I built it into my body and mind. I told myself, "No more, no more of not being ready. Just be ready!"

I was so inspired I actually shared this belief on a first date with a guy once, "I am ready, bring it on!" I told him. He never called me again, it may not have fit into his plans. OK, maybe it wasn't the best thing to share on a first date; or maybe it was. No matter what, I was determined to find the right guy who would be ready and willing to have a family with me or who would get there quickly after getting to know me. All I needed was to be open and ready.

CHANGE YOUR BELIEFS – CHANGE YOUR LIFE

How about you? What beliefs are holding you back? What's in the way of you experiencing that amazing relationship? What's that story you've been telling yourself and/or everyone else about why you can't have a great relationship or a family?

Many believe the reason they have not found love yet is because "it's just not meant to be" or "all the good ones are taken." Whether you realize it or not, these thoughts are sabotaging you. If your internal monologue is a constant replay of reasons why you are single or not happy in a relationship, those quickly become your belief system, which hinders you in finding or experiencing a fulfilling relationship.

Are you starting to come up with some thoughts and beliefs that may be blocking you?

Exercise 3: *Write down beliefs tht may stand in your way of being in a happy relationship or meeting the right person for you. How do those beliefs affect you?*

Just know that you are not alone here. Most of us have those blockers, and many of my clients discover quite an impressive list of beliefs of why they can't experience or find a happy relationship. We first identify possible limiting beliefs and then go through the alignment process to release and replace those blockers with more positive thoughts that bring a surge of different energy and life changing results!

Here are some examples of unsupportive beliefs of clients I've worked with and their new positive thought patterns. As you read it, see if any of those thoughts ever crossed your mind.

Limiting Beliefs	New Empowering Beliefs
Now is not a good time. I'll start dating **when** I have more time, more money, a (better) job, less stress, feel better about myself, after I get in shape, after kids go to college, etc.	**Now** is the time to start, and find love! The right person will love and appreciate me for who I truly am. The time is now!
I am too old.	I am a wise (beautiful, kind, etc.) person with lots of energy (experience, etc.) and love to give! I am young in my heart. It doesn't matter how old I am: now is the perfect time to find love. There is a soulmate for me who will love me for who I am.

I am overweight.	I am a beautiful person. The right man (woman) will see it and love and adore me for who I am.
I don't want to be hurt again.	Every person is a new experience. The love with my ideal man (woman) will be a completely different, new, and empowering experience.
I don't want to lose myself.	I can be myself when I'm with my true love. I can express who I am and do things I love with that person. Now I have someone to share it with.
I can't get any dates.	I open myself up to meeting new people and finding my perfect match. I enjoy going on dates! I am an interesting person and people love going on dates with me.
I hate dating.	Dating is fun! It's fun to meet new and interesting people! I can try new restaurants/activities/discover new places. Hey, I could actually meet the love of my life in the process!
All the good ones are taken.	All I need is one. And the right person for me is out there, waiting for me. I am excited about meeting this amazing person already!
You just don't understand. I have this BIG problem!	He'll love me for who I truly am and accept me for who I am/everything about me.

IS HE THE ONE?

Four months after I transformed my beliefs about having a family and meeting the ideal man, Paul came into my life. I knew he already had two children and during our first date, I asked him to tell me a little bit about them. On the second date, I asked if he wanted to have more children and he said, "I don't know." That answer wasn't quite satisfying to me, yet I decided not to push it, since it was his birthday! On our third date, I told him, "And I do want to have two children; as a matter of fact, I left my previous relationship because my ex-boyfriend didn't want to have children . . ." Paul still "didn't know," but at least I "set my expectations" from the start this time, before precious months and years went by.

I was falling in love with Paul from the moment I met him on that beautiful beach. I loved how serious he was about me: he called me every day; he wanted to be with me and took time for me, no matter how busy he was. I loved how he planned such fun dates at new interesting places: hiking, walking by the beach, trying new foods. I loved how he took me on a surprise picnic and brought a basket packed with goodies, delightful treats, and scrumptious cookies that he made himself, just for me. I loved staring at him at restaurants, watching him drive, and just being in his presence. Every day I was falling deeper and deeper in love with Paul . . . Yet, there was still that one question holding me back: would he be ready and willing to have more children with me?

Two weeks after we met, I was driving to John Gray's workshop at his ranch in the San Francisco area. Paul sent me the sweetest notes every morning. I took a sip of passion tea and got my phone to see what kind of passion was waiting for me in my inbox! And there it was:

> *"Good morning, my love. You know what they say,*
> *'Absence makes the heart grow fonder!' You're constantly in*
> *my thoughts and dreams. I hope you're having an awesome*
> *time at the ranch. FYI, I've been giving a lot of thought*
> *to the question that you asked me twice, and, well, if it's*
> *very important to you, then, yes I would. I want you to*
> *always feel happy and fulfilled. I miss you. Paul."*

That day John Gray talked about the hormones that produce happiness and certain supplements one can take to "feel" happy. I didn't need any supplements. I had the happiness hormones rushing through my whole body creating a state of complete elation! This is when I knew that Paul was "the one" for me.

EMPOWER YOURSELF

Are you ready to change your beliefs and open yourself to love? This sounds like a huge quest, yet it's possible to shift your limiting beliefs even if you've had them for a long time. How do you begin to transform your beliefs? One way of doing it is to question your beliefs.

Ask yourself: What else could be true?

Is it that you can actually find a person who really loves you for who you are? Is it that you do deserve to love and to be loved? Is it that you do know of that one person who is happy in a relationship and just maybe it could also happen to you? You fill in the blank and think of limitless possibilities here. Think of something that would actually be supportive of your goal to find a new relationship, something positive, something empowering to you, something that may be much truer than the negative things you've been telling yourself for a long time.

As a coach, I feel that belief alignment brings one of the biggest shifts to clients searching for harmonious relationships with others and with themselves. You can purposefully change your beliefs yourself, especially once you get familiar with the process and creative way of going about it. It may be challenging to do it on your own, and many find that having support is immeasurable! Find someone who can help you: a coach, a role model, a supportive friend who has more empowering beliefs than you. I hired a coach for myself who guided me in this journey to find an ideal relationship, and, since then, I've had a number of coaches who have helped me to get what I wanted in other areas of my life and business. I talk to a coach every week. Find someone who believes in you!

> **Exercise 4:** *Question your limiting beliefs, one at a time. Is it 100% true? Could there be a 1% or even a 0.1% chance that it's not ture? What else could be true then? Start coming up with more empowering beliefs. Get help from a professional coach who could help you with that.*

HAVE TOTAL FAITH

You've created your list and are projecting what you want. You are replacing your old limiting beliefs with more empowering ones. Now what? While there are a great many things you could do to attract a loving relationship into your life, aside from taking action, there is one thing that I believe has the most power! It's having *total faith* that it's going to happen, no matter what. It's quite easy to believe if everything is going well. How about believing when everyone and everything tells you: "No, it's not going to happen!"?

BELIEVING, WHEN IT'S HARD TO BELIEVE

Remember that I made that bold decision to move from NY to LA? I packed up a few belongings into seventeen large boxes and left everything else behind. There I was living the California dream and staying on a mattress at my friend's home. All I really needed was a job, new business income—or some kind of income—a home, a husband, two children, a car, and a dog would be nice too. That's about it. I know, some people ask for small things. Aside from focusing on manifesting my dream husband, I also had other goals written out for developing my business, generating more income, getting a new place to live, getting a car, etc. The car was actually at the top of that list. While living in NY being car-less was the way to go, I really needed a car in LA! After plenty of research, I decided to get a Mazda, a red Mazda.

I went to a nearby dealership, and there it was: my beautiful red Mazda . . . I really liked it. As I was visualizing how great I was going to look in that sexy car driving it to all my business meetings and dates, I got some distressing news. Apparently, my proof of income—or lack thereof at the time—wasn't sufficient to buy that vehicle, or pretty much any other kind of vehicle. I had just invested money in the new coaching business, my move to California, and quite pricey self-development seminars (which were worth it, of course). Going to Italy, Paris, London and other exciting places didn't really help financially either, although it was nice. I didn't have "a job" and my new business was not yet bringing in as much income as myself or the lenders would have liked to have seen.

Still, I didn't want to take "no" for an answer. Surely, someone was going to see my potential and give me a loan for a vehicle. I thought, "Come on, since when are there so many requirements? I made money before, I could do it again! People get credit in the US all the time!" That was my first time looking to buy a car. Yet, one dealership after another told me, "no", "no", "no", "no", "no." I must have gone to at least five dealerships with the same result.

After one of those unsettling visits, I remember sitting in a car—it wasn't actually my car, I borrowed it from my friend for a few hours—and thinking, "Wow, this is really hard. No one wants to give me a car and the money is running out and I don't even know how I am going to pay for things . . ." I was sitting and crying and wondering what to do. I had a pendant with the word "miracle" inscribed on it that I got at one of my inspirational seminars, and I was holding on to it to get back into where I knew I wanted to be in my mind. I did some meditating, visualizing, and convincing myself that I was somehow going to get the car. It didn't matter what they told me, and even though I didn't know what was going to happen, somehow I was going to get that car that I really wanted. I knew that I needed to believe and have faith no matter what, and I started to really believe it. After a while, I was crying again, not from feeling sorry for myself, but from feeling a powerful release *knowing* that it was going to happen . . . somehow.

I stopped going to dealerships for a while, and I put a nice poster picture of a red Mazda on my wall next to my action plan of how I was going to get it. I kept visualizing every day—sometimes several times a day—that I was going to get my perfect car, and I was also visualizing that I was going to get my perfect husband, of course, over and over again.

So guess what happened? When I met Paul about a month later, he just happened to have an extra car—a red Mazda!

No down payment, no credit check, no monthly payments necessary. I didn't know that he had that car before I met him or before I even fell in love with him. No, I didn't put it on my dating profile that the guy had to have an extra car for me—"red Mazda preferred"—and I don't even remember making that connection in my mind. What were the odds of me falling in love with this amazing man who just so happened to have a red Mazda—an *extra* one? It was a true miracle.

You've got to have faith. If you believe that it is going to happen, that you are going to meet that wonderful man or woman and experience amazing love, no matter how unlikely it seems to be, you will! You've got to have faith, even if it hasn't worked before, even if everything else is against it, and everyone else told you that it wasn't going to happen. Even if it seems impossible, visualize it and believe that *somehow* it is going to happen, no matter what. Faith creates miracles. Leave all your excuses and reasons for why not, develop total faith, and create a magical relationship for yourself!

BUILDING FAITH THROUGH VISUALIZING

One of the most powerful ways to build faith is to visualize what you want. When you visualize, you are actually creating what you want in your mind and that helps to materialize it in real life. Seeing what you want to happen in your mind's eye helps you to believe that it's possible and real.

Come back to your list now. Read it again and vividly see what you want your ideal man/woman to be like. Now close your eyes and visualize that man or woman as if he/she were already in your life now. Engage as many senses as possible. Feel him or her next to you, being with you, looking at you, talking and listening to you, touching your skin or hair, maybe even perceiving the scent of his/ her skin or perfume. How does he/she treat you? What do you do together? Visualize how you feel and how this person feels about you. Visualize that amazing man/woman as if he or she were already totally in love with you and you loving this person with all your heart, maybe like you've never experienced love before. Make it as real as you can. The more positive emotions and feelings you bring to this, the more powerful this visualization becomes. You don't have to be perfect at it, even a glimpse of that person or feeling is a great start and then you can repeat it again and again to live it in your mind and heart, before you even meet this person.

> **Exercise 5:** *Visualize yourself in your ideal happy relationship. DO this visualization at least twice a day until it becomes reality.*

DREAMS COME TRUE

Two and a half weeks after I met Paul, I was going to a workshop at John Gray's ranch in the San Francisco area and to another phenomenal seminar in Florida right after that. I was going to be gone for ten days, which, as Paul put it, was going to be "an eternity." He knew that I was going to have a two-hour layover in LA between my flights and told me, "I want to see you, I will come to the airport, and we will have lunch!"

"Wow, he *really* wants to see me," I thought. "That just shows that he is really into me!" I was so excited about our airport date and a bit unsure about how we were going to squeeze it into the two hours between flights. As I landed in LA, I realized that my phone was dead too. Wow, I need to charge my phone, call Paul and figure out where he is, find him somewhere, have a *really* quick lunch, and then check back in, run to the new gate, and still make it to the next flight somehow!

As I walked off the plane, I saw Paul standing right there by the gate! "Wow, how did you get in here?" I wondered. Paul replied, "I told them I wanted to see my girlfriend and get to the gate."

He said the airline agent told him, "I need to see your ticket." Paul said he didn't have one, to which she replied, "Then you can't go to the gate." "But I want to see my girlfriend," he had said.

"Well, you need a ticket to go through."

Paul told the woman he wanted to buy a ticket. When the agent asked him where his destination was, he said, "It doesn't really matter."

He bought a first-class ticket to New Orleans, just to meet me at the gate and spend an extra half an hour with me, and so I wouldn't need to check out and check in!

We found a nice little café to grab lunch. We were happy: smiling, talking, and looking at each other. Then, Paul took out a beautifully wrapped gift for me. As I unwrapped the box, I found a pretty cup inside that read: "I love you more than I've ever loved anyone else." This was two and a half weeks after we met! He knew the very first day, when we met on that beach, that I was going to be *the one*—the woman for him, the one he'll always be with.

TWELVE YEARS LATER

In 2022, we will celebrate our tenth anniversary, and it has been the happiest time of our lives. We got married a year and a half after we met and just a few months after the date I had set for my future husband goal.

It was a beautiful wedding. We now have three precious boys and a little girl! Hold on, did I actually say I was ready for that? Well, I got ready in the process. That's the power of changing beliefs: you get even more than you ask for! I must have over-meditated on that one, or Paul over-delivered, as usual, or it was just meant to be.

Michael, our eldest, his younger identical twin brothers Robert and Eric, and princess Rachel are sweet angels. The miracle red Mazda grew with the family and evolved into a larger model to fit the entire clan, including our beautiful dog. We live in a gorgeous home. I love my career: traveling the world, coaching, training and helping people to achieve their dreams and to find love for themselves. We are truly blessed. Paul is my dream come true. He is also like a magic wand that makes everything else I want happen and makes all my other dreams come true. He is the best thing that ever happened to me.

WHAT IS TRUE LOVE?

Before meeting Paul, I once got a question at a Toastmasters public speaking meeting: "What is the difference between puppy-love, infatuation, and true love?" When it came to talking about true love, I simply told them, "True love . . . once you experience it, you will know it!" I kept thinking about this subject after the meeting, and I thought: "True love . . . I don't know what to say about it. I mean, I've loved people before; I've been in relationships before; I've even been married before, and I still have no idea what to say on this topic." I thought, I should look it up on Wikipedia or something, in case someone else asks me again.

After I met Paul, I didn't need Wikipedia to answer this question. I could feel it, breathe it, and live it, and I have every moment since then. I am so grateful for Paul, and he is a true miracle to me. I could not have possibly imagined how incredible life can be when you are truly in love with a man who loves everything about you, adores you, worships you, and will do anything for you. I feel that nothing else, no matter how wonderful it is, even comes close to that.

I love who he is and how he always (always!) does what he says he is going to do and keeps his promises. I love that when he asked me where I wanted to go on our honeymoon, and I wanted to go to Machu Picchu or the Amazon jungle, and he wanted to go to Galapagos, he made plans for us to go to all three! I love how he takes instant action, follows through, and gets things done with lightning speed. I love how he reads my mind and acts on what he picks up on. I may have a quick thought flashing through my mind, "It would be nice to have some music on," and at that very moment the music goes on, like magic. Paul heard it and put on the exact album I wanted. I would stand by the car and think, "Where are my car keys? Did I leave them at home?" Instant click . . . The trunk and the car doors open. Paul already knew I was looking for the keys and had pressed the unlock button. The car battery died when I got out of a business meeting at a place an hour away from home. Paul happens to be two minutes away with a car starter in his trunk. He drives by, gets the car started instantly, and drives off to wherever he was going. I do something wrong; he defends me and says that it really wasn't my fault. I love that he is a pilot and how he takes me flying above the clouds, because "above the clouds" is how I feel with him. I love that when I shared my list with him and he saw that he got 108 out of 109 things on that list—because he didn't like to dance—he said that dancing was a stretch goal and signed up for a dancing class to dance with me at our wedding. I love that he says the purpose of his life is to always keep me happy and fulfilled, and he is certainly living that purpose.

FIND YOUR TRUE LOVE

My wish for you is that you too find your true love, that incredible feeling, that person who completely adores you and truly cares about you. Envision it, feel it already, believe it, and fully trust that it's going to happen *to you*, no matter what. Surround yourself with people who support you. Take one step at a time, little steps, big steps, and discover the joy of true love for yourself!

LOVE EXISTS

— NEELOFAR QASMI —

Neelofar Qasmi is a hairdresser, an electrical engineer, a Mars Venus life coach, and the mother of two grown-up boys. She sees life as an experience that teaches us new lessons with each moment. If time is passing her by and she's not learning, she feels that she is missing out. She sees herself as the creation of change and takes every opportunity to make life easier and more interesting.

Neelofar loves helping others in the same way that personal development gurus have helped her. She is a love advocate. Her purpose in life is to create love between people as she herself experienced it with her late husband of ten beautiful years. After following John Gray's advice, she found the love of her life again and wants to help others do the same.

THE POWER OF DREAMING BIG

When I was five years old, my parents told me I wasn't their child. They said I must have been swapped at the hospital. At such a young age, I didn't realize they were joking, and I never felt like I belonged in the household. I have two sisters and brothers, but, for cultural reasons, my parents didn't want us girls.

They always hoped for boys, which meant that I was a disappointment, an unwanted child, and that's how they treated me. My parents kept repeating that I wasn't their daughter, that I was exchanged with someone else's baby at the hospital, but I didn't let this bother me—because I had dreams.

Even though my upbringing was difficult, I never tried to leave, never caused any trouble at all. Instead, I acted like a good little girl and always obeyed my parents, knowing that I would eventually find love and leave my old life behind.

I didn't do well in school. My dad was really into mathematics; he worshipped the sciences, and he wanted us all to feel the same as him. While I did enjoy math and science, I wanted to explore other subjects, such as history, sociology, and geography, but my dad steered us away from those topics. In a way, we were brainwashed into thinking that the sciences were the only subjects worth studying. That's why I never did well in those classes, which made my homelife even more difficult. Although I was a girl, if I did well in school, I would earn my father's approval. Unfortunately, I struggled to get good grades, and I wasn't in his favor at all. But, still, I was always dreaming.

I wanted to become an electrical engineer, but my mother wouldn't allow it. In her view, girls weren't meant to be climbing to the top of utility poles, tinkering with electronics, so she forbade me to follow that dream. To her, becoming a doctor, nurse, or another science-based professional would have been a more appropriate career choice. I couldn't argue, couldn't dispute their opinion, so I accepted their decision.

At age seventeen, I found out that I was my parents' daughter after all. They'd just been making fun of me because I'm tall, and my two sisters are short, like my mom. To my mother, I was the wrong shape: too tall, too ugly, too different from her. Although their words had hurt me when I was five years old, trying to understand why I didn't fit in with my family, I never expressed any resentment, because I was always dreaming big. One day I would leave that house, and what they thought of me wouldn't matter. Once my dreams began to come true, their hurtful words wouldn't affect me at all. However, the solution wasn't so simple. In truth, those words destroyed my childhood, sullied my heart, and tarnished my earliest memories, and I had to live with the hurt and the hardship it created for a long time.

AN INTRODUCTION TO LOVE

At age twenty-one, I met Farhad. Although we'd never had a real conversation, he proposed to me several times over eight months, and each time I said no. I wanted a husband who was truthful, honest, and lovely, and I didn't know anything about this man who kept asking me to marry him.

After several failed proposals, Farhad asked my parents if he could talk to me. They agreed and left the house so we could speak in private. My sister and brother-in-law lived downstairs and when Farhad came over, I pretended to be asleep in another room. I was acting very stubborn. That evening, he stayed downstairs and watched TV with my sister and brother-in-law, and, eventually, he left. I had successfully chased him away with my lack of interest—or so I thought.

The next night, he returned, and I continued to deny him my attention. "Who is this guy?" I said to my sister. "I don't know him. I don't like him. Why has he come back?" Eventually, my stubbornness eased, and I agreed to speak with Farhad upstairs. That night, we talked for around fifteen minutes, and he said six words that made my heart melt.

"What do you want in life?"

Until that day, no one had ever asked me what I wanted. Suddenly, I felt important, and I could barely contain my excitement. "I want to study," I said. "I want to become someone. I don't want to just sit at home and be a homemaker. I want to study and work and have a career. I also want to raise kids. Really, I want *everything*."

What he said next shocked me. "Neelofar, I'll help you get whatever you want." Hearing those words made me so happy. Then he asked a second question. "What do you expect after ten years of living together?"

"I want to have a small house that's full of love," I said.

"I'll prepare it for you," he said. At that moment, I knew he was the one. It just felt so right.

I never received words of encouragement from my parents. They never told me that I would do great in life, succeed at school, or realize my dreams. My mother and father only ever put me down. But finally, someone was paying attention to me, saying positive things, and making me feel important. Within three months, we were engaged, and we didn't wait long after that to get married. Six months later, we officially became husband and wife.

During the first four months of our engagement, we would lie beside each other in bed, holding hands and talking until three or four in the morning. Well, I would talk, and he would listen. In those first four months, I told him all about my life, and he just lay there and listened.

"Oh, wow," he'd say. "Tell me more. Oh, wow. Then what happened? I'm sorry. Oh, wow."

He listened to everything that had happened to me, and, after several months had passed, he'd removed all of the pain, all of the bruises, all of the scars I had collected during my first twenty-one years of life. I emerged from those conversations as a pure, happy version of myself, someone who felt truly cherished. Farhad introduced me to love, which is something I had never experienced in my mother and father's home. I always thought that it was okay that they never gave me love because I would find it myself someday—and I did. Finally, my dreams were coming true. But, as I discovered, a dream can become a nightmare in an instant.

TEN BEAUTIFUL YEARS

Farhad and I spent ten beautiful years together, and, during that time, I gave birth to two amazing boys. Throughout our marriage, people would say things to try and bring us down, to break us up. For example, they would think that I was going to leave him because he didn't have any money. Then they'd tell me there was no way that my husband would stay with me, and I would be best to leave him now. But none of these things happened. Instead, we had a love that was so beautiful that even my dad eventually wanted to know our secret. Our detractors, including my parents, put us through hell, but they saw that our love only grew stronger. They soon understood that what we had was real, beautiful, and long-lasting.

During our marriage, we restarted life three times. In Iran, after we got married, we had nothing. We had to borrow money just to have the wedding, and my parents refused to offer any assistance whatsoever. So, from nothing, we began to build a life for ourselves in Iran, one that we would soon leave behind. Our second restart took place in Pakistan, where we stayed while waiting to get a visa to come to the United States. We left everything we owned in Iran and had to start a new—albeit temporary—life from scratch. The visa took fifteen months to be approved. Finally, we left everything behind again and came to the U.S. with little more than nothing. Once again, we restarted life in a new country, and we were happy. However, four years later, Farhad and I were in a terrible car accident. My husband didn't survive.

A few months earlier, he had told me that if I ever died, he would die two minutes later. But if he were the one to pass, I would be strong and take care of the kids. When the accident took Farhad from us, I remembered what he'd said, and I put all of my energy into raising our two boys. They're both adults now, and I'm proud of the great men they've become. But I always give credit for how they turned out to my late husband because he was such a lovely guy.

Farhad and I had a powerful affection for one another. We had nothing to hide, and we trusted each other completely. Nothing in life bothered us. We loved each other wholly, intensely, and unconditionally. Farhad was my hero, my companion, my love, and my life. In the ten years we spent together, we had many beautiful moments. My husband said that he'd watched me for two years before he proposed. He knew me and loved me for who I was. Farhad didn't marry me for my looks or for any other superficial reason—he married me for the person I was, the real me, the Neelofar he'd grown to know and love. Looking back, I can't recall a single moment when we were mad at each other. During our ten years together, we felt only love between us.

Although I survived the accident, I didn't escape serious injury. I lost both my short and long-term memory, and all I knew in the beginning was that I had two boys and a dead husband. The accident had damaged my frontal lobe and left lateral lobe, which meant I couldn't speak; I couldn't remember; I couldn't comprehend. For me, everything was brand new. I was like a two-year-old girl in the body of a thirty-two-year-old woman. When I left the hospital, I had some help from friends and also my brother-in-law, who visited for three weeks and helped with the cooking and cleaning. But they weren't there all the time, and I mostly had to take care of the kids myself. Before the accident, I had been studying nursing, but, due to my condition, I had to drop out of the course.

As broken and downtrodden as I felt, I had no choice but to begin putting in the work to overcome my memory loss and restart life again. Farhad always told me that I'm so strong and can do anything in life I put my heart into. During my recovery, I listened more than I talked. I would pick up words that other people said and try to use them myself. Words that looked or sounded alike were difficult to manage. For example, I might say, "Thanks for the complaint" instead of, "Thanks for the compliment." Repetition was the key to restoring my memory and grasp on language. I would often repeat words over and over until they stuck in my mind. During my recovery, there wasn't a single day that I stayed in bed. Once again, I had big dreams, and I knew that I would succeed, because my heart was in it.

REALIZING DREAMS, OLD AND NEW

In 2011, I began studying for a bachelor of science in electrical engineering, and, four and a half years later, I graduated. Few people thought I would see my degree through to the end, especially considering what I'd been through, but I proved them wrong. I even went a step further and completed my master's in 2020. When I first enrolled in the bachelor program, I couldn't even fill out the admission form, but a lot has changed since then. The days of not remembering where I had parked my car and not recognizing family members when they called on the phone were behind me. Through hard work, determination, and an unwavering belief in myself, I had earned my degree and realized my dream of becoming an electrical engineer.

Additionally, I've been a hairdresser for over thirty years. In the mornings, I do my engineering job, and, in the afternoons, I service my hairdressing clients in my home salon. When I told them I had earned a degree, they couldn't believe it. They knew I was busy hairdressing and raising my kids, but they had no idea that I'd also been sneaking off to university to become an engineer. Once they realized the effort I'd put in and the struggles I'd overcome, they said they would never complain about anything again. If they ever did feel like complaining, they would remember my life and what I had been through, and everything would seem okay.

My hairdressing clients always feel good after spending time with me. They call me their "therapist" and often say that they get more value from me than they do from actual therapy. I love helping others remove the scars from their hearts. I don't want to see people hurting. I've hurt a lot, and I know that I can assist others in overcoming their own challenges. Suddenly, I had a new dream: I wanted to help people find love and live happy, fulfilled lives. I didn't know at the time, but I wanted to be a coach.

After Farhad's death, I remarried, but the union didn't last. Following the end of my second marriage, I had a series of short-term relationships, and each one failed. I didn't understand what I was doing wrong, so I turned to John Gray for help. His YouTube talks drew me in, and I listened to him speak for hours each day. In one of his videos, he said, "Call my office and make an appointment for a free session." So, I did exactly that.

After speaking to Rich Bernstein, CEO of Mars Venus Coaching, I decided to become a coach. I studied, graduated, and earned my certification. Although I had been consoling, advising, and practically coaching my hairdressing clients for years, my role was now official: I was a Mars Venus life coach.

While studying John Gray's material, I began to think differently about relationships. The concepts fascinated me, and I aimed to apply everything I had learned to my own life. If I could find love again, I knew that I could help others do the same. When I did my own ninety-day plan, I wrote that I wanted to find the love of my life, publish a book, and become a great life coach. On November 8, 2021, I fulfilled one of those goals.

I got to know my current partner through the Telegram chat app. He lives in Vancouver, Canada, and he's an engineer too. When we met in California in November of 2021, I knew I'd finally found the man I'd been looking for. He's very helpful in every aspect of my life. He's also a straightforward guy who hides nothing from me. If things went well, he said he didn't want to move to New Mexico, where I currently lived. He asked if I would be willing to go to Vancouver. He also said that he didn't want his heart broken and if I was just there to mess him around, I should walk away. Like I said, he's a very straightforward guy.

We talked more and more and got to know each other better. Each night, we'd interview each other, asking questions about our likes, dislikes, strengths, weaknesses, and everything else we wanted to know. It wasn't just lovey-dovey talk; we were quite serious, and we were both honest and transparent. Gradually, we began to really trust each other. He appreciated my transparency, and I felt the same about his honesty and directness. As we got to know each other better, we realized that we had a lot in common, and, over time, the relationship blossomed.

He'd never experienced love before. When I told him my story about my late husband, he said he couldn't imagine feeling that way. However, after four months, his attitude changed. Finally, he said he felt that same powerful love for me. He'd never experienced this with anyone before. I, of course, felt the same, and we have been living together since March 15, 2022. For the second time in my life, I had found the man of my dreams, along with a great and beautiful love. Now I can focus on fulfilling my other ambitions, the two remaining goals in my ninety-day plan: to publish a book and become a great life coach.

LOVE IS IN THE AIR

For love to begin, we must first believe it exists. My experience in this area and the past adversities I've overcome put me in the perfect position to coach others. I know that love exists. It's not just some fantasy we've concocted in our heads—it's real. I know this because I've lived it, breathed it, and I'm living it now.

Love is in the air—wake up and breathe it! Relationships where two people know each other intimately are one of the most beautiful and meaningful aspects of life. When we communicate openly, we grow. I wish that we'd all get to know our partners before we sought to leave them, to dismiss them, to write them off. Communication is the key to opening the door to trust, love, and a beautiful relationship. Honest words and a gentle touch can resolve even the most difficult problems. We're all human and we all make mistakes, but patience and forgiveness are the glue that holds us together.

Because I've lived love, I can pass my knowledge on to others. I can let them know that love *does* exist. When you believe in something, you have a much better chance of finding it. I've experienced love in its most powerful form, and I aim to share that experience with others. Whenever I mention my beautiful love story to my clients, they're amazed, but they're also hopeful. Because, if love exists—and I assure you it does—anyone can find it, create it, *live* it, and that's a beautiful thought.

HOW TO SHAPE YOUR LIFE WITH COACHING

— CHRISTIAN BRAGA —

Christian Braga is an Italian business and life coach, NLP trainer, entrepreneur in the renewable energy and real estate fields, and renowned expert in gender intelligence and leadership in national and international organizations.

He is a life and relationship Mars Venus coach, certified at the highest levels of prestige. Christian has helped many couples overcome obstacles during his career, revealing the secrets of gender intelligence that allow them to rekindle love and passion and build successful romantic relationships. After achieving significant success in Italy through seminars and dedicated coaching courses, he was invited to the United Arab Emirates to share the stage with John Gray, the father of Mars Venus Coaching.

Christian has also earned the highest business coach certifications. He has trained alongside great entrepreneurs, coaches, and gurus to learn the deepest secrets of doing business. Subsequently, he has helped dozens of business owners scale their companies, achieve financial freedom, and learn how to govern their three most important assets:

time, money, and people.

Taking advantage of his great skills in business, Christian launched an enterprise in the renewable energy industry and created, in just three years, a group of multimillion-dollar companies that have become leaders in this sector.

Christian's deep-rooted life purpose guides him to be the ultimate expression of himself each day in everything he does. He is driven by an infinite source of energy, enthusiasm, and discipline that constantly pushes him to be a better human being than the day before. His passion drives him to help men and women transform their lives by awakening from a deep "sleep," taking the reins, defeating suffering, and finding true happiness.

THE GREATEST POWER IN THE UNIVERSE AND HOW TO ACTIVATE IT

Becoming a Mars Venus coach was part of a long journey for me: a personal, professional, and spiritual evolution that began more than seven years ago; a story fueled by the most powerful energy in the Universe—the energy of love—which has guided me to awaken the latent power that lies in every one of us, the power to create what we want! Through this power, we can create our own reality and achieve everything we want in life, relationships, and business.

Everyone who is open to embracing the true magic of love and is willing to live according to the laws of the Universe can achieve what I accomplished and much more! My journey from an unsatisfied call center operator, earning very little money, to a successful entrepreneur and coach living an incredible love story started when I met my wife, Karolina.

She is from Poland, and I met her in Krakow, around 1250 km from my home in Italy. On our first date, I told her, "I don't know when, don't know how, and don't know why, but I *will* marry you." Her first answer was: "You're crazy!" And she was right! We didn't even speak the same language! Over the next few months, I became obsessed with finding a way to conquer her heart and attain the financial freedom needed for us to live together and make my promise a reality. I couldn't stop visualizing the happy and loving life we'd have, and these feelings pushed me to act. At the time, I was just discovering the real power of life and how through love, the most powerful energy in the world, we can shape our entire reality.

Here's the secret: if you create in your mind a clear mental picture of what you want and live it within yourself as if it were real now, experiencing the feelings you'd feel if it were already happening, being grateful as if you had already obtained it, always acting from a place of love for yourself and others, then you can imprint that image into the intelligent substance from which all the Universe and everything within it is created. Once you imprint an image, the Universe acts in ways you'd never expect in order to bring what you've wished into reality. You just need to think about the *what,* and the Universe will figure out the *how.* Once you learn how to apply this real formula, you can achieve whatever you want in life.

For me, the first manifestation of this magical Universe came one winter day. It was about three weeks before Karolina would arrive in Italy so we could spend a weekend together. I was out of my mind with excitement! I had booked a hotel in Milan and organized a romantic weekend that would make her feel like she was living in a fairytale. One evening, while driving on the highway, my car began to smoke, turned off, and wouldn't start again. After assessing the damage, a mechanic sent me a repair quote for over €1200. Unfortunately, I only had a spare €500, which I'd planned to use for the romantic weekend. The *what* was so clear; I wanted to have my weekend with her, but I did not know the *how.*

Desperate and unsure of what to do, I invited a friend for a beer so I could blow some steam off. When we met up, he told me about a personal growth seminar he'd attended the previous month. He offered to lend me a book that night, and he recommended that I read it.

I accepted his offer, and although I didn't know it at the time, this was the beginning of my awakening. In the book, the author explains what coaching is and how to ask yourself and others powerful questions that help us transform problems into opportunities. So, I stopped asking myself questions such as, "Why is this happening to me?" and "How can I be a great man if I can't even fix my car?" and I began to ask much more powerful questions like, "What are my options?" and "How can I find the money I need to fix my car?" And you know what? When you ask your brain something, it always answers!

Some days later, it popped up in my mind that I had some old possessions I no longer needed in my garage, and so I sold them. Within about a week, I had come up with more than €3,000 and was able to fix my car. With some simple questions, I directed my focus from the problem to the solution, and I created exactly what I wanted. I learned this important lesson: the questions that we ask ourselves dictate the quality of the decisions we take. Moreover, the quality of our decisions dictates the quality of our actions, and so too the quality of the results we get from life.

Over the next few months, I became obsessed with personal, professional, and spiritual growth, reading dozens of books and listening to hundreds of audiobooks. I even skipped taking lunch breaks with colleagues and instead used that hour to meditate and do other personal growth exercises. Karolina and I lived apart for three long years, seeing each other once a month for two days and talking on the phone almost every night for at least four hours. We discussed everything: ourselves, our relationship, personal growth, and our current and future goals. But most importantly, we asked ourselves powerful questions every day about how we could make our dream possible. Again, we were creating a clear picture of what we wanted in life, feeling the emotions we would feel if it were reality, and activating the Universe to bring it to us.

During those first few years, many "aha" moments occurred in my life. By asking myself new questions and challenging my limiting beliefs, it was as if, step by step, the normal world in which I had always lived was giving way to a completely different reality. Enthusiasm, wonder, and gratitude were the bases of my daily mood. The more I was positive and grateful about what I was receiving, the more I got from the Universe.

During the next three years, my work situation completely changed. I was no longer a call center employee but rather a project manager heading a team of thirty-five people. I was able to buy a small apartment in Milan, and Karolina and I moved in together. We were so happy and excited; we were finally living our life together! But we still had something to work on. I spent eleven hours per day working at the office, and I slept eight hours so I could enjoy my remaining six with Karolina. However, we could not accept this as our long-term future. I wanted to be free to enjoy my life, working from wherever I wanted and doing what I was passionate about. So, the next questions we needed to answer were: how could we create our successful business together?

We began to fantasize about creating something of our own, starting from scratch. We opened our checking accounts and examined our finances, asking: if I quit my regular job and we use part of our savings to invest in our new company, how long can we live without earning? We calculated we could afford about nine months of our current lifestyle. Within that time frame, we'd need to launch our business and start earning to pay the bills! We had to answer several powerful questions before we began our new venture: What are we good at doing? What value can we bring to the world? And how can we improve people's quality of life? We agreed we were good at building and improving our relationship! Over the years, in fact, we studied dozens of books on love and relationships, and we learned and implemented all the techniques based on the gender intelligence strategies discussed in John Gray's books. We have frequently trained ourselves to manage our emotions, understand each other's needs, and fulfill them.

Love comes from the verb "to love"; the verb indicates a series of actions that must be performed for love to exist and persist. The problem is that no one taught us what to do, and so we learned through trial and error. And many of us are still stuck making the same errors! But suppose we understand and implement all the Mars Venus Coaching actions necessary to show love and continue to do them consistently in all of our relationships. In that case, love will not only remain forever in our lives, but it will also continue to grow while opening the doors of perpetual happiness and fulfillment.

The main issue that couples face is that men and women don't understand their differences and differing needs. Due to this, they can't give each other what they want nor express love in the most desirable way. Eventually, resentment and anger can kill the relationship. When men and women understand their differences and how to manage them, resentment and anger transform into compassion and love. Our love-focused coaching system has helped hundreds of couples overcome obstacles, unleash the power of love, and get to the next level of happiness and fulfillment in life and business.

For us, the first significant step toward real success in coaching was deciding to become Mars Venus coaches. Once we discovered Mars Venus Coaching and spoke with Rich Bernstein, cofounder and CEO, we moved forward without hesitation in investing part of our savings in the coaching training. As we studied, we learned how to really coach and how to market and sell. After just a few months, we launched our life and relationship coaching company! Today, Karolina and I have gone from seeing each other one weekend a month to being together twenty-four hours a day. Today, we travel the world year-round, living in beautiful resorts and helping men and women create the lifestyle they want to live. We still talk for hours each day about our relationship and how grateful we are for it. Whenever someone asks what inspired me to create all my success, I always provide the same answer: the power of love.

TWO POWERFUL BELIEFS THAT SHAPE MY REALITY

A belief is an idea that we strongly believe is true. We all have beliefs about ourselves and others and how we think life works. Our "model of the world" is the sum of all our fundamental beliefs, and so it dictates our thoughts, decisions, actions, and results.

Dr. Wayne Dyer, when discussing an Albert Einstein observation about the most fundamental and major decision that we must make in our lives, asked: "Do I live in a friendly or a hostile universe? Which is it? Is it a universe that is filled with hostility and anger and people wanting to hate each other and people wanting to kill each other? Is that what you see? Because when you see the world that way, that's exactly what you will create for yourself in your life."[1]

By filtering events through our models of the world, we create our own reality. No model is right or wrong. However, some are more useful than others for achieving a certain quality of life. In short, your model of the world is the set of fundamental beliefs that you start to build from when you are born until your last day on earth. We all develop our personal and unique set of beliefs, and they directly influence our quality of life.

For example, if you think that you don't deserve to be successful, that you are not smart enough, that others are luckier than you, or that you can't convince your boss that you deserve a raise, then that's exactly what you are going to experience in your life.

I had a friend struggling because he did not have a job. When I asked him why he did not send out his CV, he answered: "Because I don't have a degree and so they will not give me the job." Thus, because of this limiting belief, he was not even acting toward his objective.

During a coaching seminar, Paola, a girl from Canada, said she had dreamed of going to Italy ever since she was twelve years old. When the trainer coach asked her why she had never gone, she answered that the travel costs were too much since she only earned $2500 per month. "How much does it cost?" asked the trainer. "I don't know," Paola answered. So, our trainer invited her to get her laptop and check at that very moment. When she discovered that she could afford it, she cried.

Her belief was limiting her from achieving her dream.

The truth is that you are what you think yourself to be, and you get from life only what you think you deserve to get.

To better illustrate this concept, I'd like you to imagine that living is like playing a board game. When you are born, life gives you your version of the game and tells you that to live, you must learn to play. So, you open the box, and within you find several items, including dice, checkers, paper, and some other useful tools. Almost everything you need is there, but one essential item is missing: the instruction book. You realize that you're playing a game whose rules you don't know.

Without clear guidelines to follow, you grow up trying to copy the rules (the beliefs) that your parents, grandparents, and teachers use. They tell you what is right and what is wrong. What you should be and what you should not. Then, as you grow and gain more experience, you start to challenge some of those beliefs, change them, or create new ones. Once you reach your thirties, you probably possess your version of the "life instruction book." And the level of happiness, joy, love, and success that you experience in your life depends totally on the quality of your beliefs. Your instruction book represents your model of the world and the rules by which you play the game. And while they may not apply to others, they indeed work for you to shape your entire reality.

At age twenty-seven, I had an "aha" moment while I was reading a book. That book forced me to do an exercise (I invite you to get a pen and paper and do it right now as well. It is a very powerful exercise). So, as a first step, I had to think and list my top three limiting beliefs.

This was my list:

1. Making money is difficult
2. There isn't enough time to do everything I want
3. Having my own business and working from where I want is impossible for me

Once I listed my three limiting beliefs, I had to answer these sets of questions for each of them: Why do I think this? Who is saying this, and how do I know they are right? How do I know that this is true? What proof do I have to support this belief?

Something inside my brain "clicked" doing this exercise! Not only was it the first time in my life that I took some time to build awareness around my limiting beliefs, but I discovered that they were founded on nothing concrete.

I figured out that not only was I the one who had created all the beliefs I was playing with, but—and this is the most important thing—I could change them! So, I became interested in knowing what set of beliefs and rules the most successful people included in their own instruction manuals. For up to eighteen hours a day, I studied the gurus of personal and spiritual growth, and I followed and implemented every strategy I planned with my coach. If certain rules worked for others, then they'd also work for me, I thought. And so it was!

I want to share with you two of the most powerful beliefs that I implemented in my life and how they've drastically elevated the quality of my life and the lives of the people I work with.

1. If you change the way you look at something, the thing you are looking at changes

This belief assumes that there is not one single reality. Each of us experiences reality through the filters of our memories, experiences, and actual moods. So, everyone sees something different. Therefore, what we see outside merely reflects what's happening inside us. And here comes the magic: if we change the way we are looking at something, the thing we are looking at changes. Isn't that magnificent? Once we learn how to use this superpower, we can shape reality as we want. It's a great rule with which to play the game of life, isn't it?

Here's an example of how I used this magic power with Sara and Roberto, an Italian couple who, after nineteen years of marriage, came to us because the relationship was not working anymore. During the first couples' coaching session, Sara externalized her resentment because her husband did not behave as she expected. She said he worked all day and did not help with the children at home. As a result, she was only able to focus on those behaviors that caused her frustration in the first place. If he left his underwear lying around or failed to clean up the table after dinner, she said: "There it is again. You see, just proving again that I'm not important to you. You don't respect me!" When she pointed out his shortcomings, he would respond defensively by stating that he does many things for her, but all she sees are the things he is doing wrong. So, they would argue, and each partner would try to convince the other that they do more. Roberto added that he tried his best every day for her, but she was never happy.

For Sara, the point was that she wanted to be listened to, understood, and receive more help from him, but to achieve these results, she was trying to change him instead of changing how she looked at him.

I used a simple but powerful exercise to alter her internal perceptions and change the way she looked at Roberto. First, I asked Sara to take a blank sheet of paper and divide it into seven columns, labeling each one with the days of the week from Monday to Sunday. Then, I asked her to mark an X on the corresponding day whenever her husband behaved as she wished, even if he only performed a tiny action. Each time a positive moment occurred, she had to add an X to the sheet and show appreciation to him. Simple, right?

We continued this exercise for the next four weeks, and as time went by, the number of Xs grew dramatically. Soon, she realized that her husband *was* behaving exactly as she always wanted, and she had made no effort to try to change him. How did this magic happen? I helped her identify desirable behaviors that she couldn't see before. For example, she now noticed he was doing things like closing the fridge, preparing food before she arrived home, and asking how her day was when she arrived home. Once she began to change her focus, the resentment decreased, and she began to feel better and let him know that she appreciated the things he was doing well and the effort he was putting in to help her. Although she still complained about certain behaviors, she was also pointing out his positive actions.

The real change happened when Roberto felt appreciated for the effort he was already showing to her—even if it was very small! Finally, Roberto began to feel necessary in the relationship, and he felt he was able to make his wife happy. This sensation generates testosterone, the hormone responsible for a man's confidence. His brain will then seek more positive feedback, encouraging him to perform additional actions that make him feel good and appreciated by Sara. Week after week, Sara changed her strategy, going from complaining about his errors to validating and appreciating the positive things he was doing. And so, day after day, he began to give to her more and more with less effort and with more joy.

But how can we implement this belief in our life? Let me explain in greater detail. If, for example, one day we're happy and an event we view as negative occurs, or someone doesn't behave as expected, our happiness vanishes into thin air, and suffering appears in its place. We suffer because we believe that we must change external conditions in order to be happy. We believe that our wife or husband should treat us better. Or that our boss should understand us more. But events themselves don't cause suffering; the real suffering is created by how we perceive that situation within us. Meaning and interpretation come from within, which means we can control these variables. For example, if I tell a joke to two different people, one may laugh while the other may get angry. Similarly, an entrepreneur could view an economic crisis as a misfortune, while another in the same industry may see it as an opportunity. How many times have you at first judged an event to be negative but later, because you changed your mood or got new information, you changed your mind?

What changed? Nothing! The event is still the same; you're simply changing the way you look at it.

When something in life causes us to suffer, we often try to change the person, job, or situation that is instigating the problem. But this approach is rarely successful. Instead, we must work on our inner selves and try to understand why we're really suffering. Which meaning are we giving to that situation, word, or behavior? If we are giving a negative meaning, then we must force ourselves to stop doing that and find another more useful meaning. And there is always a more useful meaning for everything. And when you change the way you look at something, the thing you look at changes.

2. You get more of what you focus on

This powerful belief is part of the Mars Venus Coaching philosophy and is the foundation of the coaching style used by my great and esteemed mentor, Rich Bernstein. While most people know exactly what they *don't* want in life, few have even the faintest idea of what they *do* want. It's much easier to find people who complain about what's not working in their lives than it is to find those who envision what they want and how to achieve it.

I've pondered the reasons for this strange and destructive situation, and I found my answer.

First, I must point out that we live in an experiential world: a world in which to really know something, we must experience it. For example, parents who try to compel their children to not make the same mistakes that they have made soon understand that the strategy doesn't work. Instead, when a child makes a mistake, he should feel safe sharing his experience with his parents, who can turn the situation into a teaching opportunity. In order to learn, we must misstep, bump our heads, and fall from time to time. To know if something is bad or good, we must experience it.

Some months ago, I talked with Giulia, a girl from Milan who came to me because she was looking for her soulmate but, as she said, "I'm continuing to find the same kind of man, one who treats me badly." So, when I asked her what her soulmate looked like, she told me she did not know. She only knew that she did not want a man who treated her poorly. And *that* is exactly why she continued to attract this same kind of man into her life. She was so focused on what she did not like in a man and on the things that made her suffer, that she kept getting more of that. Because we get more of what we focus on!

For the rest of us, the concept is the same. Knowing what we don't want in life is easy because we've already experienced those things. We avoid leaving our comfort zone for the same reason: we know what we'd be leaving because we've experienced it, but we don't understand what stepping into the unknown will bring without taking that step. We're afraid of what we don't know because it creates uncertainty, and the devil that we know is always better than the devil that we don't know.

So, how do we know what we want in life? Lack of experience makes gaining clarity difficult.

If we'd already experienced what we wanted, we'd have a clear image in our minds, an explicit goal for our internal navigator. It's more likely to take us there when our inner navigator knows where we want to go.

The only way to get somewhere in life is to know exactly where you want to go. What are the chances that I'll get in my car and successfully arrive at my destination when I don't know where I'm going? Practically zero. I'd start driving aimlessly, wasting time and resources, and I'd eventually find myself somewhere I don't recognize or even want to be. Isn't that precisely what many of us do each day? We wake up and start living without knowing exactly what our goal is. We just know what we don't like, and so we continue to receive more of that.

We're like a sailboat pushed by the wind, a little to the left today, a little to the right tomorrow, ultimately getting nowhere or remaining in the same place we have always been.

We can't go somewhere if we don't know where it is and where we are right now. We can't achieve anything if we don't know what it looks like. We can't have a better relationship if we don't know what that means. We can't live a better lifestyle if we haven't created a clear, vivid picture of our perfect day. And finally, we can't find the man or woman of our dreams if we don't know exactly what they look like or how they behave. Coaching is the ultimate tool for solving this problem. Through the questions and powerful techniques used in coaching, you can bring clarity to your life, understanding exactly who you want to be, what you want in life, and where you want to be.

A Mars Venus coach is able to guide you through creating a clear image of what you want to achieve in every area of life. With the help of our coaching techniques, you'll be able to fully experience the results you want from life before transforming them into reality. Once you have a clear image of what you want, you can make an experience of it, and so life will bring it to you.

In our coaching program, we spend quality time each month to create a clear picture of the current situation (where you are right now), the goal to be achieved (where you want to go, what you want to have, or who you want to be), and the path that must be taken to get there (the action plan). Living this way means calibrating the navigator of your life so you can take the fastest route to success and enjoy the journey.

At the end of the day, life is simple. Most of the time, we are the ones complicating it.

ENGINEERING BETTER LIVES

— CHAHIRA TAYMOUR —

Chahira Taymour is a gender intelligent relationships and business coach personally mentored by Rich Bernstein. She comes with over twenty years of experience in corporate life and has been an active coach since 2017, helping clients and couples better understand themselves and create plans for success.

Chahira is inspired by all of John Gray's writings, especially *Men Are from Mars, Women Are from Venus*. Gender intelligence teachings have personally helped her in healing and self-discovery, as well as creating a healthy relationship with her teenage girl. Chahira has learned to fill her own self-love tank by being a triathlete, a poet, an artist, and by engaging in many other hobbies that she pours her heart into. She always encourages her clients to do the same: to follow their hearts and pursue their desires.

Chahira helps her clients understand what goes wrong in relationships and how to take part in the solution and ownership of the problem (if you are not part of the solution, you are part of the problem). She also helps people move on when necessary and grow hopeful for a better future, all in a concise ninety-day plan developed together and followed through.

Additionally, she speaks Arabic, English and French fluently and facilitates workshops in both English and Arabic. She's also good with the Venusian and Marsian languages.

PUTTING DECISIONS TO YOUR HEART

As an engineer, I immediately appreciated the clear, organized steps used in Mars Venus Coaching. The well-established system of logical processes and the availability of ready-to-use resources are appealing. The Mars Venus approach is structured, methodical, and highly scientific, which speaks to the engineer in me.

Long ago, I learned the hard way that not everything we're taught by teachers, family members and other mentors is correct or fruitful. Additionally, some of the customs and cultural inheritances we carry with us don't entirely make sense when examined closely. Often, simple things can become more difficult than they should. In my culture, this is especially true when it comes to expressing oneself among others, challenging an idea, or even rejecting one without creating a war zone. Many people wrongfully perceive women in Middle Eastern society as weak, helpless, and unable to stand up for themselves—but such beliefs are inaccurate. Some women simply need a little help understanding how much wit, strength, and power they actually have. That's where a coach can help.

I made an oath to myself a long time ago that I would pass on the lessons I'd learned in relationships and business to other people. Due to my own experiences in life—good and bad—I've developed an intense internal need to help others. I reached a major turning point in my life when I was considering emigrating from Egypt to the United States or Canada. I almost went ahead with the process and filed for a green card, but something held me back, gave me pause, and made me reconsider my decision.

I'd recently started coaching, was helping several clients, and was even being coached myself. Sometimes, when you expose a story or decision to your heart and see how it feels, you know without question what you must do. So I turned to my heart and, in doing so, realized that I didn't truly want to leave home or quit my country. But it wasn't nostalgia or anything similar that changed my mind. My past experiences have influenced me greatly, as will anyone's, and I couldn't ignore my pledge to help others not repeat the mistakes I'd made. When I really thought about it and put the decision to my heart, I realized that I didn't want to emigrate. I felt that here, in Egypt and Middle Eastern society, I could have the most impact.

In Islamic and Middle Eastern cultures, verses and teachings in the Quran and Prophet Mohamed's (salla Allah alayeh wa sallam) Hadith often get misinterpreted and, other times, mis-implemented. People bend the words to suit their own ideas of right and wrong and do so under the banner of religion. Inaccurate interpretations can lead to all sorts of issues, including the oppression of certain groups and ideas, which most often affect women. When people improperly apply the principles of the Quran and Sunnah to their lives and society, interpersonal problems can arise in relationships between men and women, with a huge impact on their intimate lives. When I considered all of this, I understood where I belonged; I felt exactly where I should be, where I could have the most positive impact. I may not be where I'm most valued, but I am where I'm most needed.

NEW ANSWERS TO OLD QUESTIONS

A lot of women are oppressed but don't immediately realize how much so until later in life. Over time, they become extremely frustrated by this oppression, and, eventually, they explode, usually after few years of marriage. In marital and family life, women aren't always allowed to freely express anger, rejection or disapproval. They are not commonly permitted to articulate their feelings or dislikes to their parents, husbands, or other people in their lives. If they do, they are labeled as disobedient and noncompliant and may even be punished, bullied, and further pushed to "swallow" it and keep moving forward. Over time, young girls form the habit of oppressing their feelings. In these cases, after they get married, the oppression becomes clear within their marital lives. Expressing yourself when you are happy or satisfied is easy, but dissatisfaction and objection can be more difficult to communicate, and I help women work around that.

In my culture, and in many others, there's an intense pressure to get married. Once you've finished school, graduated college, and joined the workforce, you're expected to take the next step and find a husband. If you don't get married and have kids, society tells you something's wrong. The pressure is always there and can cause the logical part of the mind to malfunction in certain ways. For example, women might make unwise decisions and choose to settle. They don't take the time to determine whether they're making the right choice or not, and that's not the ideal way to begin a marriage. First, you must see what happens when there's a disagreement in the relationship. If you rush into a marriage, you deny yourselves the opportunity to understand how you'll handle tense situations.

I personally went through a bad divorce, which led to a long journey of self-discovery. During my quest to learn what went wrong, I visited psychotherapists, psychologists, and marriage counselors, attempting to take ownership of the mistakes I'd made in my relationships. I soon realized that I wasn't good at disagreeing. I don't recall a single time when I objected to my fiancé or gave him a straight "no." For the entirety of our short marriage, I employed this timid approach, not realizing how sad and frustrated I had become until much later. After a messy divorce, I required a long journey of healing.

Later in life, I discovered Mars Venus and gender intelligence. The concept was mind-blowing. Finally, I understood what went wrong in my relationship with my ex-husband. Part of the problem was that I didn't communicate properly when I disapproved of something or hated another. Due to a built-in compulsion to try to be a good wife, I never objected to anything, never made a fuss. When you're in that situation and mindset, you're simply tagging along, trying to be a good person, and saying OK to everything.

Operating this way made me so miserable that I got sick. Psychosomatic symptoms caused by sadness, frustration and oppression were affecting my physical self. During that period, I was getting sick on a monthly basis. However, if someone had helped me learn how to effectively communicate my needs to my husband, the relationship could've been much healthier. When it comes to expressing disagreement, dissatisfaction, or even anger, you need to understand the character in front of you and, most importantly, the differences between you both. Then, and only then, can you learn how to convey your feelings the right way, at the right time, and say a nice "no" that achieves the outcome you want. I didn't learn all of this until later in life, but now I help others discover it sooner.

FAULTY INTERPRETATIONS OF CULTURE AND RELIGION

When I meet someone who's in an oppressive situation, I share some of my own personal failings. Many clients that are having problems with their husbands or ex-partners typically follow their father's advice. I was once accustomed to doing the same thing. Older people are wiser; your parents know better, and you should always follow their advice and accept their decisions. But none of this is true most of the time.

I learned the hard way that our parents aren't always right. They're simply advisors, and you should treat them as such. Ideally, you should hear what they have to say, listen to their advice, and process the information and see if it fits the situation. Your parents and anyone else can only offer guidance from their own perspectives, but you have your own views and reasoning that you must consider, and you cannot rely on others to provide the right answers every time. Listen and judge, but don't follow advice blindly; you should always think about the background of the person giving you the advice. You must consider all the variables, all sources of relevant information, and, finally, what's in your own heart and mind.

After my divorce, my father made it clear that we didn't want anything from my ex-husband. We could afford to pay my daughter's tuition fees for school on our own, so we didn't need any financial assistance. But I totally disagreed with this concept, which went against logic and our religious principles. In Islam, the father is responsible for the children, regardless of the marital status. While I knew that my dad was only trying to look out for his granddaughter's best interest, his desire to avoid asking for money and appearing to be a beggar clouded his judgment. Asking for help with tuition wouldn't have been begging. In fact, providing support is the lawful responsibility—in both religion and culture—of the father. I stood up to my dad and told him that I would handle the situation—and I was so proud of myself. By expressing my feelings and following my own beliefs, I allowed my ex-husband to take responsibility for his child, and the arrangement has continued happily ever since.

ALWAYS TRUST IN THE PROCESS

If you need help, you must be ready to receive it. When some clients really begin to discuss their situations and express their fears and some hidden secrets, the experience can overwhelm them. They get scared, freak out, and say they can't continue. Asking for help is one thing, but being open to receiving it is just as important. If you're not ready to help yourself, you'll struggle to make any meaningful changes. No one else can walk the path for you.

The Mars Venus process always shows us who's ready and who's not. When you're open to progression, you move on to the next step. If not, you simply don't proceed until you're ready. In the beginning of the process, we provide the client with a complimentary call to give them a taste of what coaching feels like. After that, we move on to the paid sessions.

Although some aren't ready to take that next step, many are. At each point of the coaching journey, the client must decide whether or not to keep moving forward.

After reaching a certain level of trust and rapport, most clients begin opening up and sharing important personal information. I recall one client who was crying over a partner's betrayal. Her emotional response and willingness to share such personal details was a serious breakthrough, and she was soon able to articulate and process her hidden feelings and begin exploring solutions. Previously, she'd been stuck between two decisions: to continue with the relationship or to end it. Paralysis caused by an inability to process her feelings left her unable to make a move. However, after her breakthrough, she quickly regained her confidence and her ability to make decisions. Sometimes people aren't ready to take the next step right away, but persistence and patience can achieve amazing results.

EVERYONE CAN BENEFIT FROM COACHING

I believe that everyone could use some help when it comes to achieving personal goals. When we lose focus and skew from our objectives, we need accountability, someone to answer to. Yet, we must be ready to ask for and accept such help.

Relationships are always a two-way path. Whether we're talking about family, romantic, or another context, this statement consistently holds truth. You must do your part to nurture the relationships you're in but also ensure that you receive everything you need to thrive. Relationships help us flourish as human beings, and each one deserves special care and attention.

One mistake I made with clients was letting our meetings turn into storytelling sessions. Sometimes people want to share things just to get them off their chest, which is fine, but coaching isn't meant to be a replacement for psychology. Coaches are there to help you move forward, to set targets and pursue them, and to do the necessary work to meet your goals. We'll often meet bumps and roadblocks along the way, but we have the tools and techniques required to help our clients overcome any obstacles in their path. At times, we may need to slow down and deal with a problem in a more dynamic or flexible manner, but we always find a way to keep moving forward. Continual progress is important.

Nothing in life is ever permanent. The good and the bad events will always pass. When you accept this fact, you alleviate much of the stress associated with the less-favorable moments and the depression that comes when great times end. If we acknowledge that the afterlife is where there will be no hard labor performed nor effort exerted, we can more easily accept the constant work we must do here and now and feel the urge to move ahead. For in Heaven, we shall have the ultimate rest.

EMBRACING OUR DIFFERENCE

— GABRIELLA DE LEEUW —

Gabriella de Leeuw uses both heart and mind in her work as a trainer and coach, with the objective of balancing feminine and masculine energies in people and organizations so they can work to their full potential. A licensed psychotherapist and multilingual coach/trainer in several schools in France, the Netherlands, and USA, Gabriella continues to learn and hone her skills daily.

Trained in Mars Venus coaching, (AO) business and executive coaching, intuitive coaching, and musical therapy, she has applied her vision in different environments. Widowed in 2003, she assumed both paternal and maternal roles with her two children who were still in a period of growth. That's when she met John Gray. She joined the team of Mars Venus trainers in the coaching training program, which focused on his famous book: *Men Are from Mars, Women Are from Venus*. She has taken up the challenge, while also working full time in local and international organizations. Her style of training and coaching reflects her personality where sensitivity, intelligence, nurturing, humor, warmth, and a resolutely positive outlook form a powerful and effective mix.

With over twenty years of experience in corporate and private coaching and training, Gabriella has the passion, knowledge, and experience to help others achieve success as well as the ability to assist others in reaching and realizing their full potential.

Her expertise is in the fields of gender intelligence, improved leadership, and communication. She has created several businesses inspired by the new model of working with the values of collaboration, participation, and open-mindset and attitude.

EMBRACING OUR DIFFERENCES

We've all seen the Super Mom/Superwoman in our work culture. It's a phenomenon that gets written about, talked about, and debated about. Some defend it; some are against it, and some just enjoy the argument. But none of these social debates ever address the true problems of being a Superwoman. Firstly, the model of the Superwoman is much like a square peg being shoved into a round hole for *everyone*, including men. Secondly, the model's root problem is in the way it forces us all to live; it is not that women should or shouldn't be working. I know this because not only have I taught this through my business for over ten years, but I lived it myself.

SUDDENLY A SINGLE MOTHER

My children were teenagers when I suddenly found myself a widowed, single mother. I always worked, but now I was responsible for being both father and mother to my children. Along with these responsibilities came the financial responsibility of raising two children on my own. My reaction to this circumstance was a typical one: I began to focus in the extreme on earning money, my responsibilities, and the idea that time is money. In other words, I began to function using a masculine model. I do not fault this reaction in myself to me or others; it is a primal instinct to provide for your children in order to protect and nurture them. It is a reaction that has the best of intentions and can many times have a good outcome in financial terms. However, it can have other ramifications that aren't very positive, and I found that out when I finally became sick from thinking—and functioning—in a singular, masculine way.

MAKING MYSELF UNWELL

After several years of working hundreds of hours and focusing solely on my financial picture—something I now call the Masculine Model—I became so physically ill that I literally could not function. My body was as broken as if I'd been dropped from a multistory building. In addition, I had a serious ulcer, an illness very masculine in nature. I knew intrinsically that I had done this to myself through a combination of overdrive and stress, the constant striving and never stopping, but I didn't know the mechanics behind it. In other words, I didn't know what was happening chemically with my mind and body to cause such a complete breakdown.

In 2009, I began reading John Gray's books, starting with *Men Are from Mars, Women Are from Venus*. I already had a basic understanding of how men and women thought differently—even through my intense strivings, I did always make some time to work on myself. John Gray's books led me to his seminars, and in the first one I attended, he spoke about hormones, specifically, oxytocin and testosterone, and how these hormones play an important role in everyone's well-being, particularly women's. Sitting there listening, I realized I had thrown away my feminine energy; I had traded it for masculine energy and masculine hormones in the form of testosterone. This wasn't working for me. In fact, it had made my body tired, sick, and overworked. Through John Gray's teachings, I began to realize that my children hadn't just lost their father; they had lost their mother too. This switch—giving up my femininity for masculinity—was my square peg in the round hole. With the help of John Gray's teachings, I needed to make the peg round again.

LEANING IN AS MY AUTHENTIC SELF

After having this light shine brightly into my life, I began to make changes to both how I worked in my own business and what I taught in my training business. I started applying my feminine energy into my trainings, pulling the focus from "time is money" to how creativity, intuition, collaboration, and participation lead to better working strategies and work environments. I put this same energy into my work habits and personal life, becoming once again the mother my children so desperately needed.

Following Mars Venus coaching training in the United States, France, and the Netherlands, I began reading books about personal development. I started making appointments in my agenda with myself to create more "oxytocin moments" like gardening, time and laughter with friends, body care, sharing, and caring for others.

By understanding and changing my behaviors, my partner and I immediately saw a difference when I took care of myself and allowed some me time. Now he even asks me to plan some me-time before "us time."

I tested my new approach with top managers in very large, global companies. I spoke with both men and women and found that the burnout rate was quite high with both genders, but the women especially were feeling it at a higher degree. When I spoke with these women one-on-one, I heard my former self in them. These wonderful ladies were experiencing the same thing I had and were getting lost. In talking to these managers, I found that my instincts were validated: Forcing people—particularly women—to adapt to the masculine model work ethic was breaking people down. It was time to create a better work model in which companies could truly achieve by using the best that men and women had to offer while staying authentically themselves.

THE "WORKING TOGETHER" MODEL

Some of you may think that I am saying something derogatory about women in the workplace—I am not. I believe that women have just as much to contribute as men to the working world and the world stage, but it needs to be done in a different way by *both* genders. During coaching sessions with my female clients, I discovered that it's not about *how* you feel as a woman but about how you can be *different* as a woman.

As I stated above, the masculine model doesn't work for men very well either. From what I have seen, however, it just happens to take a bigger toll on women. (Masculine and feminine is a concept that should not be confused with men and women. We should not forget that both masculine and feminine values are accessible for men and women!)

Today's business is based very much on a pyramid model: there are a select few at the top, and then the organization gets wider as you draw closer to the foundation. We all know that pyramids favor the few but sustain themselves on the many. This is not only an unsustainable model, it is an unhealthy one. While corporations may always be able to find replacements for those on the pyramid, this structure is one in which investing in a single company for twenty to thirty years is really a novelty rather than the norm that it was in earlier decades. So when I say that the pyramid is not a sustainable model, this is my point: the pyramid may stand, but it will always need new workers to do so because of burnout.

Most of my coaching clients agreed to have a quota (equal numbers of men and women in a company) in the corporate world as a first step to get women in the workplace, but something was missing; something didn't feel right. A quota gives the opportunity to play the numbers game without working on the real issue and thus pushing it out of sight. The quota seems to be a politically correct solution to a nonexistent problem, with good intentions and "bad" consequences. It's quite naive to think that the current power structures based on a masculine model will change automatically, as, in my point of view, you can only change the system from within.

So I took a different shape, one that requires collaboration and direct contact: the circle. Think about what it's like when you stand in a circle: Unlike a pyramid, you can see everyone at once and communicate easily. If the circle is going to move in one direction or another, it requires the work of all to do it, i.e., collaboration. A circle is a fluid shape, giving it both flexibility and strength. Lastly, with creativity, you can take that circle and create other shapes in order to accomplish different things, and you can do it without breaking the structure: an infinity sign, a straight line, a moving curve, then back to a circle, it's all about *working together* to achieve. And best of all, it requires working together using collaboration, creativity, participation, and intuition, all important pieces to being your authentic self.

CHANGING THE MODEL

Changing the model is how we make it better, but this is not an easy task. For decades, corporations have worked on the single model of the masculine pyramid. While there are a great many failures with the pyramid model, there has been commercial and financial success; after all, these corporations would not be profitable and able to provide jobs if they didn't have a degree of success. But is this success sustainable? I wouldn't be working if I thought that to be true.

This is what I have learned from attending John Gray seminars, my Mars Venus coach training, and my many years of experience: there is no space for a collaboration model unless you create it—so the first step toward changing the model starts with *you*. As John Gray teaches, *become your authentic self!* Go for your passion, utilizing all of your qualities and competences. Then use that passion to work collaboratively—not just in the workplace but in your personal life too. This is a model for your whole life, not just your work life.

I know this won't be easy, but this is what I work on when I conduct training for companies. Some of the companies I have had the pleasure of working with over the last decade include Texaco, Coca-Cola, Facilicom, Hapag Lloyd, Albert Heijn, just to name a few. My first step, particularly with large companies, is to start with a dialogue, asking simple questions about the person's relationships. After all, without communication, you don't have relationships.

My greatest wish is for people to start being honest with themselves and share their stories with me. I would also love for people to start working on their own models of collaboration, and tell me about their endeavors: what works, what hasn't, and what has changed for them and others. In John Gray's words, we can't continue with work and life models that require all drive (testosterone) and no collaboration (oxytocin). It is destroying our bodies and our lives. We all have so much to offer—both men and women—and when we can do it by being authentically ourselves, through passion, creativity, collaboration, and participation, there will be no bounds for us.

GENDER INTELLIGENCE

After decades of ineffective finger-pointing and quotas, a revolutionary and effective approach has come into focus for men and women leaders, one shaped by a greater understanding of our gender differences and the value revealed when we engage those differences instead of trying to ignore them. We need a new approach more than ever. How do you create balance? The first thing is to learn about gender intelligence and apply it in the workplace, apply more of a blended strategy in how you facilitate leadership sessions or learning sessions.

"Different" often translates to "inferior" in conversations about business. What if the solution is not eliminating the differences between men and women themselves, but instead learning how to recognize, value, and leverage those differences? This is what I focus on as a Mars Venus coach. In business, we are all about converging. It is about the results not about diverging, but women can bring some amazing ideas and thoughts. The biggest successes happen when both types of thinking come together.

Whether we are born with an X or Y chromosome not only dictates what reproductive equipment we've got but also how our brains are wired. Nature doesn't classify one as better than the other, but our social and business structures do.

What if the solution is not eliminating the differences between men and women themselves, but instead learning how to recognize, value, leverage, and embrace those differences?

WORKING TOGETHER

Men and women are wired differently; it's as simple as that. That doesn't mean that we cannot function together successfully in a corporate setting. By learning more about the ways men and women think, process emotions, and see the world, we can be more effective and influential toward the world around us. By being authentic and being an asset in changing the outdated model, you too can transform the world around you. This is the mission of all Mars Venus coaches around the world.

THE POWER
OF PURPOSE
— ASMA SHAHEEN —

Asma Shaheen is a life coach specializing in relationships, training, and mind map coaching. She is also a loving wife and nurturing mom. Asma is deeply rooted to the belief that any woman can make a place in this world. Regardless of color, race, culture, language, age, or status, she believes that going for our goals is the greatest chase we could ever experience. Her time as a coach brings her to believe that the world is more than what we see.

Although her journey has not been easy, Asma now believes that she serves something greater than herself. Her heart's desire is to share her inner self with the world through the essence of coaching and training. She believes that the evolution of life is what we're here for. The destination is our goal; rediscovery is our journey, and redirection is the process.

• Assertive   • Successful   • Motivated   • Accepting

Asma hopes to help and support others by spreading the message that, "Life is a gift, and, no matter how painful it gets, life will always provide us better and more beautiful pictures of who we are." She enjoys learning because we're all students of life, and we can get the answers we need each day, but only if we seek them.

LEARNING TO HEAL IN MULTIPLE WAYS

My life changed when I lost my father. At the time, I felt like I was losing my soul and was stranded in a world without support, reference, or love. During those confusing times, I asked a lot of existential questions. I felt so lost. I thought that maybe I could find myself in books, so I read, and I read, and I read some more. I thought I hated reading, but I soon realized that was a big lie I'd lived and believed for too long, almost my entire life.

Once I understood the truth—that I didn't hate reading at all and actually enjoyed it—I continued to read and educated myself in the field of self-development. Eventually, my quest for answers led me to Dr Salah Al Rashid's Academy, one of the biggest self-improvement schools in the Middle East. Joining the academy was one of the first big steps I took after losing my father, and I'm now an ambassador for the institution. During my studies, I learned the basics of self-development: belief, energy, and everything else. Previously, I'd been living blindly, unaware of the most important aspects of life. But as I continued to develop, I felt a hunger growing inside me. I wanted to read more, to learn more, to *do* more. Even now, I always say to myself: "What next?"

Soon, I discovered Pranic Healing. The practice involves energy, auras, and cleansing chakras in order to balance people's lives. When a chakra is dirty, we can see the negative energy that has soiled it. Our job as healers is to restore the chakras by removing bad energy and replacing it with positive energy that we take from God (Universe). Before a session, we always prepare the client for what could occur. Some report a physical reaction, which may include dizziness, a headache, or something else entirely. When someone is replacing everything inside you, you're bound to feel something. Generally, the process takes more than one session to complete, especially in more difficult cases. Although I don't practice Pranic Healing anymore, learning this skill was my gateway to coaching.

Before each healing session, I always talked to the client and tried to discover if there was anything behind the pain they were experiencing. Talking helped me understand their background and learn more about why they were feeling discomfort in certain areas of the body. If a specific event had caused their pain, understanding the situation was important to me to start the healing process. When I spoke to my Pranic Healing clients, I was always interested, and I loved listening to them and trying to connect their problems with their bodies, with their energy. I felt like I wanted to do more of this, and that's when I began exploring the possibilities.

My Pranic Healing teacher pointed out that what we were doing with our clients before a session was really a form of *coaching*. I loved the word—I'd never heard it before—but I knew that it was what I wanted to do. After reading the Mars Venus books, it was clear to me that they were the best when it came to dealing with relationships, so I decided to join the family.

RELUCTANT CLIENTS AND SELF-IMPRISONMENT

I once had a client who was a prisoner within herself. Her daughter was the one who initially reached out to me. She said that she needed help because her mother was struggling, didn't want to talk to anyone, and was locking herself in her room. The woman had removed herself from the world, from everyone, and I wanted to help her in any way I could. Surprisingly, she agreed to talk to me.

In the first session, she went along with everything but didn't really want to be there. She was simply honoring her daughter's request. However, over time, session by session, she began to open up and share details about her life. She said she'd gotten married at thirteen years old—she was in her fifties when she started seeing me—and accepting the husband, the marriage, the whole situation had been very difficult. But she couldn't do anything at the time because she was just a kid. When she was older, she tried to get a divorce, but her parents wouldn't let her, so she stayed exactly where she was.

One day during a session, she said to me, "I just want to fly." She had never studied, never worked, and didn't have an income of her own, but she was very talented at making organic products for hair, face, and body. She would craft these things by hand—and they were amazing. When we looked deep inside, we knew that we'd discovered her true talent. After some encouragement, she created an Instagram account to showcase the products she was making. Although she resisted at first, scared of what her family and friends might think, I convinced her to embrace her talent, take the leap, and present her gift to the world—and she did. Her daughter was very supportive and said that this was exactly what she wanted her mother to do. After more than a year of coaching, my client finally got the divorce she wanted. "I'm flying," she said. We'd taken the journey together, and she'd finally learned to fly.

The experience was challenging for me because she was an older lady who didn't want coaching to begin with. She offered so much resistance after years of living as a prisoner within herself. Deep down, she did want the things she eventually got, but she'd grown so accustomed to denying herself that accepting the freedom to truly express herself had been difficult. But she succeeded in the end. Two years ago, she sent me a picture of her with all of her products—creams, oils, everything else she'd been making—and said she couldn't have done it without my help. Sometimes the toughest challenges generate the greatest rewards.

EMBRACE THE PRESENT MOMENT

When I coach, I enable my clients to find clear purpose in their lives, release the power that dwells within, and achieve their lifelong dreams. I also aim to develop a positive process within the plan we create together to establish an interactive relationship between us. Through coaching, I motivate my clients to reach their true potential, bring about positive change, and live the lives they desire. Coaching is unlocking a person's potential to maximize their performance. It's helping them rather than teaching them. If you're going through a big transition, coaching will help you take better care of yourself and choose the right people to have in your life.

When we establish a strong partnership, I can challenge the client to recognize and build on their strengths, explore their current reality, and move forward while making positive changes. I'm more than a coach. I help clients develop fresh perspectives in all situations and support them to consider a range of options. Often, we brainstorm together and explore the depths of their intuition. I always strive to maintain the highest level of integrity and an unbiased opinion with every client, regardless of gender or background. Coaching is *my* purpose, and working with clients solidifies this truth in my mind each day.

Recently, I quit my job and began coaching full-time. Now I can focus on doing what I love. I'm also studying metaphysics at university. I've completed my bachelor's degree, begun my masters, and aim to eventually obtain my PhD. While a move to Canada forced me to put my studies on hold, I'm considering going back soon to finish what I started. Coaching is my passion and primary focus, and everything I do now is to enhance my skills in that area. There are always new techniques to understand, exercises to learn, and deep questions to ask. Knowing more about metaphysics and philosophy in general will help a lot with my clients and help bring my coaching to the next level. The more I understand about life and the universe, the better equipped I'll be to guide others to their purpose. Changing lives makes me so happy, and I'll always consider what more I can do, what additional techniques I can learn, what next, what next, what next, what next.

If you strive to create something of value, improve the lives of others, be authentic, and focus on positivity, you'll thrive in life. Each day, my clients remind me of a very valuable lesson: you must be patient. We always seem to be in a hurry, but coaching takes time, as do many things in life, and we must progress in baby steps in order to end up where we truly want to be. Sometimes, instead of asking "what next," we should slow down and embrace the present moment—because it's all we ever really have.

ROLLER COASTERS, HIGHWAYS, AND EXPONENTIAL GROWTH

— TANWEER KHAN —

Tanweer Khan is a life, success, and executive coach, who facilitates exponential growth in individuals and organizations. He has coached multiple C-level executives and teams to increase sales, employee retention, and customer satisfaction and focuses on helping people imagine the lives they want—and live them. His passion is assisting professionals and teams with exponential growth through clarity, planning and accountability.

THE QUEST TO FIND BALANCE

During my fifteen years in Saudi Arabia, I spent around eight of those doing a regular office job. If a task came to me, I always got it done, even if it meant a lot of long days and late nights. My desire to be the best employee possible drained all of my time and energy, and I didn't bother developing any other qualities or setting additional goals. At the time, I wasn't a good father, and I wasn't a good husband—I was simply a workaholic.

Because I worked so hard, my life was a constant roller coaster ride that totally lacked balance. However, when I attended a workshop titled "Strategic Visioning of Your Children," I had an important realization. While I was creating a vision for my kids, I'd not bothered to do the same for myself. How could I consider the future of others when I'd never contemplated my own? Learning that I'd been living my life without vision was quite a surprise, and I knew I had to create a plan of my own before I could do the same for my kids. As I began to consider my vision, I realized that being an employee wasn't my only role. I was also a father, a husband, a brother, and many other things. On top of that, I wasn't giving back to the community, which was something I wanted to change. I knew that I could restore balance to my life and turn that roller coaster into a smooth highway. But big changes don't come without struggle.

With a fresh purpose and newfound vision, I began running a volunteer organization that aimed to spread the word of the Quran to non-Arab Muslims across the world. By around the two-year mark, we were a team of twenty, and we all worked hard for our shared vision. And guess what? Imbalance returned to my life. The roller coaster grew more chaotic than ever, and I felt that I had little control over where I was going—I was simply along for the ride. At that point, I understood exactly what I had to do. I needed help.

That's when I approached my first Mars Venus coach, and it was the best decision I ever made.

Through one-to-one coaching, I was able to define my goals and begin the journey of truly balancing my life. The process was gradual—there's never a quick fix—but after a few months, I restored balance in my life and became a good father, a good husband, a good worker, and a good volunteer. However, as I led the volunteer organization, I noticed the same imbalances in members of my team. I wanted them to experience the same coaching that had helped me, but hiring a coach for such a large group wasn't economically feasible. Then someone gave me an idea: I should become a coach myself.

Was the solution really that simple? Yes, it was.

After I received coach training from Mars Venus, I transferred my knowledge to the volunteers, and their lives drastically improved. I soon had the opportunity to coach really influential people, helping them live better lives and have a greater impact on the community. When I saw the value that Mars Venus coaching provided and the positive change it created, I arrived at a crossroad where I had to make a decision. I asked myself, "Should I continue with my volunteer work, which is a great thing indeed, or focus on coaching people and helping them develop themselves and their teams?" Naturally, I wanted to do both, so I added another main course to my plate of life and jumped back on the roller coaster.

Once I'd gained enough experience, I realized that coaching for free was no longer viable—as time is money—and clients often took free sessions for granted. With this in mind, I switched to a paid coaching paradigm.

At one point, I was working, coaching, volunteering, and still riding that rough roller coaster through life. Where was that smooth highway I'd envisioned? Imbalance clearly still dominated my life, so I reconnected with my coach to solve the problem once and for all. Again, I redefined the lifestyle I wanted to live and used my Mars Venus coach as an accountability partner. With time, I achieved the balance I'd imagined, performing pro bono coaching at my office for executives and paid sessions in my personal/weekend slots. I started to see that, through coaching, I could create positive change and make the world a better place.

The Mars Venus tools and philosophy proved very effective, and I grew accustomed to getting results. As a coach, I loved using gender intelligence to help clients gain a better understanding of their personal and professional lives. Moreover, the alignment process helped big time to identify the real WHY behind each person's goals. Once you unearth those silver bullets, you can use them to take down any adversities that may arise. Removing emotional blocks is another powerful tool that can't be denied, and I consider it Mars Venus's biggest contribution to humanity.

Looking back, I can see that coaching helped me realize that I wasn't prioritizing myself. I was a go-with-the-flow type of guy. In addition, I had submissive behaviors and would add a lot of low-priority tasks to my plate.

Coaching made me focus on my vision, my goals, and put me on the path of excellence as I balanced my many roles. I realized that anything that takes me away from my vision isn't important, and anything that moves me toward it is. I started doing proper prioritization and a weekly review, which helped me understand much more about my behavior.

While I was spending time with my family, I wasn't giving them the attention they deserved, so I made some changes. Now, I'll often take one of my five kids to the coffee shop for an hour or two, and we'll just sit and chit chat, where I talk 5% of the time and listen to them for the remainder, sharing and caring. We take the opportunity to really talk and build a sound relationship. I also started taking my wife on weekly dates to listen to her and help her with all of her thoughts and emotional needs. Previously, I'd spent time at home, but I wasn't giving my family the quality attention they deserved. Quantity means nothing when the quality isn't there.

When you first begin to understand the multiple roles you have and which ones you've neglected, you feel bad for a time. But imbalance isn't the only issue that people face.

Sometimes unchecked emotions can lead to crazy roller coasters and chaotic times. However, once you pour attention and effort into the important aspects of your life, you gain satisfaction and feel more in control of your time. We all have the ability to define our own lifestyle and live it. I've learnt that being assertive keeps your plate free of unwanted food and focusing on life and balance is an ongoing activity. We can either choose to be driven by external variables and live stressful lives, or we can give serious thought to how we want to live, and practice focus and persistence until these things become second nature. We must keep ourselves on the track to excellence in all of our roles, and prioritization is the key to success.

In my coaching career, I've had the chance to coach many professionals and executives on their personal and professional lives. Because my coaching capacity was always full, I had to give many clients to other peer coaches. However, the people with whom I worked experienced massive improvements in their lives, and their potential was boosted exponentially.

A LION IN THE OFFICE, A LION IN THE HOME

I once had a client who was part of an executive group coaching program. He was the country head of sales and had set himself a high one quarter target that he hoped to achieve. During alignment, I discovered two challenges. First, he was double-minded. He didn't know whether to continue with his current organization or go elsewhere. Second, he had serious anger management issues, which greatly affected both his personal and professional relationships.

To address the first issue, we used the NLP decision grid to develop clarity and help him arrive at a firm conclusion. He chose to stay with his current organization. The second issue would be much more difficult to resolve and was a major barrier to him achieving his sales target, which was 40% in the first quarter of the year. Although he had a well-crafted plan for meeting that goal, his short temper was causing problems in the office.

During alignment, I'd discovered the red flag of anger and some emotional blocks. As coaches, we don't initially know the client well. During the process, we avoid mentioning the emotional blocks we uncover, and the client wasn't flagging anger as an issue for him. After the coaching had progressed, I asked him: "When was the last time you sat with your kids for an hour, discussing their topics and not yours?" He said he'd never done that.

Then I enquired about his schedule and asked how much time he gives to his kids. Through his answers, I realized that his relationship with his family wasn't good. I asked him: "Do you throw tantrums at home?" He said no. I then asked what happens when he gets home, feeling drained after a hard day of work, and the kids are making a lot of noise. "I say *QUIET*!" he said. But he didn't say it; he roared it like a lion in the jungle. I pointed out how his kids must feel when he communicated with them like this and never took the time to sit down and really talk to them. At that point, he realized that something had to change. That one word he roared as he walked through the door was damaging his relationship with his kids, so he found alternative ways to deal with the situation at home.

Once his perspective shifted, he began playing with his kids more and giving them quality time. He'd even plan activities ahead of time so his children would always get the attention they deserved—and their relationship greatly improved. On top of that, he realized that he'd been short-tempered with his wife. While I didn't work on that relationship directly, it did improve a lot once he became aware of his anger issues.

With his personal life improving, we could now focus on his professional goals. While he had a solid plan for hitting his sales targets, few of the people on his team wanted to do the work. Instantly, I knew that something was wrong. After much discussion, he finally admitted that he was never able to get a complete status update from his team. If someone delivered bad news, he'd lose his temper, and the meeting would soon end. He never knew what was happening with his team because he always exploded before anyone could deliver a complete report. To remedy the issue, I gave him tips on how to lead by coaching instead of exploding in anger at any mistake or oversight. Instead of being Mr. Fix-it for every problem, he had to coach them so they could formulate their own solutions. He followed my advice and became a more supportive person. Rather than unleash fury on the members of his team at the first sign of failure, he'd ask them how he could help. Through coaching, he changed from the angry red-faced boss to the super-supportive mentor—a complete transformation.

At the end of the coaching cycle, I was amazed to hear the news that one of his employees who was nominated to be fired became the best sales agent in a team of 127 people. When I asked him about the magic behind this huge achievement, his answer was simple: "I stopped losing my temper in the workplace."

When you experience a lot of stress in life, anger can arise, and the emotion can hold you back in your personal and professional lives, hindering your life in general. Anger is a common emotional block, and I have many more stories of clients who've overcome it and journeyed onward to success. Once you learn to recognize a barrier and understand why it's there, breaking through is a lot easier.

AVOIDING EMOTIONAL BANKRUPTCY

In any relationship, regulating your emotional bank is critical. You can't withdraw more than you deposit. If you do, you go bankrupt, and the relationship suffers, sometimes irreparably. How exactly does the emotional bank work? Let me give you an example.

If you expect love from your kids but don't give them enough of your time, how can you expect that relationship to remain solvent? When you try to take out more than you put in, the situation isn't sustainable. Eventually, bankruptcy occurs, and you're left wondering what went wrong and how you could've prevented it. Kids are an important example because they don't spell love as L-O-V-E. Instead, they spell it T-I-M-E. They want your time and your attention and consideration, which, in their minds, translates to love. But kids aren't so different from everyone else.

For any relationship to remain prosperous, each party must make appropriate deposits, and often the simplest way to replenish the bank is with time and attention. If you don't listen to your husband or wife and acknowledge the problems they've collected throughout the day, you're not depositing. However, you likely still expect to withdraw without issue.

That type of thinking leads to bankruptcy.

The same logic applies to professional relationships. You should always seek to build a strong bond with your team. Whether someone has the worst or best news to tell, you should aim to be one they contact first. If you are, you've built the right relationship with your team, and your emotional bank is well-regulated.

I always seek to support every person in my team, even the most junior members. If a marriage, funeral, or other important event occurs, I make the effort to attend whenever I can. While I do have a busy schedule, supporting my team in this way is a high priority for me. Actions such as these create real positive change, especially in a volunteer relationship. When it comes to volunteers, you're not paying them anything, and the relationships you build are a big part of what keeps them going. In such situations, you must deposit a lot into the emotional bank, but the investment is always worth the effort.

For my volunteers, I also provide workshops and help develop their skills. I try to add value wherever I can. When you ask people to work for free, you must have a strong relationship with them. Otherwise, the arrangement would never work. Many of my volunteers are busy professionals—they often work demanding jobs and have families at home—yet they continue to put in the effort. Why? Because of the relationships we've built. We even do family outings, barbecue together, and organize other enjoyable activities. The more you put into a relationship, the more you'll get out of it. That's how the emotional bank works.

Any business that integrates this rule into company culture will experience big time growth. Relationships are everything, and you should always treat people in a way that exceeds their expectations. You can't retain people with monetary rewards alone. Love, care, and consideration are what maintain that bond. You must monitor your emotional bank at all times and never withdraw more than you've put in.

XPONENTIAL COACHING AND A FUTURE OF SMOOTH HIGHWAYS

I understand the importance of coaches as well as anyone. I did, after all, experience my own journey of transformation as I sought balance in life. Without the help of my coach, the journey would've been much longer and perhaps much less fruitful. I understand the struggles that many of us face, and I'll continue to use my knowledge and experience to help others. I've already witnessed the impact I can create, and Xponential Coaching is how I take that to the next level.

As CEO and founding member of the company (Xponential Coaching), I aim to unleash the true potential of individuals and organizations and help them achieve outcomes beyond what they ever dreamed possible. I have a team of eight certified Mars Venus coaches, and I've clearly outlined our vision, mission, and strategic and financial plans for the next one, five, and ten years.

In 2023, we aim to be the top coaching organization in Pakistan. Within five years, we'll have a massive footprint that spans the entirety of the Gulf. While I've scaled back my coaching commitments to manage the company, I'll never lose the passion I have for helping people create the lives they dream of. However, I understand that I can create a much bigger impact by growing Xponential, expanding my influence, and changing the world for the better.

TURNING LOSS INTO GAIN

— KAREN LECKIE —

Karen Leckie is an online faith mentor and spiritual catalyst who helps people believe and keep moving forward. She coaches people to walk by faith in their quest for healing and live more fully in God's will.

Karen earned her master's degree *with Distinction* in Organization Development from American University. She is a certified Mars Venus coach and a motivational speaker, giving keynotes and leadership training for conferences. Karen is a highly collaborative team leader, inspiring superior performance by developing, coaching, and mentoring people.

To accompany the development of a learning and leadership culture, Karen also accelerates business outcomes and organizational performance. She works with organizations in recruiting, hiring, performance coaching, training, mentoring, appreciative inquiry, and organization development. Her passion is to see people thrive and grow in the midst of challenging circumstances.

LOSS AFTER LOSS

Loss instills a great deal of fear in people, and with good reason. It's scary. Loss of loved ones, in particular, can be devastating . . . if you let it. After my own experiences with loss during the past fourteen years, I believe a heart broken from loss can not only heal, but can grow *stronger* and attract greater love and success back in.

On December 3, 2008, I lost my mother to a long-term illness. My mother was my best friend, my confidante, and my anchor. Losing her was earth-shattering for me. I felt as if I had no way to ground myself, no inner center which I could use for direction. It was such a huge loss to me that I felt like I had been hit with my own personal tsunami that wiped away everything I had ever known before.

At that time, I was working in an innovative learning program in my school together with my principal. Students were allowed to create their own curriculum, and we supported learners in a learning community. It was a success; it even got published in several magazines. However, when the principal of my school retired, so did the program. The school shut the program down and moved back to the regular curriculum. This was an enormous loss to me, as I had watched students for whom I cared a great deal about succeed greatly by creating their own curriculum. When the program was canceled, I left teaching. I was so devastated, as I had put my heart and soul into this program. I simply could not continue.

The loneliness and grief I experienced between the two losses were simply overwhelming. I had lost the relationship with my mother and then my whole career. At this point, I started to see a counselor who gave me the support and validation I needed to take the time to grieve. This included taking additional time off so I could process all that was happening to me. It had never occurred to me that grief was a *process*, and I am grateful I had someone to point me down that path.

I felt really lost. I started looking for something that would heal me and help me start a new career. I started reading John Gray's books and found that there was a coach training program. I signed up right away. Being trained as a Mars Venus coach gave me the particular training I needed to move through my grief and transition into a new kind of life that I had never known or dreamed of before.

The Mars Venus coach training taught me the difference between how men and women grieve and also how to come out of grief and thrive. For men, the best thing to do is to build testosterone and start solving other problems right away. The best thing for a man to do is to jump full-force back into life and be in "achievement-oriented" mode. That didn't seem to work for me. I was struggling to keep it together and through my coach training, I realized that the best thing for me to do was to go into the "girl cave."

> Men need to build testosterone to relieve stress;
> women need to build oxytocin to relieve stress.
> For men in grief, the best thing to do is to jump
> into achievement mode. For women in grief, the
> best thing is to re-center and get back
> in touch with their true selves.

THE GIRL CAVE

The "girl cave" is a hideaway, a place where women go to recharge and reconnect. Some women build a "she-shed," a retreat from the world. Usually when Mars Venus speaks of the "cave," it is when a man is pulling away to regain his sense of independence. This fits perfectly because Martians love autonomy and need to pull away temporarily.

Venusians, on the other hand, go through waves. Women go through cycles with their emotions, which go up and down. Women pull away into the "girl cave" to find their true center, find out what makes them happy, and build on that happiness. Women are responsible for building up 90 percent of their own happiness. A partner or loved one can only fill the last 10 percent of the love tank. I learned this through personal experience: I had to build my own happiness. Women reduce stress by building oxytocin, which can be built in a number of ways. It can be built by going to get a massage or health treatment, by reading a book, by connecting and talking with some girlfriends.

Women like to talk out their situation, not to find a solution, but simply **to be heard**. Women love community, so connecting with a group of women is very powerful and can have amazing effects in filling up their love tank.

A LIGHT SHINING THROUGH

For me, I felt an intuitive need to build oxytocin and cleanse myself of deep unresolved emotional trauma. There was one little point of light that shone through all this chaos and despair, and it was exactly what I needed: the knowledge of how to start over. I knew instinctively that my mom was very much with me. I could feel her presence in my life, and her influence at times seemed even stronger than when she was alive. I knew that I had the strength within me to proceed and thrive.

However, a third loss was about to occur. Everything as I knew it was about to change in a moment. I went to the doctor for a physical exam, and he found a lump in my right breast. It was breast cancer. I experienced feelings around loss for a third time when I thought of the loss of health, loss of a breast through a mastectomy, and loss of future opportunities. It was too painful to consider. It seemed to threaten my identity, my femininity, and my very life.

MY CANCER JOURNEY

Many women who experience breast cancer go on a "journey." The journey may be to find themselves, to become stronger, and to get in touch with what is really important in life. I began a journey to discover my true self, and I traveled to Brazil and Peru. I felt that my breast cancer diagnosis gave me permission to live . . . and live the way I really wanted to, for once in my life. I went on a journey to discover me, my talents, my gifts and what I was meant to contribute to the world.

My "retreat" or "girl cave" expanded into four years of searching. I was searching to reconnect with my mother. She had gone to Peru on a yoga journey, and I felt that going there would get me in touch with her spirit. She loved to travel.

For me, I needed to pull away from the regular pace of life and slow down enough to listen to and process the intense feelings I was having. It is a woman's responsibility to create a sense of balance so she can be receptive to love and support. It is important to receive love in general but not become dependent on any one person for love. Women need to become responsible for building their own support network. I realized this because in my life I had become very dependent on my mother for support, and I had to learn how to build more support by depending on other people as well.

This is what I learned from John Gray, and it was very helpful for me. It is important to be compassionate to yourself as women—or to the women in your life—by learning these important ideas:

- When women move out of their feelings too soon, they sabotage the natural healing process.
- When a woman doesn't recognize the importance of exploring her feelings, she will either bury her pain by giving too much to others, or she will withdraw from relationships and become overly self-reliant.
- On "Venus"—a woman's natural home—a woman must decisively allow herself to take time for herself and open up to receive support from others.
- By allowing ourselves to fully process the four emotions of grief—anger, sadness, grief, and sorrow, in this order—the grief diminishes, and we are able to fully let go and open to love, forgiveness, and acceptance.

SEARCHING FOR MEANING AND PURPOSE

At first, I didn't know exactly what I was searching for. I continued to experience a very strong need to "get away." This need to get away was a driving force for me to want to escape life as I knew it, and I went on a trip to Brazil to see a famous spiritual healer.

The thought of going through traditional cancer treatment created a lot of fear inside.

More terrifying, however, was the thought of not having anything to live for.

VALIDATION FOR MY EXPERIENCE

Mars Venus training teaches the important differences between men and women, not to change anybody, but simply to be aware of what is. You can't fight biology, and you can't go against nature. Our biological systems are designed differently. I felt validated knowing that I had embarked on a perfectly natural process for me. This gave me the confidence to heal my inner wounds.

Since, in a woman's brain, intense experiences become connected due to the stronger connection between the two hemispheres, everything is connected to everything. The corpus callosum is like a superhighway between the right and left hemisphere and is one-third larger in women than in men. Men's brains are like isolated compartments, while women's brains are like spaghetti. Everything, including memories, emotions, and thoughts, is interwoven together. Thoughts and emotions become mixed together and engrave deep patterns in the brain. When a woman experiences a trauma or intense experience, it brings up every other time in her life when she has felt betrayed by life or by her own self. This connected to my personal experience because I felt like I had multiple traumas and I needed to unravel these patterns in my brain.

> Men's brains are organized like isolated compartments, while in women's brains, everything is connected to everything by a larger corpus callosum. When a woman experiences deep trauma, it brings to her memory every other time in her life that she has been betrayed or experienced loss.

The Mars Venus coach training has a practice that while simultaneously being a coach, you are also a coachee. While you have clients, you also have a coach who is coaching you. You have to know what a client would experience and the ups and the downs of what that feels like. You have to feel what it is like to be riding high and then get hit with a situation that shakes you to the core. You have to realize that as you progress on the path, you will reach many "upper limits" that you need to break through to reach the next level. Coaching helps in releasing a lot of limiting beliefs and replacing them with more empowering beliefs. Coaching helps you break through upper limit after upper limit to reach your desired goal and destination.

Knowing that in a grieving process women need to slow down and get in touch with their intuition helped me to honor my own process and allow life to emerge naturally. In coaching, there is an emergent learning journey that starts with the relationship between the coach and coachee. The coach determines the process and holds space, and the coachee determines the speed. The client can go as fast or as slow as they want, based on their comfort zone. Every time a client stretches out of their comfort zone, the coach will always be there to "wrap a warm, cozy blanket" around them and make them feel safe again.

The client is always in charge of their own speed and their own journey within the process to reach their desired state of transformation. I now encourage all of my clients to be in an emergent process, which is not necessarily a simple, linear process, although the left, logical side of the brain wishes that it was. It was important for me to be committed but not attached to any one outcome so strongly that it affected my inner balance. I had to listen to my body and intuition during my journey, and I gathered internal and external resources to guide me.

> The coach determines the process; the coachee determines the speed. The coaching process emerges as a journey, where the client determines their own goals that they want to achieve and can become empowered to be in charge of how fast or slow they want to go.

THE IMPORTANCE OF COMMUNICATION

One thing I have learned, through much trial and error, is to communicate more. Coaching pushes you to have weekly conversations as you progress through life or business. This brings to the surface things that you normally might not have reflected upon, and having a coach allows you to go further than you would go yourself. Without a coach, you would get to the edge of your comfort zone and not proceed further. A coach enables you to be brave and move through any internal resistance that might be holding you in the status quo position. Coaching enables change and transformation.

REDUCING STRESS AND INCREASING OXYTOCIN

One benefit of my coach training experience was the amazing support network we created among all of the coaches. We constantly inspire each other to go further and tackle challenges that we probably would not take on alone. Stress can be a huge factor in our mental and emotional health. With cortisol levels at an all-time high in society, women need to learn how to reduce stress by building oxytocin. As a Venusian, I learned that oxytocin is a bonding hormone and can be built in so many different ways!

It is our responsibility, as women, to learn how to build our own oxytocin.

Talking and being heard, without the need to provide solutions or fix anything, is the biggest oxytocin builder. By just listening, you will raise a woman's oxytocin levels, therefore, lowering her stress. Oxytocin is at work when you cuddle a puppy or hug a friend. It makes women more trusting, generous, and more in love. It's a neuropeptide. It is a protein-like molecule that your brain cells use to communicate with each other. It is a hormone that plays a role in sex, childbirth, bonding, social interaction, emotions, and many other functions.

In his books, John Gray gives one hundred ways to build oxytocin for women. Here are just a few:

1. Join or form a new mothers' club.
2. Take care of children in some capacity.
3. Feed the hungry.
4. Read magazines about fashion and people.
5. Attend inspirational, spiritual, and religious gatherings regularly.
6. Keep updated on the lives of friends.
7. Watch your favorite show with a friend.
8. Listen to inspirational music.
9. Talk with or call a therapist or coach.
10. Study a new culture and taste its cuisine.
11. Spend time at the beach, a river, or a lake.
12. Learn to ski, play golf, or play tennis with friends.
13. Enjoy wine tasting with friends.
14. Hire someone to help you remove the clutter from your house.

TRANSFORMING THROUGH PAIN

Getting through my journey with cancer made me stronger, more powerful, and able to receive love, peace, forgiveness, and understanding into my life. I learned that in cancer, and in facing difficulties in life, you need to go into the thing that you are afraid of. All of the preparation that I did by setting up a strong support network and asking for help was instrumental in getting me to the place where I felt courage. I turned my pain into an awakening. I turned the dark days and suffering into an opportunity for brilliance. The nurses commented that they had never seen anyone so glowing and happy throughout the entire treatment. I came out glowing on the other end because of the preparation I did, physically, mentally, emotionally, and spiritually. I knew that I had an entire network of people, near and far, who were rooting for me and wanted me to live, thrive, and be happy.

COACHING CLIENTS TO BREAK THEIR UPPER LIMITS

When I left my first career, I pushed myself to start my own business as a coach. Facing my own demons gave me the experience needed to inspire and coach others to break through their limiting beliefs, or "fictitious restrictions," about what they thought was possible to achieve.

In addition to life coach training, I also took business coach training and started coaching small business owners and entrepreneurs to grow their businesses. You have to face your inner demons in order to succeed in business. Entrepreneurship is the biggest self-development tool on the planet. When you start a business, who you are at your core is reflected back at you through your interactions with the world. What is happening in your life is mirrored in your business. A lot of the time, how you do one thing is how you do everything.

What I learned during my cancer journey was to have the strength, persistence, and perseverance to navigate any obstacle that comes my way. Through Mars Venus, I had the tools, the support system, and the coaching methodology to support entrepreneurs and business owners to their greatest successes. I became a better coach because of it. In addition to helping business owners to increase their sales and focus on the bottom line, I also knew how important it was to focus on their health and reduce stress.

CRISTINA: CLIENT STORY

A client of mine, Cristina, had been hesitant to leave her job and start her own photography business, so she worked full time and did her photography part time. She wanted coaching to help create higher-end service packages so she could charge more for her services. At the same time, I realized that while Cristina needed help with her business, she also needed help in her personal life. I taught her how to handle her stress. For entrepreneurs, the working hours are very long, and making enough sales is most often a challenge. Every single month, entrepreneurs worry about cash flow and in times of deficit, while waiting for the next sale, life can be really difficult emotionally and mentally. I coached Cristina on the importance of oxytocin for women and how women can only lower their stress by producing the hormone.

Money, focusing on the bottom-line, and success are all needed for entrepreneurs, but these also build testosterone. This is great for men, but not for women. As a result, Cristina made sure to keep up her workouts at the gym, make massage appointments, and make time for her female friends to offset all the testosterone building she had to do as a woman business owner. So while I coached her on her leads, her sales conversion, and ideas to generate higher ticket sales in her business, I also helped her with her life and work-life balance.

We worked on developing new packages and programs for her clients. She does newborn photography, and she is planning on publishing a book about children with pictures of her clients and their kids. When I started coaching her, she got the confidence to run her own business full time.

In the ninety-day success plan that we wrote together, Cristina realized the importance of scheduling time for nurturing, bonding, and de-stressing in her calendar. This served as a measure to keep her stress in check and also allowed her to be in the optimal state of mind and health so that when she was spending time in and on her business, she was able to radiate abundance and health. This attracted more clients to her and kept her previous clients reinvesting in themselves through her photography services. Keeping her stress low meant that she could serve at a higher level and provide top-notch services for her clients.

Exercise 1: *What do you want to accomplish in the next ninety days? Write your plan down and hire a coach to help keep you accountable as you implement your plan.*

CYNTHIA: CLIENT STORY

Cynthia had just returned from maternity leave, and she was having trouble with her sales. She called me in to get a vision for her business and to help her get back in the working world after being off for three years with her three children. We worked together on a plan, and it helped her in selling more in her marketing campaigns.

Together, we created a ninety-day success plan that would keep her accountable to implementing that vision every day for her marketing role. Before she went on maternity leave, her sales had been at a certain level. After returning, Cynthia was having trouble keeping the discipline needed to develop new leads, follow-up, close sales, and manage her time. She also wanted an accountability partner to maintain her workouts at the gym, which she was able to fit in before and after work, depending on the schedule of her children's pickup times. Once I coached Cynthia through the vision process, she tied certain rewards in with certain achievements. For example, her goal of closing more sales would allow her to save up and be able to attend her sister's wedding. Tying the achievement into things that made her happy allowed the vision to activate her oxytocin.

Women's *happiness* increases when their *oxytocin* increases. Also, women manage time differently from men, and I was able to work with Cynthia to allow more flow into her life and guide her to be compassionate with herself, while at the same time maintaining the high level of accountability that she wanted.

Cynthia was able to work on developing leads for her business while also focusing her vision and motivation to push her to keep going. Our coaching sessions were held in person, and we were able to bond over tea, creating oxytocin and providing a little retreat from her busy days. Building in time for her workouts was also important as a stress-buster and a time when she could put herself first.

Exercise 2: *In business and in life, you need to build in time to recharge your batteries and balance out your stress. What three things can you do in the next ninety days to reduce your stress?*

BRUCE: CLIENT STORY

Bruce wanted to start his own internet marketing training business after being a music teacher in his first career and later being an anti-bullying speaker in schools. We developed a plan on how to get new clients, package his programs, and make offers to the audience in his workshops. We created a ninety-day plan on how he was going to attract clients to his training workshops. Bruce had enjoyed so much success in his anti-bullying workshop business by generating leads online through internet marketing that he had been flown to the Caribbean—all expenses paid—to deliver a workshop. We focused on replicating the success from one business to the new business and getting the word out.

I coached Bruce to brainstorm ways to market and attract participants to his workshops. The main part of our coaching was to maintain focus and keep him on track during the implementation of the plan. Knowing that men need to build testosterone to reduce stress, we focused on timelines, targets, and results as a way to keep momentum. Bruce is not only a terrific internet marketer, but he is currently growing his public speaking business. We focused on landing more speaking opportunities as a way to grow his profit.

Bruce led several workshops during the time that I was coaching him. Each workshop had better attendance, better conversion, and better results than the last in terms of learning outcomes. Bruce developed a solid curriculum, more robust workshop delivery, and was able to generate more leads from a local networking association in his area. He hired an assistant to help out with the search engine optimization to handle the increasing load of clients that he started serving in his new business.

Due to the focus on reducing stress through our coaching and other resources, Bruce also utilized optimal nutrition techniques from John Gray's expertise. He kept himself in peak state mentally by utilizing motivation and empowerment practices from several self-development tools, all of which helped his business to grow. After everything he learned, Bruce started to grow his "mindfulness" business, and he now hosts a very successful podcast called Mindfulness Mode that helps people reach new heights of calm, focus, and happiness.

> **Exercise 3:** *What do you want to create in the next 5-10 years? Write your action plan and call a coach to help you in implementing your vision.*

LESSONS LEARNED ALONG THE WAY

I truly believe that a heart broken from loss can not only heal, but it can grow back stronger—if you allow yourself to go through the four emotions of the grief process. By allowing yourself to grieve properly, you open up your capacity for love in ways you can hardly imagine. You simply have to listen to your intuition and your body and get the support you need to grieve fully and successfully. Though it can be a very painful process at times, it can also be both rich and fulfilling. You can go through the "dark night of the soul" and come out into the light on the other side. Taking the time to get the help you need, grieving the loss, and becoming whole all help you to open to love again.

Rushing the healing process doesn't heal you faster; it actually holds the process up. Healing a broken heart is like healing a broken bone: you must get help, reset the bone, and protect the bone in a cast. The healing for your heart is the same thing, just with different tools for resetting and protection. Take the time to figure yours out, listen to your intuition, and then give yourself the permission to follow the process.

Once you have slowed down, listened to your true self, and gotten in touch with your deepest "why," then life starts to have more meaning. Hire a coach to help get you out of your comfort zone and break through your upper limits. When you set out on a path of excellence, that is when you will have more blockages put in your way. It is important to have a support system to soothe you in the tough moments, but also to push you further than you would have gone by yourself.

LOSS TURNS INTO GAIN

So, how did I turn loss into gain for myself and my clients? What is the secret sauce? Is there one factor that outweighs any other in the struggle to turn pain into awakening and brilliance? I would say the number one factor is transforming your attitude: the belief that it is possible. Through the loss of my career, I learned that I could step into a new career as a coach. Through the loss of my mother in the physical form, I learned to trust that she is with me deeper and more powerfully now, and I feel her presence guiding me to live my highest potential. Through my cancer journey, I learned that I am stronger than I ever knew. The qualities that I had developed in myself (strength, courage, overcoming fear) are qualities that I now help clients to develop in their life and business.

I learned that some transformations take a long time, and it is important to be patient. I learned how to ask for support and help. I learned how to receive love on a deeper level. I learned that you have to love yourself first before anyone else will love you. I started trusting more. I let people help me. I let people support me. I had to let go of my identity of being "broken." I had to let go of the story that I don't deserve love. I learned what true family love is. I started to believe that things were possible. I realized that I am very powerful. I went on a journey to discover my true self, and I now know myself on a level deeper than I ever thought possible. I know that I can and do make a difference in clients' lives and I can inspire people with my story.

I learned how to show up fully as myself. I learned that we don't lose ourselves by being open and opening our hearts. In fact, we receive more of life. I learned that how I choose to see things is how they end up being for me. I can choose to see things as a loss or as a gain. The choice is mine. I learned how to break down the "lone wolf," "independent woman" identity that I held on to so strongly. I learned how to break down the walls around me. I learned that it is OK to need people. In fact, needing people makes you stronger. You can't do everything alone. I learned that if it is true that in a woman's brain everything is connected, and you cleanse out the "broken down, dead end, failure" type thoughts that you have about yourself, you can start to build new brain connections. Then the new connections of positivity will grow exponentially.

Through the cancer journey, I tapped into a deep strength, persistence, and perseverance to navigate through any obstacle in life and business. I learned to coach my clients to honor their own journey of achieving their goals and greatest desires. Once the tides turn and, rather than a series of losses, you have a series of successes, success breeds success. I learned that you can't outgive God. In giving, you receive. Also, the more you give, the more you receive. By opening your heart and giving love, you receive more love than you ever could imagine. Abundance, prosperity, success, and love all start with gratitude in your heart. That is when you make the greatest difference in the world—when you know yourself, own your own journey, know your own strength, and live a life full of purpose and meaning. Live life fully; every day is worth you living in your brilliance. Every day is worth turning loss into gain.

ASK THE RIGHT QUESTIONS, GET THE BEST ANSWERS

— MONIQUE SARUP —

No matter the situation or what life has thrown at you, everyone deserves to love themselves and live with true purpose and passion.

As a mindset coach for youth and young adults, **Monique Sarup** has a mission to help women dare to create the lives of their dreams. She assists her clients in realizing their true potential through goal exploration and works with them in mapping out practical steps for reaching targets. Supporting her clients every step of the way, Monique believes that no dream is unreachable—it's just about uncovering the right path to get there. She understands the pressures and challenges that young people face today and helps them "find their spot" in life and the world.

Using leading-edge self-development techniques and personalized coaching methods, Monique helps young people gain confidence, self-esteem and life skills so they can move forward in a way that fulfills and motivates them. She empowers her clients to live life on their terms, providing them with the skills to manage and overcome hurdles as they arise.

Having commenced her own self-development journey at the age of nine, Monique knows the importance of young people understanding their minds, emotions, and unique purpose in life. She has "walked the talk" and actions her own advice and mindset techniques in her day-to-day life.

Her coaching sessions have often been described as both "fun" and "life-changing," and that's exactly what she sets out to do—change lives without compromising on the good stuff.

Monique lives in Mount Macedon with her husband, Sanjay, and their daughter, Zara.

AN UNCONVENTIONAL CHILDHOOD

My personal development journey began at a remarkably young age. Mum and Dad are both life coaches, and they raised my sister Chloe and I in a warm and nurturing environment that fostered self-development, self-education, and constant growth. Due to my parents' tireless care and attention, I had a happy and fulfilling childhood, and I always felt supported in everything I did. I never had to experience trauma or suffer from neglect, which I thought was a fairly normal way to grow up. However, I soon learned that not everyone had the same nurturing childhood as me. Outside of my warm, cozy bubble of love and unconditional support, some kids lived in a much colder world of pain and neglect.

When I was nine years old, Chloe and I attended a self-development event for kids aged eight to twelve. Being in that large room with all those other children was an eye-opening experience. Suddenly, I had been yanked out of my protective bubble and thrust into a world where kids had to deal with divorce, trauma and, sometimes, abuse. Many didn't know what love, safety, and support felt like. They hadn't experienced these things and if they had, it was only in small, fleeting doses. I realized then just how lucky I was to have had such a happy childhood. Many of the children I met were hurt, but none were lost causes by any means.

Over the course of several days, I watched in amazement as coaches worked to empower even the saddest and most traumatized kids in the program. Using the right words, actions, and tools, the event's leaders were able to instill new, positive, more fruitful mindsets in those who had suffered so greatly. Each hurt kid in that room had the potential to heal, grow, and move beyond the traumas of the past, and I saw so many successfully take those all-important first steps. I saw firsthand the power of coaching.

Until then, I didn't know that most people don't get the same opportunities that I got growing up. Not all kids have coaches for parents, parents who understand the value of continual development through exploration and self-education. Most kids don't get to attend the "Unleash the Power Within Youth Leadership Program" and walk across hot coals while Tony Robbins himself holds their hand during one of his infamous fire walks. Not everyone receives the support they need early in life to grow to their full potential, discover their purpose, and work towards realizing their wildest dreams.

Seeing those dejected kids transform before my eyes sparked something in me. Although I hadn't suffered my own trauma or neglect, I wanted to help others overcome the mental health hurdles that life had placed in their paths. From then on, I continued my self-development journey with renewed passion and purpose, knowing that everything I learned wasn't just for my benefit, but also for the benefit of those I wanted to help. I would make the most of the amazing opportunities I'd had growing up and pass my knowledge, insights and tools on to those who needed them most. Coaching would be my calling.

DISCOVERING MARS AND VENUS

When I finished high school, I took a gap year to break routine and experience something new. If I was going to help a diverse range of people, I needed a diverse range of life experiences from which to draw. So, I left the familiar comfort of home and ventured out alone, flying to the United States to seek out some of the best trainers in the world.

Ultimately, my search brought me to Dr. John Gray. I was familiar with his work, and I knew that the methods he taught were not only effective for coaching others, but for managing your own life as well. So, I applied for the

Mars Venus life and business coach training program, hoping to take the next step in my self-development journey. I was eighteen years old at the time and hadn't accomplished anything of note; I hadn't made any headlines, but I was determined to learn every valuable skill that the experts were willing to teach. I knew that the Mars Venus methods were top-tier when it came to dealing with relationships, whether they be romantic, business-related, friendships, or anything else.

Everything in life stems from our relationships, and learning how to manage them well is a superpower that can't be matched. When I applied to become a Mars Venus coach, I was ready to learn the magic behind the methods—and I wasn't disappointed.

After being accepted into the program, a whole new world of insight and understanding opened up before me. I learned so many powerful tools that I could use to help my clients, but I also acquired skills that I could apply to my own life and relationships. As I immersed myself in the world of coaching, my purpose grew clearer and my passion burned brighter. The spark that had ignited my desire to guide others to their goals and help them through dark times became something much more fierce, and I knew for certain that I was on the right path.

At age eighteen, I officially became a Mars Venus coach—and I was ecstatic! When I returned to Australia, I got my first coaching client, and the next part of my journey began.

GETTING BIG DREAMS OFF THE GROUND

I once had a client, Anna, who had a big dream: she wanted to be in the Olympics. Clearly, she had a firm goal—even if it was a lofty one—but something was standing in her way. It certainly wasn't a lack of ambition. Was her dream too big or unrealistic? No! Others had made it to the Olympics before, so getting there was definitely possible. In fact, I'm a firm believer that *anything* is possible. Achieving her goal would take unshakable commitment to the task. Did she lack dedication? No! She certainly had the drive to see it through. So, what was holding her back? Anna's biggest barrier wasn't the difficulty of the task at hand but her lack of belief in herself. While she was ambitious, she lacked confidence.

Before we began planning her path to the Olympics, I had her envision what being an athlete at the Games would look like, and she pictured it perfectly:

Anna arrives at the stadium for her big moment. In the locker room, she takes the time to prepare herself, warm up, and settle her nerves. She's more excited than nervous. Finally, her moment comes, and she walks out to the sound of a cheering crowd in a packed Olympic stadium. They know her name, and they know how hard she worked to get here. Everything has been leading up to this moment and after years of training and dedication, she's ready to give it her all.

After the event, she celebrates with friends, family, and teammates. She hugs her mum, her dad, her brother Ben, her best friend Steph, and her coach who pushed her so hard—sometimes too hard!—in every training session. She returns to the locker room where she showers, changes, and prepares for what's to come: a night of celebration with those who came all this way to see her reach her goal.

Anna visualized everything clearly and in great detail, even down to the sponsors she would have and the uniform she would wear. Visualization alone doesn't get results, but knowing exactly where you want to go is the first step of any successful journey. Anna saw her destination as clearly as if she had already arrived; now, she just needed a map to get there. So, we began planning her route.

We mapped all of the steps—big and small—needed for her to get from where she was to where she wanted to be: the Olympic Games. This is where a "goal circle" can help you gain clarity surrounding the steps needed to reach your destination. Here's how it works:

1. Write your goal in the center circle.
2. In the outer circle, list small steps you can take towards that goal.
3. In the second circle, add greater, more significant steps.
4. Begin working towards your goal, starting with the small, easily-achievable actions and moving on to the bigger steps when ready.
5. Reach your goal!

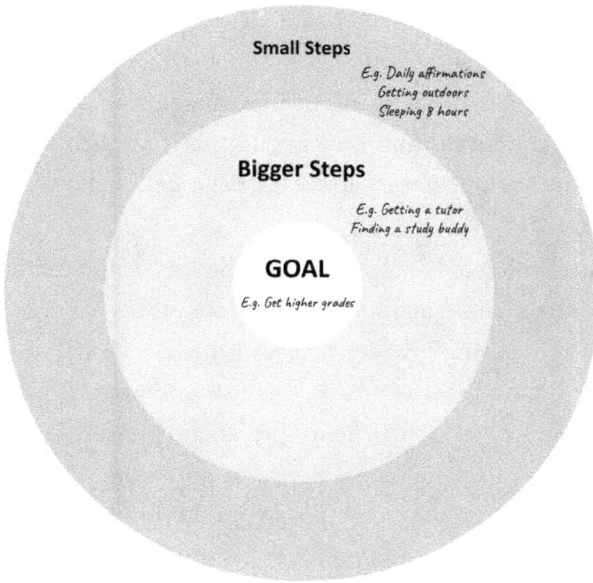

Small Steps

E.g. Daily affirmations
Getting outdoors
Sleeping 8 hours

Bigger Steps

E.g. Getting a tutor
Finding a study buddy

GOAL

E.g. Get higher grades

GOAL CIRCLE

Allowing clarity on your
ultimate goal

Once we knew the path forward, we came up with practical solutions for each step involved. How would she make time for extra training? How would she find a world-class coach? How would she get sponsors to support her on her journey? These were all important questions that needed answering. A map isn't much use if you don't know how you're going to get from point A to point B. So, we solved each problem one by one and eventually had a complete action plan in place. Her journey to the Olympic Games was ready to begin.

To give Anna some perspective, I booked her a helicopter lesson at a local flight school. As well as being a fun and challenging activity, the lesson was an analogy that would help her better understand the journey to come.

The helicopter represented her dream to compete at the Olympics. But do you think she could just hit a button and launch into the sky? Of course not! Before takeoff, she had to perform a rigorous pre-flight check before she could even consider getting in the air. If she missed a single step, she risked having the helicopter—her Olympic aspirations—crash and burn. Takeoff itself wasn't a quick and straightforward process, either. Before attempting to fly, she had to learn the functions of each gauge, paddle, and lever. Without knowing how everything worked, there was no way she could achieve the outcome she wanted: to get in the air.

Finally, it was time to fly. With the help of her instructor, knowing that she had performed all the right checks and understood the controls, she put everything she had learned into practice, and slowly the helicopter lifted off the ground. She was in the air.

That first flight was always going to be a little shaky. However, with practice, Anna could master the controls and learn to fly on her own. When I coach, I don't want my clients to rely on me long-term. I want them to learn to fly on their own. As a coach, I don't provide answers—I ask questions. I'm not there to offer tidy little solutions to all of my clients' problems. Instead, I guide them to find their own answers to their most important questions. Through coaching, I equip people with the tools they need to fly on their own. I'm sure we've all heard the "teach a man to fish" analogy. And it's so true!

At that flight school on a sunny afternoon, Anna learned what it would take to get her dream off the ground, and she has been flying high ever since.

MY MENTAL HEALTH MISSION

Once I started coaching, I made it my mission to spread awareness and educate others about mental health. There's so much information out there—online, on TV, across social media—about having a healthy body, but a lot of Western medicine focuses on our physical condition and fails to consider our mental state.

Before you can have healthy relationships with others, you must first have a healthy relationship with yourself. You are the only person in your life who can never leave, and you must be happy with who you are before you can wholly commit to others. Investing one hundred percent in any relationship, whether with friends, family, colleagues, business associates, or a romantic partner, is difficult when you don't love yourself. Self-love is the first step to any successful relationship, and working on yourself is vital. How often do you do something just for *you*? We can't just live to serve others, not if we want to live happy and fulfilling lives. Your relationship with yourself is the foundation on which all others are built, so make it strong, sturdy, and capable of bearing great weight.

If you're unsure how to start nurturing your relationship with yourself or would simply like some more ideas, here are ten great ways to connect and check in with yourself:

1. Take a walk in nature
2. Take ten long, deep breaths
3. Go outside and move the way you feel
4. Do a superhero pose for two minutes
5. Detox from social media and the news
6. Spend at least thirty minutes on a creative hobby
7. Spend time with supportive loved ones
8. Take a long, hot bath
9. Participate in yoga, Pilates, or tai chi
10. Say three things that you are grateful for each day

When I met my now-husband, Sanjay, I was still working on myself, and I wasn't ready to commit to a serious relationship. I was honest from the outset and told him that I needed to love myself and be really happy with who I was before I could fully commit. Many of us get so caught up in giving—to our kids, our partners, and everyone else in our lives—that we forget to take care of ourselves. We fail to stay on top of our own mental health, and, as a result, all of our relationships suffer. How can you be your best for others when you're not at your best? I always take time out for myself and focus on doing the things that I love. When you take time for yourself, you have more to give to others in your life.

As the saying goes, "You can't pour from an empty cup." When you feel that you've got nothing left to give, anxiety, depression, and other mental health issues emerge to fill the void. These aren't the things you want filling your cup! When you pour from a cup of anxiety, you spill that negative energy on those around you, and it seeps into all of your relationships. In order to thrive and live a happy life, you must fill your cup with something sweet.

When life gives you lemons, make lemonade! Life isn't always rainbows and butterflies. Mental health is something that requires work every day, much like physical health and fitness. For example, if you lose five kilos, it doesn't mean you can go back to your old ways—sitting around, eating cake, and not exercising—and the weight will stay off. You must continue to work on your health to ensure that it stays where you want it to be. By continuously working on your mental health, you can improve it every day, but if you abandon it for months at a time, it can suffer and slide backwards.

Think of a yard. You can't just mow the lawn and trim the bushes once—or even once a month—and expect it to remain tidy. Leave it too long, and it becomes an unmanageable mess. Like a yard, mental health requires constant care and attention—mowing, trimming, pruning, fertilizing—to stay neat, vibrant and healthy. There's no one-time fix. You must continue to do the work.

To help stay on top of your mental health, try setting yourself at least one goal a day and watch how this changes your outlook and attitude. For example, making your bed or not looking at your phone for the first hour of the morning are simple actions you can take to achieve something early. By completing just one simple task in the morning, you feel a sense of accomplishment, which primes the brain to want to achieve more throughout the day. It's a simple trick that gets amazing results. Give it a try, and start the day with a win!

After learning to love myself, where I was, and where I was going in life, I was ready to give Sanjay my complete commitment and the love he deserved. On top of that, Mars Venus equipped me with some of the most powerful relationship tools available, and referring to them every day has helped me and my husband continue to strengthen our love and our relationship. We now have a baby daughter, Zara, and, after eight years, our relationship is as strong as ever.

It's amazing what you can achieve when you have the right tools. You'll never have a perfect relationship—perfection is a myth!—but you can certainly have a great one. Mars Venus allows you to see both sides of all situations, which is incredibly important when it comes to navigating any relationship. The skills I've learned over the years have helped me in both coaching and life, and they can help you too.

EQUAL PARTS STYLE AND SUBSTANCE

I mainly coach women aged thirteen to thirty. Because a lot of my clients are young, they're often struggling to find their purpose in life. Setting goals is difficult when you don't know what you want to achieve. I experienced similar setbacks between high school and university. Sure, I was pursuing coaching at the time, but I still wanted to invest in my education and earn a degree—I just didn't know what it would be! After taking the time to consider my ideal path through life, I knew that I wanted to run my own business, so I settled on a bachelor of commerce.

When I see clients struggling to find their purpose, I ask a lot of questions. A good coach will never just give you the answer. The ideal solution is always buried somewhere within the client's own mind, but we need to work together to dig it out. If you're struggling to identify your own purpose in life, stopping to acknowledge that you're stuck is the first step. Don't keep powering through, repeating the same old routine. Stop, acknowledge that you're yet to find your purpose, and start asking questions.

Here are some to get you started:
1. What do you love doing?
2. Can any of the things you enjoy become a job?
3. If you could have any career in the world, what would it be?

If you keep asking questions, you'll eventually unearth the right answers. But if you continue to go with the flow and don't take the time to stop and think, you may end up in a place you never wanted to be, creating confusion and, later, resentment. When you know your destination and get to plan the journey, you can enjoy this life a whole lot more. Don't work to live, live to work on something you love.

Another big problem that many of my young clients face is social media. If you're not on it, you're missing out—or at least it can feel that way! Sure, social media is great for connecting with people, and it's an invaluable tool for businesses, but negative consequences arise when we don't use our online time in healthy and productive ways.

On social media, everyone's lives can appear perfect, but it's an illusion. Even if I'm having a shitty day, I can post a nice photo with a positive caption, and all anyone sees is that. But reality rarely matches our social media feeds, and faulty perceptions of what life should look like can negatively affect our mental health. When we can't meet those impossible, idealistic expectations we see on the screen, anxiety finds an opening and moves in.

I've helped clients with eating disorders who, due to the influence of what they saw on social media, always wanted to be thinner. People in this situation often see anorexic girls online who they idolize and want to mimic. Social media plants unrealistic expectations in their minds, which leads to them creating incredibly unhealthy—and potentially dangerous—goals.

Clearly, social media isn't going away. If anything, it's becoming a bigger part of our lives, so avoiding it isn't an option for most people, especially those of us who run businesses or want to stay connected with friends and family. As always, the quality of our relationships is key.

Here are some tips for maintaining a healthy relationship with social media:

1. Don't check social media first thing in the morning. Challenge yourself to hold off for as long as you can.

2. When you're spending time with other people—friends, family, partner, kids, *anyone*—avoid checking social media and your phone in general. Instead, take the time to connect with the people who are right there in front of you.

3. If you find yourself mindlessly scrolling, stop and acknowledge the fact. Bring awareness to what you're doing and consider whether your time would be better spent elsewhere.

4. Remember—what you see on social media isn't reality! It's fiction, and that's exactly how it should be treated.

Our lives consist of many different relationships, and the quality of those relationships can dictate the quality of our lives. Communication is key. There are two sides to every story and two sides to every relationship. If you want a romantic date night, just ask! If you need some alone time, say so! If your partner forgets to take out the trash, remind them!

Movies portray love and relationships as perfect, but that's not the case in everyday life. When you throw in work, study, kids, gym, housework, sleeping, eating, and all of those other commitments, life gets busy. Sometimes just sitting down, communicating your feelings with one another, and sharing your expectations can make your relationship run a whole lot more smoothly.

Effective communication with yourself, your partner, and others is the key to relieving much of life's anxiety. If you do feel anxious about a relationship, you should stop and consider why you're feeling that way. What's the story you've constructed inside your head? Is it accurate? Or is it a work of fiction? If you're having trouble unraveling the stories in your head, a coach can help. Once you've taken the time to analyze the situation, only then can you know whether your concerns are justified.

If a problem does exist, communication is the key to solving it. Addressing issues when they arise is much better than letting them pile up inside, weighing you down and fueling anxiety. When you don't hoard your problems, you carry less weight, and you'll skip through life with a lighter step.

I want to spread the word of coaching and mental health to the younger generations. Some people are on months-long waiting lists to see a psychologist when a coach may be able to fill that void. I'm not suggesting that psychology doesn't have its place—it most certainly does—but not everyone can wait six months for support. Some people may not even need a psychologist in the end when coaching gets them to where they want to be. The option to hire a life coach is always there, and that's the message I want to spread.

When I coach, I put a huge amount of effort into my clients, not just during our sessions but around the clock. Some coaches simply attend to their clients for the hour or so they're with them. They have a chat and collect their fee. However, I work with people twenty-four hours a day, seven days a week. I'm *always* on call. If a client needs me at 3 am on a Sunday morning, I'll be there. If I'm on holiday and a client calls for support, I'm answering the phone. If a client puts their trust and faith in me, I'm there for them whenever they need me, day or night. Our problems don't stick to standard business hours, and a great coach will be flexible and understanding of her clients' needs. I still maintain a healthy work-life balance, but my clients know that support is only ever a phone call away.

LOVE THE PLAYER, LOVE THE GAME

— REEM SUWAYD —

Reem Suwayd came to Mars Venus Coaching with a passion to help women find and design the lives they want and deserve, and to discover their strengths as Venusians. Gender intelligence and self-development have been her focus since she read *Men Are from Mars, Women Are from Venus* as a young girl. Her background in computer science, business, and art allows her to understand a lot about the human brain and how it works.

Now she is a master coach, corporate trainer, and social media director with Mars Venus Coaching. After years of coaching and helping people live their dreams, she now wants to help coaches succeed, find their uniqueness, and unleash their abilities to change the world one relationship at a time.

UNITING ART AND SCIENCE

In college, I studied computer science, business, and art, each subject granting new insights into the way the human mind works. Even so, one question frequently occupied my thoughts: how is it possible that great people can make each other miserable? Eventually, I discovered *Men Are from Mars, Women Are from Venus*, and, from that moment on, my life was never the same.

Within the pages of that book, I learned the lessons that no one teaches in school. Most of us tend to think that a happy relationship is something that happens to us and not a thing we create, shape, and perfect over time. I soon realized that this was a faulty belief that had little grounding in reality, with no logic to it at all.

The mind works very much like a computer and can even be programmed in similar ways. Certain inputs trigger pre-programmed patterns or responses that often lead to predictable results. This is true for both computers and the human brain. My computer science teacher used to say, "If you put garbage in, you'll get garbage out," and that's as true in life as it is in programming. If you read, watch, or eat garbage, the end results are fairly predictable. Our minds are just like computers, and we can program them in any way we please.

While our brains may operate like machinery, they're also much more than that. Because I studied both computer science and art, I understand the human mind more completely, both the left and the right portions. Art is less about logic and pre-programmed patterns and more about feelings, fun, and the chaos of life. Art exists outside the bounds of rigid rules and learned behavior. Art is the perfect complement to science. When you embrace both aspects of life, you'll understand yourself, others, and the universe a whole lot better.

COACHING, THE SHORTCUT TO HAPPINESS AND SUCCESS

Whenever I had questions about life, my quest for answers often led me to coaching. I didn't always find the answers I sought, but I did learn how to ask better questions. Once I understood that I wanted to be a coach and help others find success and happiness, I spent a lot of time searching for and researching coaching schools—and Mars Venus stood out from the rest.

Coaching is a systematic process, and every aspect of a coach's journey, including marketing, sales, and handling clients, is a part of a well-designed system you learn to follow. Utilizing such a structured and logical approach appealed to the computer scientist in me and drew me further into the Mars Venus universe. I also welcomed the flexibility of the program. All of the resources we need are available on a specialized website we can access at any time. Due to the nature of the Mars Venus online system, we can meet, train, and coach remotely, which means that our location in the world is never an issue. When I considered all of these factors, I knew I'd found the right coaching school for me.

But what is coaching? It's powerful. It's a lifestyle. It changes the lives of both the client and the coach. Many people believe that coaching is about facilitating change, but it's not. A coach can't help you become something you're not. However, they can help you rediscover your true self, which is always there waiting to be unleashed. A coach can help you remove the dust, the obstructions, and anything else that prevents your true self from shining. That's what coaches do best.

DIGGING OUT EMOTIONAL BLOCKS BY THEIR ROOTS

I once had a client who I initially thought was struggling with fear. She seemed afraid of so many things, which made progressing in life difficult. Every time she wanted to take a step forward, fear held her back. Whenever she wanted to try something new, such as start a business or travel, that inexplicable terror kept her rooted in place. It took many sessions before I understood the real issue.

One day, when I was asking her about her childhood, she kept repeating the phrase, "I feel confused." At a young age, someone in her life had made her feel afraid. During the incident, a major problem had resulted in a lot of yelling, and, since then, confusion surrounding the event had dominated her life. Although she'd say she was afraid, she was more confused than scared. Whenever we tried to set a new goal in her life, she'd repeat that same phrase: "I'm confused."

My client carried her confusion for a long time, and removing such a large and familiar emotional block wasn't easy. When she wrote a feeling letter and revisited the incident that had left her so confused, she explained all of her emotions—anger, fear, guilt—but couldn't understand how she could bring herself to express love for the person involved. "I'm confused," she said. "How can I love this person?" We went through the process a couple of times, and eventually she had a breakthrough. Finally, she understood the root of her emotional block, was able to express love for the person involved, and the confusion in her life passed. While she does still experience some fear, it's not beyond the normal amount one expects. Identifying the root of an emotional block is always crucial to removing it and helping someone move forward with their life. If you don't specialize in this type of coaching, you may not understand that states like confusion can stem from fear, and trying to find the cause of a client's problem could leave you the one confused.

SIMPLICITY AND OTHER USEFUL TOOLS

A great coach is someone who can make deep changes seem simple. Simplicity is one of the most powerful tools in the coaching toolbox, and small, focused steps are much more effective than those that are big and complicated. If you climb a ladder one step at a time, you'll rarely fall. When changes are gradual, you receive less resistance from the client. The journey is more joyful, even if we do struggle at times, and simple steps eventually create a deep impact. That's why I simplify almost everything I teach. Because of this, my clients feel great and motivated after each session and can clearly envision how to achieve their goals.

Clarity is crucial to success, and complex goals can be difficult to see and seem impossible to reach. I always help my clients recognize exactly WHAT they want, but I also encourage them to view that thing from varying perspectives. Sometimes we get lost in life, and we just need someone, like a coach, to help us find the light so we can continue on our path.

Your WHY is your drive. When you have a clear purpose, nothing can stop you from moving forward. In Mars Venus Coaching, we always focus on the WHY because we understand the importance of doing so. With a clear WHY that aligns with your heart, you can create a plan that allows you to reach your goals and live your best life, the life you dream of, the life you deserve.

Planning is both an art and a science. You can learn about the scientific aspects from many different places, including the internet, books, workshops, and courses, but no one can teach you the art aspect better than a coach.

Playing the planning game can be fun but if you only focus on the science, the process can be very stressful. That's why art matters.

While science lets you create a plan that's robust and logical, art encourages more feeling and flexibility. For example, you may set a difficult goal that you hope to achieve in 90 days, but the artist inside knows that it's OK if it takes a year, or even more. You know you're going to try your best to meet that deadline, but at the same time you don't feel overwhelmed by the pressure. You're free to focus your thoughts in other directions and move them away from fear of failure.

Science allows us to create smart, specific deadlines, and art offers much-needed flexibility. It's OK to change something—or even everything—as long as you're not doing so out of fear. Sometimes during the coaching process, you'll experience an inner change and need to alter your plan to accommodate the new version of you. The scientific side of planning doesn't recognize this so easily. You can't explain it with science; you have to feel it like art. Science crafts the plan, and art gives it life.

Accountability is one of my favorite Mars Venus coaching tools. Why walk alone when you can have a friend to walk with you? Now imagine that friend is trained to hold you accountable, and, no matter what, he or she will always be there to help you stay focused, brainstorm, and remind you of who you really are and why you want to walk this path.

That's what a coach does.

Clarity, planning, accountability—the concepts may seem simple, but simplicity can be a powerful tool. I coach women more than men, and many of them are very hard on themselves. They feel overwhelmed. But when they see words like "fun" and "simple," they become more motivated, which is why I like to take complicated concepts and simplify them as much as possible. Sometimes having just one clear goal is the best way forward. Small steps can lead to big things, and simplicity is a simple and effective tool for success.

SHATTERING PATTERNS

Due to my background in computer science, I understand how to recognize patterns. We all have patterns of thinking that take us to the same unfavorable results over and over again. But a coach can be the pattern breaker and inspire clients to shatter the chains of thoughts, actions, and emotions that no longer serve them. A coach can be the catalyst that speeds up the chemical reaction—the change—and turns lead into gold.

In Mars Venus Coaching, we perform alignment in the beginning, and the client answers a series of questions. Often, even after a year or more has passed, the same patterns are still there, begging to be broken. I've even noticed the same behavior in myself at times. I journal, and, when I go back and read previous entries, I realize that some of the patterns are still there, like they're built in, imprinted in our brains. An event occurs, triggers a programmed reaction, and we behave the same every time. Often, we don't even realize it's happening. It's funny how closely the mind resembles a machine and how relevant computer science is to understanding how the brain works.

Most patterns have a root cause, an origin. For example, feeling worthless as a child could lead you to care less about certain things to protect yourself from re-experiencing those negative emotions. It's a survival mechanism. You don't want to feel worthless again, so you decide not to care, but such a mindset can make setting and achieving goals difficult. In coaching, when we discover the root of an impractical pattern, the client writes about it, and we ask the question: what if the same thing happened now as an adult? They soon realize that they have the power to effect change, to shatter the patterns of the past. We hack the system, and it works. What happens when you break a pattern? You get new and exciting results.

AIMING FOR ALIGNMENT OVER BALANCE

As a trainer and coach, running a business changed my life. It gave me the ability to create the reality I always dreamed of and stoked my passion for giving and living. A great business owner—or leader—longs to make an impact, is a genuine giver, is passionate about serving others, and strives for innovation.

But too much passion, too much motivation, channeled into any undertaking can lead to discord. In business and life, there's no such thing as balance. How can there be? You can't make everything equal. It's just not possible. Even so, many of us still seek balance, an impossible state to achieve. But maybe balance isn't what you want. Perhaps its *harmony* you long to feel. Some things you can do today; others you can leave until tomorrow. Some things need more time; others need only a little.

Realizing this changed my life. For the first time, I was able to focus on my career and not feel guilty. Today I might have a long meeting, but tomorrow I'll spend time with my kids.

Each critical facet of your life doesn't sit perfectly in line with every other and never will. There's give, and there's take. There's push, and there's pull. Some things hold more weight, while others are light and trivial. Life got much easier for me when I understood this, and the concept works with my clients as well. Running a business or building a career takes a lot of time and effort, but learning to replace the idea of balance with the notion of harmony, a more flexible goal, will relieve much of the stress and guilt that can arise when seeking stability.

LOVE THE GAME

In life, there's always a way: a U-turn you can make or a new path you can take. Coaches help others discover that new way, that shortcut to success, that concealed entrance to happiness and growth.

Relationships are the magnifying glasses that highlight the bright and dark sides of each individual. If we're happy, at peace, and enjoying life, relationships will help grow these aspects of ourselves. But if we live in our heads and allow negative thoughts and emotions to control us, relationships will amplify this too. Like magical mirrors, relationships reflect what's inside us. No matter how much we want to blame our partners for our problems, they're merely a reflection of us, and we can only cast blame at ourselves. Relationships heal the soul; they're the fertilizer of life, and nothing makes us grow stronger.

Life, however, is a game. If you don't grow, you die. If you don't move, you lose. You can't stay on the same level for long. New challenges are always there to take you to the next stage of your journey. If you trust your role in the game and its creator, you'll play well and experience great joy. You'll have fun. The more challenges you face, the more enjoyable the experience becomes. If you play well, you'll live a fulfilled life brimming with happiness. Who wouldn't want that? But you can't play well if you hate the game, which is why love holds so much power.

COACHING AND AFFAIRS

— MICHELE FESTA —

Michele Festa is a certified coach and trained side-by-side with John Gray. As a coach, Michele mostly works with couples (individually and in groups). Michele is also a certified psychologist and psychotherapist, practicing since 1972 throughout Europe.

Michele is a former president and CEO of the European Association for Humanistic Psychology (EAHP). He has taught and worked with famed US psychologist Rollo May and with noted British psychiatrist R. D. Laing.

In his practice, Michele has supported thousands of individuals, executives, and couples to actualize their potential and has brought to life the principles of collaboration, respect, empathy, discipline, and love.

His working style is direct, focused on the here and now, spontaneous, authentic, and supportive for the development of the real personality.

Throughout Michele's career as a psychologist and psychotherapist, he has found the methodologies of John Gray to be the most effective, specifically in the areas of couple's communication, gender intelligence, breaking through gender barriers, cross-cultural coaching, interracial marriages, and facilitating transition in family-held businesses.

> *To forgive*, *is to **release another** from*
> *being responsible **for how we feel**.*
>
> ***Women*** *enjoy being **Respected, Understood,***
> ***Admired and Cherished**.*
>
> ***Men*** *enjoy being **Appreciated, Accepted,***
> ***Needed and Trusted**.*
>
> **John Gray Ph.D.**

SUSAN AND STEPHAN

"This *thing* here—my husband—has had an affair, and now he wants me to be understanding and *forgive* him!"

This is how I met Susan and Stephan in their first coaching session.

Susan, thirty-eight, was a successful psychiatrist and psychoanalyst. Her husband, Stephan, forty-six, was a marketing manager working for an international organization. He frequently traveled abroad with his legal and copyright executive, Gabby. Gabby, I later found out, was twenty-nine years old, and a brilliant and attractive young lady with whom Stephan had an affair.

The trouble first began when Susan started to notice her husband was often unavailable for phone calls while he traveled. He would say he was busy whenever Susan would call him during their normal chatting hours. Because of this, Susan felt compelled to look through her husband's emails and text messages. When she did, she found conclusive proof that Stephan was having an affair with Gabby.

As I listened to Susan tell the tale of why they were here in my office, I started to gather information about each spouse. I knew I needed to organize sessions according to what each spouse needed to become an effective member of their marriage.

FOREVER CAN HAPPEN

In my years as a coach, I have seen many couples who believe the devastating impact of infidelity determines that they, as husband and wife, can no longer stay together. They suppose that their desperation, misery, and pain can never be removed, and this level of betrayal is the end of everything they ever believed about love. But through John Gray's Mars and Venus Coaching philosophies and methodologies, I have seen that it is not so.[1]

True, the pain of infidelity can leave one feeling off-balance, out of control, and experience a debilitating pain and rage that they have never experienced before. However, it is not the end of everything. There can be the proverbial light at the end of the tunnel!

THE ROOT OF THE PROBLEM

After Susan's opening line, I decided to speak with her first. She clearly had many things she needed to get off her chest. As we spoke, and she started to relax, Susan continued her story.

"After questioning Stephan about his new nightly ritual of turning off his phone, he told me that he was having sex with Gabby. We have two children, both under five years old. I want to accept his explanations and his promise not to see her anymore, but I feel deeply hurt and humiliated! I feel like I cannot trust him anymore. In fact, just to hear his voice bothers me! And if he tries to touch me, I feel . . . *nauseated*."

I felt a lot of empathy for Susan. She was still in love; she wanted to save her relationship and protect their two children. However, her dignity and self-esteem had been hurt, deeply.

I must admit that I also thought Stephan had not earned so much devotion and altruistic love (coaches also have feelings and it's their duty to recognize them, before they can constructively coach their clients).

Next, I spoke with Stephan and got his side of the story. "Susan has been tense and insulting me, with any pretext, since the birth of George—our second child, two years ago," Stephan began. "She also stopped wanting to have sex with me. She'd think of any number of excuses: she is sick; the children are sleeping in the next room; she feels embarrassed; she is preoccupied with work; her mother, her sister . . . the list goes on! I tried to be understanding, to be patient, but it was difficult. Gabby saw that I was starting to become depressed, and I readily accepted the sympathy and understanding that she gave me. I even thought that I could relieve my marital pains with a platonic relationship: a pure, innocent affection."

During my talk with Stephan, I learned that Gabby was also married. It was about one month ago that their affair began during a two-week seminar in Berlin. "Because of my children," Stephan continued, "and also because I still care for my wife, I admitted to Susan what had happened in Berlin with Gabby. I told Susan I wanted to stop seeing Gabby, even though she was in love with me and I also felt responsible for her suffering. I'm so sorry, and I know that I have been disloyal. At the same time, I just don't think I can go back into the routine of Susan: always nervous, insulting me . . . even when the children are around."

I felt a lot of compassion for Stephan and for the suffering that was active all around him. Stephan never learned how to communicate constructively at various levels, from the romantic to the intimate and from the tender to the passionate.

ON DIFFERENT PLANETS

I could have started working with Susan and Stephan like a typical couple's psychotherapist, since I am also a certified psychologist and psychotherapist, but I assessed that John Gray's coaching approach would get more adequate results. This approach would give the desperately needed practical and direct support to Susan, Stephan, and their children.

Susan and Stephan needed, in my opinion, to find a rapid way to heal the pain, reestablish trust, and discover the different "languages" that men and women use to communicate.

According to John Gray, men and women are often seen as coming from two different planets. As discussed in his book, *Men Are from Mars, Women are from Venus*, Venusians are accepting and enjoy sharing not only their ideas but mostly their emotions. They like to do things in harmony with other people, from shopping to cooking and leading a team to creating a common vision. Because of their brain composition, women have easier access to their emotional and rational hemispheres. Women's emotional part of their brain is twice as big as men's. It's activated eight times more than men. Therefore, they are not only able to multitask but also capable of evaluating more accurately the impact of their decisions, from a realistic *and* from an affective/emotional point of view.

In Venusians, the hormone oxytocin is not only responsible for the biological functions in reproduction—childbirth and breast-feeding—but also allows them to be more involved in emotional, cognitive, and social behaviors. Venusians with adequate oxytocin activity can relax, trust, and develop a bonding not only with their children but also with their partner.

Martians are more solitary and competitive. They perform better with compliments. They are generally more naive than Venusians in romantic, erotic, and sexual fields. The hormone of testosterone in Martians is mainly responsible for their sexual arousal and makes them more competitive, not only while doing sport but also in the workplace and in the family setting.

Generally, testosterone is very active in the "courting" phase, and after the "honeymoon phase" ends—one to three years into the relationship— testosterone levels decrease. And this is when Martians have the opportunity to transform an attraction into a mature, responsible love. Studies have shown that Martians with high testosterone levels are more likely to divorce.[2]

I illustrated the model and the guiding spirit in which I was proposing to work to Susan and Stephan. Our work would proceed for a certain period of time. While we worked together through the coaching process, there was to be no major decision-making unless there was a discussion in my presence. Most of the topics included:

- moving out of the house,
- sending children to stay with relatives or boarding schools,
- changing job, and
- economic/financial/legal situation (if necessary, refer to the "Spousal Elective Share" or similar arrangements, according to local laws).

During this time, there was also to be absolutely no:

- manipulation of children,
- disrespect and violence (whether that be physical, emotional, sexual, or psychological), or
- dating other partners (unless clearly stated and accepted by both and for both).

When both Susan and Stephan agreed and understood the terms, I explained philosophies that I would be using to help them bridge the gap that infidelity, anger, and resentment had caused. As illustrated by John Gray in *Men are from Mars, Women are from Venus*, men and women have very different perceptions of one another. Utilizing the teachings of Gray, I was confident that I could guide Stephan and Susan on how to communicate at a deeper, more constructive, and more intimate level.

HOW COACHING WORKS

Working with couples utilizing the philosophy and methodology of Mars and Venus Coaching is one of the most challenging activities on which someone in the life coaching professions could embark. At the same time, it is one of the most rewarding, professionally and emotionally.

Mars and Venus Coaching is much more efficient and efficacious than other interventions I have experienced as a professional coach. Today, people want *instant relief* from their troubles before solving the deeper problems and becoming equipped with knowledge and tools to help them know themselves better.

The methodologies used in Mars and Venus Coaching effectively motivate the couple to clarify the dynamics and communication type of their relationship without getting too much involved in past traumas, hurts, or pains. Even though the coach may show respect and sincere empathy, there needs to be a clear boundary between coaches and their coachees; Mars and Venus Coaching provides that.

OBJECTIVES AND LOYALTY

Coaches, in my opinion, have the responsibility to start where the clients are, regardless of the specific prevailing school or philosophy to which we may also adhere. As the old saying goes, "When someone is drowning, don't teach them how to swim, but give them a life jacket."

When I begin an intervention with a couple seeking help, my first step is to clearly communicate the conditions and the objectives of the intervention. This equips the partners themselves with an understandable responsibility and power for the evolution of their marriage.

I find it more constructive to work with both partners individually *and* as a couple. I had to learn how to manage my loyalty to all three:

1. the wife
2. the husband
3. the couple

THE STRUCTURE

In couple's coaching, I generally meet the partners for ten sessions. Each session is structured into three hours and three parts: First, I meet with one of the two partners for forty-five minutes. Then, I meet with the other for forty-five minutes. Finally, I meet with both the husband and the wife together for an hour and a half.

This gives me the opportunity to listen to both sides of the story, to know how each partner is really feeling, thinking, or judging the same situation, and to listen to the homework they were given in between sessions to support the couple's evolution.

These modalities have given me very good results in working with hundreds of couples, from various countries and cultures, in the last twenty years.

TIME AND COST

Depending on the level of the conflict and situation of the couple, the length of time it would take to coach a couple varies. Typically, I coach in one of three ways:

1. One meeting of three hours, once a month (with weekly reports) for ten months.
2. One, three-hour meeting, every week for ten weeks.
3. In a critical or urgent situation, a more intensive method could be applied: the first option for ten weeks and then the second for ten months.

Coaching must have the objective of solving problems, not creating them. Therefore, often we adopt the "Sliding Fee Model" based on the client's ability to pay.

We set aside 10 percent of our income to finance "scholarships" for deserving or needy clients. Many clients—anonymously and voluntarily—contribute to this scholarship fund to help disadvantaged clients.

DIFFERENT NEEDS

John Gray states that "women are motivated when they feel cherished, while men are motivated when they feel needed." According to Susan, she wanted to be able to look behind the eyes of Stephan. But after their initial relationship, she felt that either he was avoiding eye contact, or—if there was eye contact—she would feel loneliness, emptiness, and boredom.

Susan wanted to be heard *beyond* Stephan's ears. She craved moments of fun, playing, dancing, and cuddling each other. Susan asked Stephan directly—more than once—for this kind of complicity. She told him that the lack of this was making her feel useless in the relationship and left her with no sexual desire.

In one session, Susan quoted *The Little Prince* to show how she wanted their relationship to be: "To me, you will be unique in all the world. To you, I shall be unique in all the world."

Stephan had different needs. He felt he needed a woman who would enjoy his company, especially when he was tired and returning home from a long trip. He desired a life partner who would be tender and accepting, just as Susan was when they were first married. Stephan sincerely tried to understand the requests of Susan, but he just could not detach himself from his logical mind.

He felt that since his logical way of thinking made him a success in business, it should also make him a success in society and in his couple relationship. Many people had told him how pleasant his company was and how much they enjoyed his jokes. After playing the part of the efficient business executive, whom everyone liked and respected, he found himself growing jealous of his children for all the caresses they received from Susan.

After some discussion, we discovered that Stephan and Susan got married under the auspices of the "hormone force" and some pressure from their parents. When they first met, they both felt an immediate attraction to one another: physically, passionately, and emotionally. Their parents belonged to a particularly rigid church that had very little tolerance for too much intimacy before being married. The combination of these two elements contributed to rushing into marriage.

Through the years, Stephan and Susan had become so focused on their activities and social engagements they were unaware that a cloud had fogged their vision with apathy toward their own needs, romance, intimacy, the requests of their partner, and care for them as a couple.

Now that we knew the problems and what led to Susan's constant insults toward Stephan as well as Stephan's affair, we could start to rebuild the relationship from the ground up.

PEACE TREATY

I began my sessions by asking Susan and Stephan to positively state their goals for a desirable relationship. The goals had to be action-oriented. For example, they should not state their goals with vague terms, such as, "I don't want a relationship where there is no respect for my needs." Instead, the goals should read something like, "I want a relationship where there is clear and serene communication, where I can abandon myself into the arms of my partner, where the desire for sexuality would be the natural and spontaneous evolution of the interactions we would have had throughout the day. I want—within six months—a relationship where respect and trust would naturally pervade our interactions, exchanges, and communication. If all this happens, I will see my children less tense and happier."

Their goals had to be SMART (specific, measurable, attainable, realistic, timely), and they needed to think of a series of small ways in which they could evaluate their progress.

The message of John Gray is that by teaching in a practical way *how* to have an appropriate blend of love, patience, gentleness, compassion, and caring, most couples would have a more joyful and meaningful life.

It may sound like an oversimplification of an obvious quality, but when we work on tender, soft, and often neglected feelings, it is as if we are performing open-heart surgery. We take what was once an unhealthy and unstable heart and give it a new lease on life, with the ability to love, care, and empathize. It takes personal and professional training, experience, warmness, humbleness, patience, stamina, risk-taking, enthusiasm, courage, and leadership to obtain this. Every valid Mars and Venus Coach is able to tackle this task.

LOVE IS A DISCIPLINE

Love without discipline could sabotage all efforts to evolve from roommates to soul mates. All good intentions have a momentary life and dissolve when the first real or painful problems arise. This is why I had Susan and Stephan do some homework. An assignment often given to couples is "The Feeling Letter."

Following a plan developed by John Gray, partners are instructed to write a letter to the other partner with whom they can express freely anything they feel: anger, sadness, fear, regret, and love. The letter may then be shared with no one, or only the coach. This is because they have to feel sincerely spontaneous and put down on paper the best and the worst, the compassionate, the shameful, the vulnerable, and the bully. With the "prescription" of secrecy, we often obtain this.

During the individual sessions, the letter is reviewed with the coach and often it goes back for multiple edits. This writing and rewriting are important parts of the coaching work. The level of spontaneity and patience—or impatience—is essential feedback for all those involved, partners and coach.

After two months, Susan wanted to move out of the house. She called me and asked for an urgent appointment for a couple's session. The session opened with Susan communicating that she wanted to move out. Our contract stated we would meet for ten months, and during our months of work, there should not be any major changes to the relationship, e.g., moving out or divorce.

Susan felt that she could not regain her trust in Stephan. Stephan was devastated and did not know what to do to get Susan to stay. He sounded sincere when he told me that he had completely stopped all relations with Gabby.

During the couple's session, the desperation they both felt helped Susan and Stephan to clarify to one another their specific wants and needs for their marriage and for their family. Each one found the requests of the partner valid and pledged to work for their realization.

Often, hate and love are part of the same chain of emotions. Imagine a line where at one end there is hate and at the other there is love. The couple's and the coach's work consists of moving love to a 51–60 percent level, after that, very often, love reaches such a significant place that hate is almost totally anesthetized.

No one wants to remove the lid from Pandora's box. The end result of that keeps the family compromising until everyone is miserable. Then, the members go outside the family to seek validation for their emotions. This is why honest communication is important.

I suggested Susan and Stephan keep a daily journal. They were to write no more than five lines, recording their emotions, and then email it to me every evening. The purpose was that they were to train themselves to express their *authentic* emotions, to remind themselves that they are in a ten-month program that takes place at least 99 percent outside of the coach's office.

We agreed that at least twice a week they would have practiced the "Active Listening" technique in which one partner speaks for five minutes, and the other listens and then repeats what the other has said. They are not allowed to comment, question, or judge. Then, they reverse roles.

After twenty minutes of this communication method, it is recommended not to elaborate or explain anything to the partner for at least twenty-four hours. "Active Listening" is one of the many tools proposed by John Gray. It has the objective of listening with the "third ear" to what your partner is saying, regardless of whether you do not agree, feel misunderstood, or feel gratified. The purpose is to convey feelings and encourage you to really listen and look with your entire being.

Every month we had our four consecutive sessions, and they began to develop less fear toward their partner, a little bit more confidence, and some satisfaction in intimate situations.

The real indication that they were on a good path was the comments that came from their children: "I love to be with you two, together." "I don't feel afraid of the dark anymore." "My teachers say that I have become more attentive."

EVER AFTER

Stephan, Susan, and I worked constructively together for ten months. Eleven years have gone by since they first came to see me, and a few months ago I received an email from them. They were happily and joyfully together and invited me to participate in a dinner in Paris to celebrate their wedding anniversary. They were going to have a small ceremony in which they would remarry as soul mates.

My gift to them was a book by John Gray with a card saying,

Thank you for being committed to love, because as women and men love each other more—and we learn to connect in this most challenging time—we truly are stepping through a threshold to make a better world.
With more women in the workplace, more women in government and men participating more in housework, we can create a World based on mutual respect, inclusion and appreciation of differences.

This Mars and Venus coaching methodology is one of the most powerful and yet one that potentially could be assimilated by many people with emotional and intellectual attitudes. If we look at what made this coaching successful, I will give credit to the attitude that John Gray exhibits with his trainings, teachings, and writings. His main message is not about if there is love but how you can manifest it.

NAVIGATING THE NEW DATING PARADIGM

— OKSANA IRWIN —

Oksana Irwin is a lifelong student of life. She acquired her credentials via ever-evolving growth, evolution, and self-mastery, and the result you see today is due to decades of learning and teaching, fiascos and breakthroughs, big falls and big comebacks.

Along her journey, she gained deeper access to her truest and most authentic self. She uses this access to help her clients with transformations and the overcoming of limitations so they can break through self-imposed glass ceilings, leap into limitlessness, and attain new heights in all areas of life.

After graduating from Kyiv University with an accounting degree, Oksana realized that this wasn't her calling. Her creative and untamed mind was seeking challenges, and her thirst for life and adventures led her down the entrepreneurial path.

Along the way, year after year, decade after decade, Oksana has been continually studying and learning about the human condition. Quantum physics, karmic energy, universal laws, neuroscience, psychology, physiology, hormonal effects, gender intelligence, epigenetics, triggers and responses, and generational consciousness are among the areas that she has studied during her lifelong quest for knowledge and her own evolution.

Oksana helps her clients manifest their dream lives of success, harmony, and fulfillment by finding and treating the root cause instead of endlessly treating symptoms. The Mars Venus success methodology that she teaches leads her clients to newfound insights so they can move forward with clarity, focus, confidence, and momentum.

Oksana has a reputation for helping her clients tap into their power, unlock their confidence, and create extraordinary results in their personal lives, their intimate relationships, and their careers.

She is a catalyst for people to:
- Find love and create polarized and harmonious intimate relationships
- Fall in love with themselves, gain power and confidence, and create and maintain boundaries
- Establish self-care regimes, gain vitality and energy, and reduce internal stress
- Reconcile and revive broken and stale relationships
- Remove friction in relationships and create peace, harmony, passion, and aliveness
- Determine when it is time to leave toxic or unfulfilling relationships and create a follow-through plan
- Create breakthroughs in existing careers or create new opportunities and success in new endeavors
- Improve their communication, emotional intelligence, and stress management
- Live fulfilling lives that they absolutely love

PART 1
FROM RUSSIA WITH LOVE

Over two decades ago, I moved to Canada to meet my soulmate to whom I was married for almost twenty years. When we first connected, we lived on opposite sides of the world: he was in Canada, and I was in Ukraine. We met via one of the first online dating sites at the dawn of the internet (wow, it's hard to imagine now how we lived without it). At first, we wrote letters, sent faxes, and used a landline to connect. We really were the pioneers of international online dating. Our love story felt like a fairy tale or something out of a Hollywood movie. He flew across the world to meet me, and it was love at first sight. It was so romantic, fun, new, unknown, exciting, and adventurous. I was thirty, and he was forty-one. We had our whole lives in front of us.

To get to know each other, we spent two weeks traveling, and, when he left to return home, I knew he was the one. I came to Canada three months later, and, from that point on, we were inseparable. Even though we lived in a tiny old rental at the time, we felt like we were on top of the world, because we had each other. Three months later, we got married, and a lot of skeptics didn't believe that our marriage or love would last. But we both knew that we were truly soulmates who'd found their counterparts and come together from different parts of the world.

Most of our marriage was just as happy, fulfilled, and exciting as the beginning of our love story. Together, we built businesses, traveled the world, and had incredible success—and some big falls—during this part of our life journey. We were there for each other as true warriors, partners, and passionate lovers. We had an unbreakable bond between us. We were full of love and life.

For most of our marriage, we had a beautiful and exciting time together. However, after my husband's second back surgery, he was prescribed a cocktail of drugs to help deal with the pain, and the medication took a toll on his mental health. He became depressed, started drinking more, and the light went out inside him. Before his back issues, he'd been a very active man who loved skiing, fishing, and other outdoor activities. Unfortunately, in the later years of our marriage, he severely deteriorated, and I struggled to recognize the man I'd married. It was a sad loss for me that I needed to grieve.

When our relationship ended after eighteen years, I felt lost and was completely unprepared to be single in the new dating and relationships paradigm. My role in the family business concluded alongside our marriage, and I found myself without a plan or vision to create a new life in this new age.

PART 2
THE AWAKENING

When I first started dating after my two-decade-long marriage ended, things weren't working out for me at all. Everything I thought I knew about relationships seemed wrong or outdated, and I struggled to even meet anyone interesting let alone form a meaningful relationship.

During my marriage, life felt fulfilling and full of excitement. My husband and I had a lot in common, and we ran multiple businesses together. We also had a house in Costa Rica, planned to build a dream home there, and were on track to early retirement. However, when my marriage ended, everything else ended as well, and I needed to grieve what I'd lost, heal from within, and reinvent myself on so many levels, personally, professionally, and spiritually. The emotional pain I went through opened me up to an awakening and put me on the path of spiritual growth.

When I read *The Celestine Prophecy*, the book changed how I related to the world and became the starting point for my spiritual journey. Discovering spirituality, connecting to my higher self (soul), and learning and embodying energy work was nothing short of life-changing for a girl who was born into a communistic society, completely cut off from her spiritual connection and gifts for most of her life. Ever since my awakening, I've studied quantum physics and energy work extensively and become a spiritual and intuitive leader for a lot of my clients.

When I first began down this new path, I had to heal myself, work through my trauma, and reinvent my mindset. Along the way, I dealt with shadows, old programming, limiting beliefs, fears, and insecurities. To be successful in dating, I also had to learn new relationship skills and seek to understand men, myself, and the differences between us. Only once I understood the fundamentals of a healthy relationship could I thrive in the new dating paradigm.

PART 3
LEARNING TO DATE AGAIN

Dating was very challenging for me at first and didn't seem to be working. I dated online and offline and, while I went on a lot of dates and met a lot of men, the experience disappointed and frustrated me. I felt like I wasn't in charge of my love life. Nothing made sense when it came to men and dating, and, after a couple of failed relationships broke my heart, I decided to make a change.

My second heartbreak had been devastating and wasn't something I could logically explain. Struggling through my pain, I tried to talk to friends and the personal development coaches I was involved with at the time, but nothing they said helped. That's when I realized that something was missing. Clearly, I was failing to understand certain things about men, dating, and relationships. I kept hitting the same wall of disappointment and frustration when men didn't treat me with respect, when they acted like I was a commodity. They were never serious about me and didn't want to commit to anything real and lasting. Out of pain and frustration, I turned to Mars Venus relationship coaching. I didn't know what else to do.

As I gathered and applied new ideas about men and relationships, my reality transformed, and I started to feel more in control of my love life. With new information to guide me, dating became more positive. The more I learned about relationships, the better and easier everything got. For most of my life, I struggled with not having any answers to why things can get so hard in a relationship. I'd frequently ask: How can I get him to understand me? How can I make him want me? Why didn't he do this or that? Mars Venus answered all of those questions and solved my relationship dilemmas. Better yet, I now had tangible solutions that made my relationships work. After spending so much time not knowing why things weren't working out, why I wasn't attracting the right men, and why I wasn't able to create something meaningful and lasting, my love life quickly grew smooth and predictable. There were no more rollercoasters, anxieties, or doubts. I now had a practical step-by-step plan that I'd not had access to for most of my life. For the first time, I felt like I was in control.

Finally, I could relax, trust myself, make better choices, set firmer boundaries, and start having fun with dating instead of stressing and worrying about acceptance, rejection, validation, and what men will and won't do. I felt more at ease and in control because I knew how to produce the results I wanted in both dating and my relationships. As a result, men were now treating me with respect and appreciation. They were interested in *me* and wanted to spend time with *me*. To them, I was different and special compared to other women, and I had a lot of high-value men swirling around me.

PART 4
MEETING THE ONE, BECOMING A COACH

One year after learning and applying the Mars Venus relationship tools, I met someone with whom I completely clicked. We connected online through Tinder, and, as I found out, we'd actually been in proximity the whole time. He lived half a block from where I worked, and we frequented many of the same social places, but somehow we'd never met. That, however, was about to change.

During our first date at a casual restaurant, we clicked immediately, and I knew he was the one. I applied my Mars Venus philosophy and was amazed at how much it helped me navigate the early stages of our relationship. I always understood what to do next and was able to lead us all the way to a loving and meaningful union. We've since created an amazing and fulfilling life as a couple, staying together all this time.

Following my dating success, I began sharing my knowledge with friends and coworkers, helping them with their relationships. When things started working for them too, I was stunned and knew I was on to something. Once I realized how effective and necessary my help and advice were, I decided to take things seriously and consider a new career. That's when I started my coaching business.

When I first read *Men Are from Mars, Women Are from Venus*, I didn't have much confidence or belief in myself, and I was nurturing the hope that reading a chapter each night would change something. Ever since then, I've been a fan of John Gray's work and have been applying his insights to my own love life. Most of the Mars Venus teachings were counterintuitive to what I thought I knew about relationships, yet they were very effective. Often, ideas ran completely opposite to what I thought I knew about the opposite sex and relationships in general. I also realized that the mainstream information and common advice that everyone—including me—was using didn't match the successful and effective lessons provided by Mars Venus. Clearly, my coaching services were needed.

RESCUING RELATIONSHIPS

Maritsa, a young woman from Pennsylvania, was three months pregnant when she first reached out to me for help. Due to the rapid deterioration of a five-year relationship, she was full of anxiety, fear, frustration, and even hopelessness. She felt like she was sinking in quicksand. She and her partner, the father of her one-year-old child, were no longer living together and had very little engagement with each other, only interacting when it came to their daughter's needs. They were both hurting and feeling disconnected, and she was losing hope of ever getting to a place of love, intimacy, and certainty.

According to Maritsa, their relationship had been in turmoil since the beginning, and she never felt loved, taken care of, or content. For over five years, she and her partner had struggled to get on the same page and establish a level of commitment where she could feel safe. She wanted to be confident in her relationship, knowing that her partner would be there for her and her children. In addition, she longed to trust him and not have to worry about him leaving her or looking at other girls. The constant anxiety was excruciating and drained her mentally and emotionally. She spent years trying to get her partner to be closer to her and understand her better, but instead he pulled away more and more.

Maritsa was contemplating calling it quits because she'd run out of ways to make the relationship work, and she didn't know how to get her partner to love her, listen to her, and understand her. She couldn't get him to fully commit and want to evolve together as a family. While she was looking for intimacy, connection, and understanding, her partner was acting distant, cold, and aloof. Regardless of how much she tried to get his attention, he acted indifferent, absent, and lived in his own world. He wasn't even sure if he wanted to be with her. All of this was breaking her heart.

I remember how fragile and lost Maritsa felt when we first met. But, after just a few sessions, things started to change for the better. As she began applying Mars Venus tools and strategies to her relationship, the resistance between the couple began to fade. For the first time in their history, he was becoming more open and communicative, more receptive, more caring, more appreciative of her company, and more interested in her ideas and what she had to say.

Within a few months, as she continued to apply Mars Venus strategies, her relationship positively evolved. There was less resistance and more flow, less distance and more connection, fewer disagreements and more unity. Now, they had much more fun. They laughed, watched movies, played cards, took their daughter to exciting places, and spent time together as a family. Their relationship started to shape up the way she always wanted it to be. The interesting part of the shift in their dynamic was that *he* was the one who initiated a lot of these things that they used to argue about or that she had to "inspire" or "convince" him to do. Now *he* was initiating their time together, leading their relationship, and being present and involved. Suddenly, he was doing everything she'd always wanted him to do, and she didn't have to call or text him a million times; she didn't have to nag or beg him for attention, because he was genuinely interested in doing things and sharing his time with *her*.

The reason for this dramatic shift was Maritsa herself. She changed the way that *she* was showing up in the relationship and was taking responsibility for her part and transforming her ways. Once she understood gender intelligence, feminine and masculine energies, and how polarity impacts intimacy, connection, and men's desire to pursue and lead, all she had to do was surrender to her feminine side and create space for him to step up. One person can create an enormous change in a relationship simply by modifying their own behavior. When a woman has the right tools, she can shift the dynamic and alter the entire relationship. *She* has the power. The fundamental knowledge and Mars Venus philosophy that I taught Maritsa were effective tools that she could work with and apply to her struggling relationship.

Although Maritsa's story has a happy ending, a lot of people are out there struggling, ending up in divorce courts and spending the rest of their lives fighting over money and children because they don't know how to handle basic family conflict. They don't know how to inspire the desired action in their partner, how to create attraction and polarity in a relationship, or how to understand and fulfill each other's needs. All of these lessons are available through the Mars Venus philosophy and teachings, and so many families around the globe are benefiting and can benefit from this wisdom.

Maritsa did the work on *herself*. She shifted her relationship mindset, learned how to manage her emotions and triggers, and adopted effective tools and strategies. With my guidance, she changed her perception of men and relationships, evolved her communication techniques, and acted with a newfound certainty, confidence, and feminine charm. Maritsa changed the way she perceived her partner and adjusted her pre-conditioned views of men. But the biggest shift happened when she really *understood* her partner and *his* needs instead of just focusing on her own. When she shifted her focus, she realized how unconsciously she'd been hurting him and pushing him away for all those years. Understanding gender intelligence and men's biological, physiological, and psychological makeup allowed her to shift her relationship simply by changing herself and her own behavior. Her partner naturally responded to her feminine ways and radiant energy, which created polarity and reignited the connection between them.

SECRETS OF FLOW AND ATTRACTION

One of the biggest secrets I've learned is that no matter how much work we do on ourselves, whether it's trauma healing or personal development, relationships can be difficult and frustrating when we don't know the concepts of gender intelligence. When we don't understand our partners and we try to make them be more like ourselves, we unconsciously reject them for who they are, making them feel inadequate and wrong. This creates resistance in a relationship. Instead of trying to change our partners, we should seek to understand them and appreciate them for who they are. When we do this, it makes them feel seen, loved, needed, special, and appreciated, creating flow in the relationship instead of resistance. We bond more closely and feel safe to be ourselves.

People fall in love because of how the other person makes them feel. If you make someone feel understood, valued, appreciated, and good about themselves, they'll attach that feeling to you. The opposite is also true. If you criticize or try to change or fix your partner, they'll feel rejected, as though they're not enough. And if they associate that bad feeling with you, they'll start resenting and avoiding you. At our core, we all want to be loved and accepted for who we are. We want to feel safe with our partners, knowing that who we are is enough.

Another secret that made a profound difference in my life—and in the lives of my clients—is how feminine and masculine energy influences our attraction and creates polarity and passion in a relationship. I teach women how to embody feminine energy, which makes them naturally radiant and magnetic to their partners and to others as well. When women embody their feminine side, it reduces internal stress by increasing oxytocin and estrogen levels while reducing cortisol. Combined, the effect makes women more calm, radiant, and naturally attractive to men.

HEALING AT A DEEPER LEVEL

Besides being a Mars Venus coach, I'm also an intuitive coach and a healer. I help women release their old wounds and reprogram their limiting beliefs, which gives them the ability to rebuild their confidence and get quick results in their relationships and life. Often, in my experience, something they were struggling with all their lives can be released in just a couple of sessions, completely setting them free.

For instance, problems like abandonment, codependency, anxious attachments, and not feeling good enough can be swiftly transformed, as we work on the subconscious level instead of taking years to reprogram the conscious mind. In most cases, my clients achieve their desired results faster than they thought possible. Combined with Mars Venus relationship fundamentals, energy healing creates a powerful container that equips my clients with confidence, clarity, and a plan of action that uses proven, effective skills and gender intelligence techniques.

I've been a life and success coach for many years, and I've helped clients achieve countless incredible results in their personal and professional lives. Our ability to meet our goals stems from our belief systems, our subconscious programming (cybernetics). So often we have beliefs that hold us back and keep us from living our dream lives. But the results that my clients achieve through coaching and healing are permanent, and they get to keep them for life.

BECOME A MAGNET FOR YOUR DREAMS

When I was single, coaching helped me avoid dating the wrong men. I'd experienced many heartbreaks before, but the Mars Venus teachings, particularly gender intelligence, helped me move beyond the pitfalls of the past. Now, I teach ambitious single women how to date and avoid heartbreak by understanding men, their intentions, their language, and the way they think and act. I show them how to articulate their values in a feminine way, how to magnetize the right kind of men, and how to activate polarity and the energy of attraction intentionally and not just rely on chance.

Understanding—and appreciating—the differences between men and women also gave me the freedom to be my authentic self, honor my feminine side, and become more relaxed and present in my relationship. It allowed me to better trust myself and my decisions because, for the first time in my life, I felt like I was in control and could create the results I wanted.

Mars Venus teachings have also helped me stabilize and balance my hormones, which has significantly reduced my internal stress, lowered my anxiety, and allowed me to be in my feminine energy, glowing and radiant, overflowing with oxytocin, and positively magnetic to men. When I was dating, this gave me the confidence I needed to not feel like I had to overcompensate, doubt myself, or compete with my partner and other women. Suddenly, I had the unfair advantage of being a magnetic woman that men naturally gravitated to and respected, appreciated, adored, and loved. The Magnetic Woman later became the brand name I used when teaching other women how to activate their "it" factor and become the magnet to their dreams.

FORMING GENDER-INTELLIGENT RELATIONSHIPS

When women become more masculine and men become more feminine, relationships get depolarized and lack the level of attraction and desire that can only exist with polarity. A lot of potentially good relationships fall apart, not because they were never meant to survive but simply because people don't have the right tools to make them thrive. One of those essential and fundamental tools is the teachings of gender intelligence.

Most couples who don't practice gender intelligence end up competing, arguing, disconnecting, getting frustrated, trying to change one another, not appreciating each other, and, at the end of the day, not fulfilling their own needs. They don't understand what's happening in their relationships and don't know what needs fixing. In many cases, they end the relationship feeling angry and resentful when they could've thrived as a couple if they'd had the right tools.

By introducing gender intelligence, we restore the balance between feminine and masculine that creates polarity and a natural pull towards each other. When both partners have the right tools, the relationship grows more peaceful, easy, intimate, passionate, connected, and fulfilling because they're able to meet their own and each other's needs. I teach my female clients how to understand men, concepts like "cave time" and the "rubber band effect," and other behaviors they're struggling to grasp. I also teach women how feminine/masculine polarity ignites a man's motivation in a relationship and makes a woman feel seen, safe, and appreciated.

Many of my clients are ambitious women who've created a lot of success in life and achieved amazing results. Yet, when it comes to their love relationships, it's the *one* area they can't seem to conquer. Sometimes women come to me in great distress, feeling disempowered in their love lives, like nothing is working and they completely lack control. But after grasping gender intelligence, they realize that everything they thought they knew about relationships was in fact hurting them and creating additional challenges in their love lives.

I teach women how to ensure exclusivity and monogamy without having to resort to fights, threats, ultimatums, or experience heartbreaks fueled by fears and disempowerment. Magnetic women articulate their standards and needs with grace and power, which most quality men appreciate and value. I teach women how to activate the natural flow of polarity, intimacy, passion, and bonding in a relationship that fulfills both parties' needs. Gender intelligence helps partners understand each other and avoid judging each other's differences, which creates deeper intimacy between them. The right knowledge empowers couples to better their relationships instead of unconsciously damaging them.

Most people try to solve their relationship problems by arguing, blaming, complaining, pointing fingers, threatening, manipulating, withdrawing, or using other damaging strategies. But powerful and effective tools do exist, and anyone can create loving, supporting, and fulfilling relationships that overflow with passion, intimacy, and understanding. This is how all relationships should be. By teaching men and women about gender intelligence and how to create intimacy, understanding, attraction, and polarity, we solve a lot of the problems that people struggle with today.

TAKE THE JOURNEY
WITH ME

— SOPHIE TAN LI KOON —

Sophie Tan Li Koon has a degree in nursing and spent her mid-twenties working in wards. After attending Money and You KL in 2019 and a Crack Your Strengths Program in 2020, she discovered her innate empathy and desire to focus on people. Sophie is a sincere listener who guides others through their issues and to their goals. Due to her empathetic nature, she excels at sensing people's true needs.

With her wide range of tools, she assists her clients in discovering their hidden talents. She is a conscious giver who always receives. Sophie is constantly upskilling in order to give more to herself and others. As well as being a Mars Venus life and business coach, she's also a reiki healer. Sophie believes in abundance from the Universe.

SOME ROOTS RUN DEEP

For several years, I offered guidance to friends and helped them with their issues. At the time, I didn't know this was coaching. Whenever someone came to me for advice, I'd always provide it and do my best to set them on the right path. During this time, I didn't even know what coaching was, and I certainly didn't think I'd become the first Mars Venus coach in Singapore.

I grew up in a small family that consisted of me, my parents, and my younger brother. My childhood wasn't good, as my father shouted a lot. He was a traditional man who grew up in an era when kids were just meant to keep quiet, to be seen and not heard. My father used words to control us. Whenever we'd go out as a family, he'd get angry and shout, and I grew fearful of him. When we were at home, the situation was much the same.

Due to my upbringing, I developed depression later in life. At twenty-six years old, I was diagnosed with dysthymia, and I couldn't differentiate reality from illusion for about eight months. Although the results of my father's abuse weren't immediately evident, his early treatment of me planted the seed that grew to become my later diagnosis and troubles in life.

Because I wanted to break free of my father's influence, I began to carve my own path through life, choosing to study nursing. After graduating, I worked in wards, assisting and interacting with patients each day. Nursing helped sharpen my communication skills, as we had to be attentive and communicate as clearly and factually as possible. As a child, listening came naturally to me. I'm primarily an auditory learner. During my nursing career, the time I spent connecting with patients helped enhance this innate ability. Listening is still one of my greatest strengths.

After six years of nursing, I resigned during the SARS pandemic of 2003. In the one-year period that followed, I didn't work at all and battled with depression. I tried medication, but it didn't work. Finally, after a year of rest, I began to feel better.

Eventually, I married a man I'd known since we were both sixteen, and he helped me heal a lot. Even so, we never got to the root cause of my problems, which meant that symptoms would always reemerge in one way or another. When the COVID pandemic began in 2020, it was a very emotional time for me. While some people were able to work from home, my job at the time required me to attend the workplace. The world felt empty, and I struggled mentally with the sudden change in circumstances. Clearly, the time had come for real healing. I'd dig my past traumas out by their roots and break their hold on my life.

FINDING THE COURAGE TO CLAIM MY NAME

Alex Low was my Feng Shui instructor, and he taught me Feng Shui of the house for non-landed (macro) and divination (minor) issues. My teacher always emphasized not being superstitious or believing in myths. Feng Shui is more of a scientific study than something mystical and has nothing to do with religion. Later, my knowledge in this area came to influence my coaching.

For example, during a session, I'll try to discern the client's belief system and where it comes from, the source. Superstition can be a block in coaching, so identifying beliefs early on is important. When I see macro issues, such as a person's environment, I ask the client if they want to do something about it. I do the same for minor problems.

Sometimes people get stressed and can't differentiate between the two types of issues. When this happens, I help my clients understand the category of the problem they're dealing with and ask if they want to take specific action to fix it. In these sessions, the practice of Feng Shui and coaching combine to complement each other in amazing ways. Soon, another important teacher entered my life.

In April 2021, I attended an online program called Evolve XP that offered a thirty-minute clarity session. I chose to book with a coach named Jacy Wee (Mars Venus Coaching Asia) and signed up for some additional sessions, hoping to resolve my current problems, including my communication issues with family. During our first coaching session, Jacy told me I have a great capacity to love people and that I should open my heart and mind to coaching. I knew I had empathy—sometimes too much—and this could be a problem. If you give people too much help, they won't know how to help themselves. Jacy argued that I had the exact traits needed to be a coach. Even so, I couldn't agree. "No!" I said. "I don't want to be a coach." And we left it at that.

Jacy also recommended some other methods, including Reiki, to help me heal. The timing was perfect because I had a friend who was offering Reiki services. After following Jacy's recommendations, I did notice some positive short-term changes, but I never felt completely healed.

Over time, I learned to manage my issues much better, and I felt happier. Eventually, Jacy asked me to attend a Mars Venus seminar titled "How to Be a Coach." After attending the event, I told her that I'd changed my mind: I did want to be a coach. I realized that I'd already been coaching people. I'd already helped many of my friends find value in life, and I absolutely had the qualities of a coach. Now I believed it. So, I signed up for a life and business coaching course with Mars Venus and met the next of my great mentors, Richard Bernstein. Now I'm officially helping my own clients overcome their struggles. I still experience issues in certain areas myself, but I've gotten much better at handling them.

Around twenty years ago, I gave myself the English name, Sophie, but I'd never had the confidence to use it. In September 2021, I claimed the name as my own and put it on my ID card, making it official. Life is short, and we don't have time to let doubt and uncertainty paralyze us and keep us from our path. Coaching made life more manageable. Coaching gave me the courage to claim the name I created for myself.

Coaching is my path to the future.

MY FATHER'S TRAUMA

Recently, my father passed away from liver cancer. His behavior before his death was unusual and should've indicated that something was wrong. When someone knows they're going to die, they start thinking about the relationships in their life. I understand this now. My father and I started talking more, and I realize now that he regrets his actions: how he treated his wife and children. He traumatized us, which is difficult to forgive and forget. But he himself experienced trauma when he was young.

When my father was six years old, my grandfather asked my grandmother to move from China to Singapore. My father was an only child, and he was excited to be going somewhere new. They traveled to Singapore by boat. This was over sixty years ago.

When they arrived at their destination, my father saw my grandfather carrying a baby and holding a young girl by her hand. He soon learned that they were his stepsiblings.

Evidently, my grandfather had a second wife in Singapore, but she'd recently committed suicide after finding out about his other family. My grandmother had come with my father to help look after the other two children. Right after my grandfather's second wife committed suicide, her family got angry and beat him badly. Clearly, he survived, but his injuries left him incapable of raising the two kids alone. My father held a lot of inner anger for my grandfather, who beat him every day until he turned seventeen. When you're treated that way as a child, you can become a very angry person. That's what happened to my father, and he didn't release that anger until the day he died.

Intergenerational trauma has stalked my family for decades—but no more. I will be the one to sever the connection and free us from its influence. I will be the one to break the chain. I will be the one to finally end it. On my father's deathbed, he acknowledged the effort I'd made to be different from him. This was a defining moment in my life.

GROWTH REQUIRES ATTENTION AND CARE

When my healing and transformation really took hold, my husband pulled me aside and said he wanted to talk. "I don't know you anymore," he said. "Who are you?" "I'm your wife," I said.

"I don't understand you anymore. You're so different."

He was right. I wasn't scolding people as much, and I'd even stopped quarreling with my mother-in-law. Even though the changes were positive, my relationship with my husband grew rocky. He said that my aura was different, and he didn't recognize the woman he'd married. Often, big changes, no matter how positive, can be jarring to those who aren't ready to receive them. Accepting the person I'd become took my husband some time—and my transformation was far from complete. That was in June, 2020.

While I was treating some people better, I was still ordering my kids around before the COVID-19 pandemic. If they screamed and shouted, I screamed and shouted right back. If they did something wrong, I scolded them. If they made me angry, I expressed that anger. At the time, I didn't notice that I was subconsciously doing these things. I was operating on autopilot. Thankfully, my experience with coaching taught me to listen more rather than react. With this mindset, I've been able to have much better relations with my kids, and I communicate in more productive ways. Relationships are like plants. They need to be watered and cared for. A strong relationship is one that has been grown and nurtured with love and attention.

GUIDING PEOPLE ON THEIR JOURNEY

Coaches motivate. They encourage their clients and point out their blind spots. Coaches offer new tools and ideas, many of which provide shortcuts to success and advantages in life.

Since 2019, I've been practicing gratitude, persistence, self-motivation, and patience each day. These things are important if you want to stay grounded, remain consistent, and continue moving towards your goals.

Before I see clear results, I always struggle to believe that success is possible. Growth often involves asking the mind to do things it has never done before, and this can be the most difficult part of progress. Even after learning so much, I still feel disheartened at times, and persistence coupled with perseverance are the keys to canceling these feelings out.

As a coach, I've noticed that people tend to blame others when something unpleasant occurs. They keep complaining about how the world has wronged them, and they fail to see the situation from a practical perspective. Some people want to make big changes in their lives. But when we formulate a plan, they procrastinate and ask for a quicker fix.

Most worthwhile changes happen gradually, and often growth isn't something you can rush.

I work with clients who are committed to taking action and willing to be responsible for their own changes. A person must be ready to move forward and embrace the path ahead. I encourage my clients to take the journey with me.

In coaching, miracles happen during conversations; positive outcomes abound, and new ideas emerge about where to focus mental energy. They say that time heals all wounds. But time alone won't remedy every past injury. For deep healing to take place, you must take steps to facilitate the process. Nothing worthwhile comes without effort, and time is only a small part of the equation. However, with the right tools, you can accelerate the healing process. When I coach, my clients learn a lot in a short amount of time. Life is short, and the right guide can get you to where you're going much faster.

UNDERSTANDING STRESS

— RICHARD WANN —

Richard Wann's long corporate career and life experience have prepared him to be a successful Mars Venus coach. His skills and education have not only helped others, but have helped his own personal relationships flourish.

FIND MY ROLE

As a safety and security training director for two corporations and a major insurance company, I have traveled a lot. My wife was the rock of our family and stayed home. Our marriage had been a traditional marriage; I carried the financial responsibility of holding down a job while my wife managed everything domestic: our children, the house, and everything in between. I did what I could when I was home before I left again for another workweek. Over time, as it happens with many people, the marriage became one of apathy; it didn't thrive, grow, or move forward. The saddest part of this decline? I didn't see it. I didn't see the indifference, the lack of communication (which emanated from me). The "relationship" part of our relationship drifted away through non-communication, life distractions, and frequent absences.

When did I find out how bad things really were? My wife had planned a three-week trip to another state to help a lifelong friend with life and health issues. I thought that was the only purpose for her trip. However, after three weeks went by, I learned she had left me and our marriage with no intention of returning.

MY PERSONAL MARS AND VENUS WAKE-UP CALL

While the wake-up call was something I needed, what my *marriage* needed was insight and understanding. Our first steps to help repair our marriage were through traditional therapy and weekend retreats sponsored by our church. These provided improvements, but they proved to be temporary. I came to find that there were real answers and lasting help right under my nose.

During our separation, I found my wife's copy of *Men Are from Mars, Women Are from Venus* by John Gray. In it, I found that my wife had used a yellow highlighter to mark the problems I had never been able to see or understand.

As I read the book, noting all that my wife had highlighted, it was as though I was seeing things clearly for the first time. It was amazing to me. After a lifetime of work and marriage, I finally started to truly learn the differences between men and women and why the genders act and behave differently. Most importantly, I learned why my most important relationship had fallen apart.

Soon after my wife returned home, we attended one of John Gray's three-day workshops on health and fitness. We were amazed to learn how constant and consistent life stress can cause serious health issues, and how these health issues create problems in relationships. The workshop also made a profound and exciting impact on our understanding of why and how the sexes react and behave differently to stress and stressful times. Learning these physiological and psychological differences were the key that opened a door for us, and it is a key we began to share with others.

My wife and I attended private sessions with John Gray. We explained why we were there and what we hoped to accomplish through coaching. In these sessions, John educated us on the differences between how men's and women's brains work. A man's brain tends to focus on one item at a time; they see a problem and work on a solution for that singular problem. A woman's brain, however, can focus on multiple dilemmas at a time and decipher answers. Without communication within the couple, these differences can lead to frustrations, dissatisfaction, and anger. Without realizing it, my spouse held resentment against me. When my wife would get upset, she would metaphorically bring out her list and remind me what I did wrong. According to John Gray, that was part of our problem.

"As soon as you decide to stop adding to your list," he explained, "you'll see a noticeable difference in your relationship with your husband." I saw that she was taken aback by this. Soon, however, I started to see a difference in how she communicated with me. Gone were the complaints and eye rolls. Instead, there was acceptance and gratitude. It felt as though we were back to the days when we were courting. I felt like her knight in shining armor; I worked harder for her and our marriage.

During our sessions with John Gray, he told me that I need to be more attentive to my wife, be appreciative when she does something for me. "If a husband does these things for his wife," John Gray said, "it helps her to build the hormone oxytocin, which helps her to feel loved and cared for."

Another important aspect of the female recollection of hurtful memories is that it often leads to health issues. The buildup of these lists of grievances over the years also builds anger, which contaminates one's heart and mind. This can inhibit one's ability to cope. Over time, a woman's inner dialogue can change to constant negativity about her husband: "He no longer loves me"; "How could he treat me this way?"; "Why am I still with him?" Eventually, her "anger bucket" will overflow. In the same way, a man's inner dialogue can turn to thoughts like, "She's never happy!"; "All she does is complain; I don't need this!"

The husband becomes frustrated because he has no memory of saying or doing these awful things. Then, when he tries to use his natural ability and desire to "fix things," he ends up making it worse, for him *and* her. This produces the natural reaction of desiring solitude, storming off to his cave for peace and quiet.

This is a fairly accurate scenario that plagued my wife and me for fifty years. It was not until we realized we have different needs and different ways of thinking that we were able to come together. Many couples fail to understand the fundamental differences in the way men and women's brains have developed throughout the history of mankind. In the days of cave dwelling, the man went off in seclusion to hunt for food while the women cared for the children and talked to each other, learning and nurturing the first abilities in multitasking.

We began to realize from John's sessions that many of our problems or difficulties were caused by the tension between us. This was especially evident when I made certain life decisions without her consent. Up to that point neither of us had been aware of the misery we had caused each other due to not communicating. Our relationship started improving, and my wife began to experience health improvements, and not just physically. The health of our marriage has improved and is much more serene and intimate. We are enjoying each other again.

During our sessions and through reading *When Mars and Venus Collide*, I also understood that I needed to become a better communicator in order to move my marriage from an idle one to a functioning one. The methodologies rapidly brought to my relationship a sense of balance we never had.

COMMUNICATION THROUGH MARS AND VENUS

I am grateful that my wife and I have learned what it is to truly support, cherish, and love one another. Because of what I have learned through the Mars Venus methods, implementing those practices into my marriage, and the knowledge I have obtained through becoming a Mars Venus coach, I feel a sense of excitement at the prospect of helping others improve their lives and relationships. I look forward to teaching and learning, one workshop, one session, and one experience at a time.

HAVE FAITH IN CREATING A BRIGHTER FUTURE

— LENA JO —

Lena JO is the first and—at the time of writing—only Mars Venus coach in Sweden. She has a genuine heart and passion for helping people reach their fullest potential and live the life of their dreams. For over thirty years, Lena has worked with people in crisis and supported them on the path to another way of living, another way of physical, mental, and relational health, another way of being people of faith.

She began her career as a physiotherapist, helping brain-injured people with recovery. However, after a car accident left her with serious back pain, her life went in another direction, and she became an educated pastor. Eventually, her new path took her to faith-based, life and business, LifePower, gender intelligence coaching with Mars Venus. Lena is an accomplished speaker, author, artist, and founder of Daughter to the King, a network where women can discover their special calling and grow in it.

She has been married to her supportive husband, Sven, for over thirty years, and together they've raised their three children, Josef, Sofie and Lukas, to become exceptional individuals who follow their own dreams.

DEALING WITH LIFE'S CONSTANT CHANGES

It was New Year's Day, and I was sitting in front of my Christmas tree, enjoying the scent of spruce and thinking of the coming year. What would it bring? What was my mission? What would I have to work on to become the person who'll bring positive changes to my own life and the lives of my clients? Changes are what life is all about. We think that everything is going to stay the same, but it never does. Instead, we get a constant chain of changing events that become the reality of our lives. We just have to learn to cope with those changes.

Sometimes, a change is good: a new home, new child, new job. But other times, a change can be devastating: a separation, bankruptcy, or the death of a loved one. Every change affects us in some way. Even good changes can make us feel down when they come too quickly or too often. Therefore, we must learn how to deal with all of life's constant changes.

That's where I come in. I help people deal with change, create space, and make dreams come true. We always need a dream to keep us on track. With ancient wisdom, the great book says, "Where there is no vision, the people perish" (Proverbs 29:18). Start dreaming for the future, start dreaming about who you want to become, start dreaming about who you can help, start dreaming about whose life you can change for the better.

A dream (or vision) board helps keep your dreams alive and triggers your subconscious to make them happen. The practice involves collecting pictures and writing words and sentences that represent the outcome of your vision for the future. Once you've created your dream board, you should put it where you can see it every day, pray about it, and make acclamations as if you've already realized your goal. It works like a miracle, and, eventually, many dreams do come true, often in mysterious ways. By the way, you shouldn't try to figure out or decide *how* it will happen. The creator will see to that.

WHERE SCIENCE AND THEOLOGY MEET

Happiness, success, and fulfillment always come down to who you are as a person, how you can relate to other people, and how you cope with your life as it is *now*. Putting old grudges and traumas behind you is also important, as is loving yourself. "Love your neighbor *as* yourself" (Mark 12:31). When you don't see your own value and worth, loving yourself is difficult. And if you don't love yourself, loving others is almost impossible. You can't give what you don't have. To be able to relate to others in the best way, it helps to understand how the human brain functions. Here's the beautiful part.

As a pastor and LifePower coach, the Mars Venus concepts have given me a biological and scientific explanation regarding the biblical truths about humans, about men and women and how to deal with them in the best way, according to gender. This world relies on relationships to thrive, and gender intelligence gives us freedom in relationships and doesn't—as some claim—fetter us in old-time gender roles.

"When God created mankind, he made them in the likeness of God. He created them male and female and blessed them. And he named them 'Mankind' when they were created" (Gen 5:1-2). Here we can see that "mankind" consists of male and female parts and that both represent a piece of God. Together, the female and the male components of the creator complement each other and complete the painting of humankind.

I live in Sweden, one of the most secular and emancipated nations in the world. My country has gone so far that you're almost not allowed to say that gender differences exist—everyone is the same. But thank God that the science behind gender intelligence tells a different story. It shows us that the male and the female brains are built in quite different ways and that these physiological differences give us distinct gifts and ways to handle life, stress, leadership, caring, daring, and decision-making. In order to get the best results, whether in business or life, we need both genders. A company with a single-sex leadership team will only ever see one part of the equation, but teams that contain both male and female leaders will have the best of both competencies. To learn more about gender differences and how they affect us, I invite you to join me in one of my workshops on the subject.

WHAT TRUE LEADERSHIP LOOKS LIKE

What is leadership? Let me tell you a story. A friend of mine was in Israel and had stopped at a nice spot for fika (coffee and food). As she sat, she saw a shepherd leading a flock of sheep and lambs over the green pastures. The shepherd went before the sheep, calling them and leading the way. It was such a peaceful sight. Soon after, another shepherd went by, but this time the flock was in front, and the shepherd stayed behind, pushing the flock along with his stick to herd them in the right direction. My friend thought it was odd that one shepherd went before and the other after, so she asked a local man, "Why the difference?"

The man looked at her and said, "The first one was the shepherd of the flock. The sheep knew him. They trusted him and recognized his voice when he called them. He simply had to go before the flock and show the way. The other so-called shepherd wasn't a shepherd at all but the butcher taking the sheep to slaughter. He had to go behind and push them in the direction he wanted them to go because the animals didn't know him. They didn't recognize his voice, and they certainly didn't trust him."

It's the same with leadership. There's a difference between a leader and a boss. A boss decides what you should do, but a leader has earned the trust of the flock. He goes before everyone else and shows the way by example. That's what a leader does. Which one are you, the boss or the leader?

Leadership is a skill that you can learn. But you must first work on your own personality and grow as a person before you can lead. When a true leader leads well, no request feels like a demand. In fact, being led by the right person can feel like a privilege. You receive new energy; work ethic rises within, and you genuinely want to do your best.

You may even enjoy doing whatever it takes to get the job done.

This brings to life a memory from when I was a little girl. I had friends over to play, and I knew that when they went home, I'd be the one to clean my room. I hated cleaning my room. So, what did I do? I invented a game. When the time for my friends to leave drew close, I set an alarm clock. The clock would start to chime, and we'd have to clean up the entire room in as few chimes as possible. Everyone cleaned as fast as they could, and I led and did as much as the others—but we all had fun. With the invention of the game, I no longer had to clean my room alone after my friends left. It was a win-win situation. That's what real leadership is: creating a win for everybody.

MY NORMAL ISN'T YOUR NORMAL

As a LifePower coach, my first goal is to help you gain clarity. From a very early age, I knew I didn't fit in. I've always had my own way of looking at life, and I've never been *normal*. Born in the early sixties, I had what I thought was a typical, normal life with a caring mother and father. When I came home from school, long before I entered the kitchen where my mother was baking cinnamon rolls, the fragrance tickled my nostrils. I still remember that feeling, and I thought that this was what family life should look like: a stay-at-home mom waiting for her children with freshly-baked cinnamon rolls when they arrived home from school. To me, life never felt hectic. I was safe and secure in the knowledge that my parents loved and prioritized me, and I knew that this was what I wanted for my children when I grew up and started a family.

In the nineties, when I had three children of my own, *normal* wasn't the same as it had been in the sixties. Modern taxation systems made being a stay-at-home parent difficult.

Now, society claimed that I had to realize myself in order to have a good, *normal* life. When a child turned one, most parents would put their precious little boys and girls in childcare so they could go out and realize themselves and earn money. Everyone wanted that stylish home, that new car, that holiday abroad—and the health of the family suffered. I didn't want that type of normal. My dreams were different, and my convictions didn't match society's expectations about what a fulfilling family life was. I imagined a life that would give my children security and a foundation they could build upon to become strong, independent adults who followed *their* dreams to *their* normal.

To achieve this, I had to pay the price.

Science shows us that a child needs to be close to an affiliate, often the mother or the father, for as long as three years to become a secure and trusting person. I wanted my children to have that start in life. I also wanted to know that my children would be able to tell me if someone wasn't treating them well. Very few one-year-olds can do that. In addition, I wanted my children to be brought up with my Christian worldview, even though I lived in the most secular country in the world. I knew that a municipal daycare center wouldn't provide that sort of education. I also didn't want to rush my children up and out the door every morning. Instead, I wanted us to have time to snuggle and talk and just be together. So, I stayed at home; I baked with my kids, and they got to experience the fragrance of fresh cakes and cinnamon buns each day. We didn't have a fancy lifestyle, but we did have a good life. My sons didn't get the new bicycles with multiple gears that their friends had. Instead, they inherited their bikes from their sister. Not so cool, but they had a mother who was there for them when they hurt their knee, wanted to show a beautiful bug they'd found, or just preferred that I sit, read, or pray with them.

I understood the value of what I had. This was *my* vision of a family life. This was *my* normal. At the time, our economy wasn't great, and I knew that my retirement plan didn't look good. But I was so sure that this was the life I wanted for my family. As time went by, certain things changed, even with the economy, and I didn't have to fear retirement anymore. I'm glad I made the decision to live life on my terms. I had faith that my creator would show me the way, step-by-step, even if I didn't know at the beginning where the path would lead. Now my children are all grown up, secure, exceptional, and following their dreams.

When it comes to making decisions, you have to listen to your gut. You have to know who you are and where you want to go. And maybe, you'll have to make adjustments along the way. I know I did. Eventually, I realized that I wasn't my mom and that I had to do something other than just stay at home to feel good and fulfilled. After I completed some university courses, my husband took one day off a week so I could work. I wasn't my mom; I was me, and I needed to go out into the world from time to time. As I said before, the nineties weren't the sixties, and very few moms stayed home.

When my oldest son was about three years old, he said to me, "Mommy, I need to have some friends." During the day, there were no kids at home to play with, so I understood my son's appeal, and I had to adjust. I found a good Christian daycare center that we both felt good about—but I have to admit that I cried the first day I left him there. I had to adjust *my* dream in order for my child to get *his* dream and normal life. So, who are you? What's your mission? What's *your* normal?

ASK THE RIGHT QUESTIONS, RECEIVE THE RIGHT ANSWERS

"Before I formed you in the womb, I knew you. Before you were born, I set you apart (chose you) and gave you a holy mission" (Jeremiah 1:5).

As a LifePower coach of faith, I believe these words are true. I believe that before you and I were even formed in our mothers' wombs, we were planned for; we were on the dream board of the creator; we were chosen to be on this planet at this time, and we each have a mission to fulfill. Big or small, we all have a part to play in the universe. It doesn't matter if your biological parents didn't want or nurture you. You're a part of the creator's vision, a part of his dream, and you were surely planned for.

I'm here to ask the right questions so we can draw out the real you from your inner being and discover what you're destined for, what your normal is. Sometimes, during our journey through life, we stray from our mission. Something happens that puts us on hold. We may feel discouraged, devastated, or even traumatized for different reasons. When this happens, the first thing you should do is seek clarity. As a faith-based LifePower Mars Venus coach, I've noticed that the clients I'm allowed to pray for gain clarity fastest and in the most miraculous ways. It's as if the creator gives them thoughts and memories about how a problem first hooked into their soul.

Forgiveness is the second part of the healing process. Saying that you forgive someone is easy, but actually forgiving them is much more difficult. Perhaps you can't forgive in the beginning but when you seek to *be* forgiving, you begin the process inside you. Sometimes, it's another person that has hurt you and inflicted trauma. Other times, it's yourself you must forgive.

When we connect to people through relationships, we bond in different ways and create something like a soul tie to the other person. Some soul ties are positive, and some are negative. When you experience the latter, the connection has to be broken; otherwise, you'll walk around, dragging that person and their negative energy with you wherever you go. From a faith perspective, whenever I encounter this issue, I always pray to God to cut the soul tie and heal the old wound.

TAKING THE FIRST STEP TO YOUR NORMAL

Perhaps you've noticed that some things "run in the family." In certain families, everybody is healthy and caring. In others, people suffer from things like addiction, divorces, or perhaps being bullied. We call this generational impact.

However, prayer can free you from an intergenerational hangover and help transform you into who you really are. You don't need to hold on to all of that generational baggage. In fact, you can start a new life by lifting trauma from your inner being and seeing the future in a new light, with fresh possibilities. You can see exactly who you are and understand why you react as you do. Gaining clarity of the past helps, as does understanding how your gender-based brain works.

When I sat in my chair that New Year's Day, I didn't know what would happen in the coming year. I didn't know that I'd suddenly lose both my mother and my only sister: the sister I'd thought would stay with me my whole life, with whom I shared a history. I didn't know that I would have to cope with things I'd never experienced before. And I didn't know that I would have the opportunity to speak at a Global Woman Summit. I didn't know what changes the new year would bring. But, as I sat in my chair, I was preparing. Preparing for a future I knew nothing about. Preparing to cope with times full of change. I didn't know what changes would come, but I knew there would be some. There always will be.

Are you prepared for changes when they arrive? Will you continue to plan for the life you want to live in spite of—or because of—all the changes? How do you want to live your life? What's normal for you? What's the dream you long to follow? You don't need to be politically correct, and you don't need to be molded by the templates of society if that's not how you want to live. You don't need to be normal in the eyes of others, but you do need to find out what's normal for you. With these insights, we can build your life dream board and begin working towards realizing your vision. Soon, you'll understand who you are, as a man or a woman, and why your fellow travelers on the journey of life behave the way they do. With this understanding, you'll be more accepting and have better relations in both business and life. You just have to take the first step, and perhaps that step is to contact me as a faith-based, gender intelligence, LifePower coach. I wish you a blessed life, and I pray that you find *your* normal and that you'll become the person you were destined to be, long before you were created.

BE THE LIGHT IN SOMONE'S LIFE

— EMILY MACLEOD —

Emily MacLeod is a Mars Venus coach and thought-leader for high achievers seeking deeper fulfillment in love and life. She brings a wealth of experience from a career spanning twenty years in events, business, and technology. She has also served on the Algorand Foundation Grants Committee review board.

Before joining Mars Venus Coaching, Emily graduated from PAX Programs Incorporated, gaining a deeper understanding of gender differences and relationships. Life and relationship transformational coaching was a natural progression of her passion for helping the world one relationship at a time.

AN ORGANIC PATH TO COACHING

For me, becoming a Mars Venus coach was a natural progression. Before I even considered coaching as a career, people who needed help always seemed to find me. I would assist others in different aspects of lives, and I even guided one young person during her transition from a senior role in banking to launching a company that revolutionized charitable giving. As I helped more and more people, I began to wonder: Is this my gift? Is this what I want to give to the world? I knew I had to explore these questions.

I performed a deep dive into my own transformational journey before I even considered coaching. Due to intense bullying, high school and college had been a real challenge for me. Even some of the teachers joined in on the ridicule. Once, the headteacher told me I wouldn't amount to anything. Later, a college lecturer suggested I should stop studying business and choose something else—but I ended up passing with merit. I actually succeeded all throughout school. I got good scores in the sciences and played team sports well, so the negativity was strange and painful. Twenty years passed before I was ready to acknowledge these experiences and begin the healing process. During my transformation, John Gray's methods helped a lot.

However, past traumas take time to heal, and I didn't realize until later in life how much I'd held on to those early experiences and how much they'd affected my confidence. When you've faced certain challenges at a young age, self-worth issues can follow you through life and affect all of your relationships, whether romantic, professional, or platonic. If not acknowledged and addressed, such problems can hinder career development and stunt personal growth. That's why discovering the Mars Venus methods was such an important step for me. The feeling letter, for instance, really helps unblock whatever's inside you and preventing you from moving forward. But the process takes time, and you can't fix everything in a single moment.

During my transformation, I completed all of the available PAX courses, from Understanding Men and Women to the Heart of Partnership. I also did the Being Extraordinary Intensive program, which was life-changing. Gradually, I began to understand the importance of filling my own tank first, not running on empty, and setting myself up for success. Because the course ran on Los Angeles time, I was often up until 2 or 3 am doing night classes. Part of the program involved helping other students do healing work using the Sedona method. Assisting my classmates gave me so much joy and fulfillment—each session left me on a high—and the positive feedback I received made ignoring my calling difficult.

At around the same time, I started reading John Gray's books and enrolled in his Insiders program. People continued to come to me for help, which made me realize they were attracted to something I had to offer. In *Mars and Venus Starting Over*—my favorite of John Gray's books—he recommends not jumping into helping others too soon after performing your own healing. I took that advice onboard and waited before making any firm decisions. Six months later, I still felt that becoming a Mars Venus coach was the right thing to do. Although my path to coaching hadn't been linear, I'd arrived at my decision organically. I knew I had to take that next step so I could share my gift with the world. And so I did.

SMALL STEPS ALWAYS LEAD SOMEWHERE

One of my early clients had already achieved a lot of success in life, but they knew they could attain more—they just didn't know how. We discussed their short and long-term goals and divided each one into small, manageable activities they could complete on a weekly basis. This method is usually effective at moving clients towards their objectives, one step at a time. When you have dreams and ambitions—no matter how big or small—breaking your goals up into bite-sized chunks is often necessary to prevent getting overwhelmed. However, this strategic approach doesn't always work on its own.

While trying to complete their weekly activities, my client would sometimes get overwhelmed, frustrated, and, at times, angry. We discussed the problem during our sessions and used certain techniques to help remove blocks, working through emotions and getting back on track to the original goal. When clients acknowledge and release past hurts, they create space that enables greater clarity and transformation. As my client grew and met their goals, I felt increasingly proud of them and the changes we saw each week. Not everyone is brave enough to lift the lid on their life and emotions, daring to work through their problems and truly heal. Feelings from the past no longer hold my client back. They can now clearly see themselves achieving their dreams, and they're on a path to success in their chosen field.

When someone gets stuck, we work together to find a way to keep moving forward. Tracking measurable goals and setting weekly targets—in most cases—helps prevent clients from getting overwhelmed and provides a sense of progress. As a coach, you hold clients accountable and push them along to their chosen destination, but they have to commit to the process and be willing to do the work. You can motivate someone, but you can't force a transformation if they're not ready to accept it. One question I encourage my clients to ask is, "Would your future self thank you for this?" And, often, the answer is enough to let them know if they're doing the right thing.

RESULTS ARE ALWAYS THE GOAL

Although we often appear confident on the surface, underneath we may not be as sure of ourselves as we seem. This is true for many of the people I've coached. Due to my own experiences, I've gained a deep level of compassion for my clients, which helps me walk alongside them on their journeys. I know when to push, when to pull, and how to be their champion throughout the coaching process.

Because of the diverse career I've had, I'm able to connect with different people from all walks of life. My mission is always to support clients in attaining their highest ideas, inflaming their passions, and achieving their loftiest goals and, thereby, their dreams. I'm not a chit-chat coach—I'm analytical—and I prefer to see measurable results, which is why Mars Venus appeals to me. The methods are rooted in data, analysis, and research derived from Dr. John Gray's pioneering work in relationships. Concepts are tested in real-world coaching sessions and are shown to demonstrably improve people's lives in practical and scientific ways. Because I have an analytical mind, I like to do my own research, and I continuously expand my knowledge so my clients receive cutting-edge help tailored to their specific circumstances. A method that works for one client may not work for another, which is why I adapt my approach to suit the person in front of me. I believe that anyone can achieve their dreams if they have the proper support and knowledge needed to succeed.

The structure and strategies we use at Mars Venus help clients see regular progression and also allow for pivoting if something isn't working. Endless chit-chat isn't the aim. As coaches, we're constantly measuring progress and working towards the client's goals. Coaching isn't meant to be a therapy session. Unfortunately, however, some people would rather vent about their problems than work towards genuine progress, which isn't suitable for a coaching session. In some cases, I have to recommend something alongside coaching, such as therapy, so we can focus purely on realizing the client's dreams.

Increasing clients' awareness of themselves broadens their horizons and expands their lives. They burn bridges that led to their old selves, and, like a phoenix rising from the ashes, they emerge as someone new and improved. Committing to a coach and seeking true transformation takes courage, and often clients must lift the lid on things they've pushed deep down inside them for a long time.

But our clients are never alone on their transformational journeys. I support them with the wealth of experience I've accumulated after a diverse career and an interesting life. If required, I can also tap into the 600+ Mars Venus coaches worldwide, and we all have regular coaching calls with the company's founder. Even as coaches, we never walk the path alone. Ultimately, I want to help people soar to success, no matter where their jumping off point is. When you coach someone, you see them transform right in front of you, and it's an amazing experience. Most people need someone to hold them accountable, and a coach can be that person, walking alongside them and accelerating their journey to success.

EFFECTIVE TOOLS FOR ATTAINING SUCCESS

Part of my life philosophy comes from the saying, "Some people die at twenty-five but aren't buried till they are seventy-five." I know as well as anyone that it's never too late to grow, never too late to alter course, and never too late to undergo a massive transformation. Even if you've felt less than lifeful for a number of years—or even decades—a few steps in the right direction can help put you back on the path to fulfillment.

Success starts with your own health and wellbeing. Diet and exercise are the foundations of happiness and fulfillment. I don't mean that you should run marathons and only eat healthy food—although you can if you want—but gaining a better understanding of health and nutrition, exercising at a level that's right for you, and getting into a routine will improve your experience. You can make life work for you rather than you working for it. And if you ever slip up or need a well-earned break, you'll have the ability to get yourself back on track and, if required, get to the root cause of any issues that are preventing you from maintaining a successful mindset.

One day when driving home from work, I was feeling stressed and couldn't calm myself down. As I drove, my emotions only heightened, and I didn't understand what was happening; I couldn't identify the root cause. When I got home, I did some introspective work and realized I'd been eating poorly for the last twenty-four hours, binging on sugar, and not giving my body and mind the nutrients they needed. Once I understood the root of the stress I was experiencing, I took steps to remedy the issue, recorrecting my diet and restoring a more productive mindset. I don't force dietary advice or recommendations about physical activity on clients but if the topic comes up naturally, I do discuss it with them and point out where they could make positive changes. Some people don't understand how much nutrition and exercise can affect their lives—the massive impact it can have—and, while you can't tell others what to do, you can definitely point them in the right direction.

One tool I always recommend to my clients is the daily practice of a gratitude journal.

When it comes to success, routine and consistency are key. This type of journaling anchors people to their progress and helps stoke the courage and power needed to keep going when things get challenging. The gratitude journal is also a valuable reflective tool that allows clients to pause and see how far they've come and what has changed over time. Sometimes simply recognizing the progress you've made can keep you moving forward.

TREADING A NON-LINEAR PATH TO THE FUTURE

After studying business at college, I ended up working in hospitality and catering. I excelled in the industry, but the hours were unsocial, so I moved on. Since the age of twenty-five, I've been in the business world, and I served on a committee that approves grants for grassroots technology startups. Being asked to join the grants committee was a defining moment in my life. When I first expressed appreciation for the organization's work, Silvio Micali, Algorand's founder and Turing Award winner, said that he wanted me involved because I had a heart light. As a member, you read startup proposals, study innovation, and decide whether to approve or decline funding. You change people's lives for the better. Even if you can't approve a request—if the startup isn't quite ready—you can still offer feedback and advice. You can still provide something of value. I'm still in the startup space, and I'm looking to grow my coaching business there.

I also did consulting work for the AI and Blockchain Warya Telefonica accelerator, interviewing a selection of their most successful startups and creating investor books for them. The people I spoke to all had inspiring stories, which I loved hearing. I believe that stories, woven into each other throughout time, make us who we are as humans. As C.S. Lewis said, "There are no ordinary people." Everyone has a story worth telling.

My faith is important to me, and I wouldn't be the person I am today without it. I have a daily morning devotional routine of reading scripture, reflection, and prayer that sets me up for my day. I'm also part of a core group of twenty people who grew a church plant, which has since grown to a congregation of over 200 with a thriving multicultural community.

Before COVID struck, I was delivering Faith and Work events with the Center for Faith & Work – Redeemer Presbyterian Church, New York, and many speakers would attend, each bringing their own inspiring stories to tell, from losing a critical investor to surviving the attack on the twin towers. Stories are powerful. I feel privileged to have heard so many, and I'll keep each one in a sacred space of trust.

To balance working on Mars and returning to Venus, I do oxytocin and estrogen-building activities such as Venus talks, painting, singing, helping harvest botanicals at a local business, and keeping free space in my diary. I also train in classical dressage, and Mars Venus Coaching helped me win first place in the international Dressage Anywhere Retrained Racehorse competition, which was an incredible experience. I previously didn't compete due to the performance pressure I put on myself. Each movement in a British Dressage test is judged and scored out of ten, and there are between 200-280 marks available in a four-minute test. My desire to perform each movement perfectly caused competition nerves, and, thereby, I would forget my tests under pressure. But having my own Mars Venus coach empowered me to overcome my fears and win. The type of dressage I do is more about mastering the practice as an art rather than doing it for glory and competition. Even so, winning felt like a lifetime dream come true, and I couldn't have done it without Mars Venus Coaching. Clearly, even coaches need coaches.

I'm now focused on growing my coaching business and helping others thrive. On reflection, I see how my non-linear path was setting me up for success in coaching. Without adding all the strings to my bow and taking the time to find my gift—or allowing my gift to call me forth—I wouldn't be in the best possible place to grow my business and help others succeed. My main aim right now is to focus on my clients and build a business to give career opportunities to those like me who've experienced trauma or difficulties in their lives.

We live in a distracting world with many stresses, and setting aside time for a coaching session each week to focus on yourself isn't selfish; it's self-care. When you have someone who believes in you, you can, in turn, believe in yourself and work towards achieving your dreams. The gift of encouragement, no matter how small, can change someone's life. It's why coaching is important to me. You might be the only one who believes in a person, and you have the power to change their life for the better. The world may feel like a dark place sometimes but if you can support someone and be the light in their life, you'll make their existence, and yours, that much brighter.

MARS AND VENUS CREATING HEAVEN ON EARTH

— ADRIANE HARTIGAN-VON STRAUCH —

As New Zealand's and Bali's very own Mars Venus love and business coach, **Adriane Hartigan-von Strauch** is a quantum intimacy and dating expert, matchmaker, visionary intuitive and relationship healer, as well as a homeopathic and vibrational medicine consultant, specializing in transformational therapies and spiritual and personal development techniques globally. She is also a prominent creative entrepreneur and an international award-winning film editor and independent film producer.

Born in Munich, Germany, Adriane has facilitated many public events and sacred seminars over the last thirty years. She frequently presents on television and radio and at national conferences to international audiences, educating on topics that include attracting and manifesting love, relationship healing, illuminating quantum intimacy, the healing art of Jin Shin Jyutsu, Raja Yoga heart and mindfulness meditation, Oneness in Business, and the Oneness Phenomenon for global awakening and transformation.

Since November 2020, Adriane has been an internationally accredited and licensed Mars Venus love and life coach, personally trained by Dr. John Gray and CEO Richard Bernstein. In March 2021, she also became a certified Mars Venus business and executive coach.

Her key personal and professional lifetime coaches and mentors, next to John Gray, include Dr. Bruce Lipton, Tony Robbins, Marisa Peer, Bob Proctor, Lisa Nichols, Brandon Bays, Mary Burmeister, Shakti Malan, and Master John Douglas.

Adriane is an interactive, passionate, and highly spiritually-awakened coach, therapist, and consultant. She integrates complementary and gender intelligence based coaching and healing methodologies and techniques, offering a highly personalized approach tailored to each client and unique audience. With consciousness and compassion, and through accessing divine intuition, Adriane works with each individual to build beyond their inner knowing and strength in *living love authentically*. Her first book, *Illuminating Quantum Intimacy*, is in development to be published in late 2022.

THE QUANTUM FIELD OF RELATIONSHIPS

Do you believe in astrology? I do. From a very early age, I was conditioned to integrate the names of star signs and planets into my vocabulary. My mother, Ulrike, was an opera singer and had a great love and passion for looking "into the stars" in order to analyze and perceive her very own and other people's fates. Looking back at the mid-seventies when I was a teenager, there were no computer programs or digital tools that showed how astrology really worked or what exactly is revealed about oneself in written paragraphs. Daily or weekly horoscopes included in newspapers were the easiest way to learn whether your star sign had lucky, challenging, happy, or conflicting times attached. Even today, countless people all over the world enjoy reading daily horoscopes that focus only on their star sign. Those who seek more in-depth understanding consult astrologers, particularly when it comes to love and core relationships.

I'm grateful to have interviewed and communicated with Dr. John Gray frequently, and I recall when he informed me and our audience that the metaphor and the inspiration for *Men Are from Mars, Women Are from Venus* came to him during an astrology course. As I'd recently developed more of my own astrology skills, John's personal remark made complete and utter sense. A very respected astrologer friend revealed in a recent workshop, Astrology in Relationship, that he believes that John Gray's mother was an astrologer and ran the astrology bookstore in Houston for many years. Early on, astrology certainly influenced John's creative process as a writer and speaker.

In order to relate Mars and Venus to something so human, one truly needs to understand the frequencies and qualities of these two unique planets. The inborn and energetic differences between our two primal genders living mutually on planet Earth match the cosmic forces of the sky in truly magnetic and magical ways. Planets that constantly change their relationships to one another are shaping the uniqueness of each horoscope and transit in astrology. The sacred geometry of every greater constellation explored reveals secrets between the stars, our human characteristics, and our life circumstances and tendencies overall. The wisdom of planets relates to Greek mythology, the relationships of the ancient Greek people, and the heavenly energies they believed in. Each planet is named after a god or goddess from ancient times. However, the Romans, who worshipped the same gods, gave the planets Roman names.

Venus is named after the Greek goddess Aphrodite. Her traits are femininity, beauty, sensuality, and artistic creativity. She is often the brightest light in the sky on a clear night. Expansive, confident, and attractive, Venus always reveals our relationships to art and love, as well as our attraction to others in the most intimate ways.

Mars is named after the Greek god Ares, who was deeply masculine, hot-tempered, and fast-acting. He is the fiery and temperamental red planet and very dry by nature. Mars and its positioning in an astrological chart can uncover the ways we act and react to people, situations, and life's challenges. The planet also relates to human strength and our ability to move forward in life. Mars knows how to get what Venus conceives internally and desperately wants, but she can't have it without the essential and instinctive forceful ability of Mars to make it happen. Both bodies exist in polarity, striving for mutual fulfillment. Venus needs Mars to feel received, and Mars needs Venus to actualize his dreams and desires in a physical way.

As with most complex organisms and organizations, a large number of other specialists and co-workers are necessary for functionality. External forces truly affect those that are internal, which means the environment and extended relationships that couples surround themselves with are just as important as the love felt between individuals. In my work, I describe this as a quantum field of relationships. For Mars and Venus to create impact, happiness, and material wealth together, they require close relationships to other planets in Heaven. The following planetary companions offer support for men and women in our need to better understand each other's differences.

First, there's Saturn, named after Cronos, Zeus's father. The two gods, father and son, were often in a power struggle with each other. Saturn is the second largest planet in the sky, astrologically reflecting our human capacity to ground ourselves in the material world. Every twenty-eight years, the planet returns and has a strong encounter with our sun and birth sign, causing a reality check on every level of our so diligently created human existence.

Next, there's the farthest object in our solar system, Pluto, named after Hades, the god of the underworld. The planet takes us into the non-visibility of our spiritual, subconscious, and karmic human forces, reflecting on how we heal and renew ourselves in times of change and during unexpected tower moments. Anyone who has experienced an ugly and unwanted divorce in the past will understand what Pluto reveals to us.

Finally, there's "the magician" of the sky, Neptune, named after the Greek ocean god Poseidon. The planet appears bright blue and resembles the oceanic waves of Poseidon's domain. This highly motivated and expressive planet reflects our dreams, desires, and the perpetual longing to find answers regarding what's missing and still possible to attain in our lives. While understanding the role the planets play in our relationships is important, there is, of course, much more to the story of love.

EIGHT FLAVORS OF LOVE

After years of working in film and the arts and also being a homeopathic and vibrational medicine consultant, I began my role as a love coach well before earning Mars Venus licensing and accreditation. Since the beginning of my coaching career, I've called myself a Quantum Love Coach. Why? Because my passion and connection with the spiritual, unmanifested, and cosmic resonances of love and relationships have fascinated me since early in my adult life. The polarity between the divine feminine and the divine masculine that create quantum intimacy holds a magical attraction for me. At first, I wanted to understand and upgrade the levels of emotional and erotic frequencies in my own marital relationship. Later, more and more, I awakened to the realms of love, sexuality, spirituality, and cosmology that are truly and ultimately inseparable.

Do you believe in love? I do. What does love truly mean to you personally? Even more, what does love mean to humanity? Ancient Greek philosophy mentions eight types of love that exist within the greater realm of relationships. Let's discuss each one.

AGAPE: UNIVERSAL LOVE

Agape is a selfless and highly spiritual type of love, involving enormous empathy and compassion for everything that exists in life and beyond. This kind of love means that we accept, forgive, and trust others and see the world as part of a greater universe. Many of us who practice meditation or are on a spiritual path base our human values on this all-embracing type of love. Those who have religious beliefs or simply embrace goodness tend to cultivate this love as universal kindness and respect. Often, we extend these gifts knowingly to others without expecting anything in return.

PHILAUTIA: SELF-LOVE

Aristotle said, "All friendly feelings for others are an extension of a man's feeling for himself." Philautia refers to our ability to love, respect, nurture, and care about ourselves in a healthy and ecological way. Knowing boundaries between our own wants and needs and the wants and needs of others, particularly our lovers and partners, is a quality that influences every area of our lives positively and profoundly. Self-love has become a trendy lifestyle practice; however, humanity in the 21st century struggles to keep relationships alive. For a greater and fulfilling life purpose, we must learn the lesson of self-responsibility.

PHILIA: DEEP FRIENDSHIP

Philia represents the love between friends, which for many of us is just as important as arousing and romantic feelings. Plato, the Greek philosopher, said that Philia can mean love between equals: an integrated love that connects to the mind and the heart equally, a love between two people who have shared hard times in the past. The concept of platonic connections or relationships relates to Plato and his ideas. Ultimately, platonic love is based on the belief that physical attraction isn't necessary. Anyone who has experienced Philia knows that the love in a deep friendship can be engaging, powerful, and often lasts a lifetime.

STORGE: FAMILY LOVE

Storge is the love shared between family members. It differs from Philia in the way that it is reinforced by blood, invoking early memories and familiarity. Storge is a compassionate, protective, and cellular love that's deeply rooted in memory. We are born into our families, and many of us love our family members instinctually and unconditionally. Due to parental conditioning, Storge often influences how we act and react when entering romantic and intimate relationships, unfortunately not always in a positive and heart-based way.

LUDUS: PLAYFUL LOVE

Ludus is a highly playful and affectionate love—with no strings attached. The inner child comes out to play in innocent and unpretentious ways. Ludus can also be the attraction and excitement we feel when we have a crush or when we're first getting to know someone, before falling in love. It's a joyous, flirtatious, and teasing love, often expressed in the early stages of a relationship or by first-time lovers. However, it can also refer to the playful affection between children or teenagers. In order to maintain this love, many coaches emphasize adding more variety and laughter to the relationship.

PRAGMA: ENDURING LOVE

Pragma is a long-lasting love that has endured and matured over time. This kind of love often involves compromise, patience, and tolerance within a relationship. Staying in love—rather than simply falling in love—is the main focus. Pragma also translates to practical love, referencing the kind of love grounded in duty, commitment, and the material and worldly aspects of life. For Pragma to become long-term love, both parties must make a commitment to each other and honestly follow it through. Prioritizing our relationships can create mutual success for all parties

MANIA: OBSESSIVE LOVE

While some might argue that Mania isn't really a kind of love, the Greeks did use this word to describe obsessive love. Jealousy and selfishness are the characteristics of this love type, and it usually involves feelings of codependency and the fatal belief that another person will heal and complete us. One could also describe Mania as an energetically toxic or emotionally addictive relationship in which one person or both partners become overly attached. Mania can be difficult to come back from. However, if you do overcome it, you'll develop a healthier emotional intelligence and clearer sense of boundaries. Hanging on too long or beyond the end of a connection can prevent you from fully experiencing the other seven flavors of love.

EROS: PASSIONATE LOVE

Eros, named after the Greek god of love and desire, is romantic and passionate love. In Roman mythology, Eros is the equivalent of Cupid. It's an intense and fiery form of love that arouses sensual and sexual feelings and deep physical attraction. With Eros, lovers forget their boundaries and become very physically and emotionally intertwined. Due to the way it made people lose control of their hearts and minds, the ancient Greeks considered Eros to be a dangerous type of love. For many, this intense attraction can burn out relatively fast and cause a relationship to end forever. However, some manage to transform Eros into a deeper love of friendship and endurance. For most of us, Eros is by far the most desired form of love, as it speaks to the deepest and most passionate parts of ourselves. But, as certain biographies illustrate, not everyone is destined for a sexual love relationship, and some of us navigate life without ever establishing an intimate connection with anyone.

If you've experienced a relationship with the opposite gender or a same-sex partner, you likely know how to embrace most of love's various forms, understanding the entire concept as the greater matrix of love. The Greeks related their eight types of love to almost all stages of human evolution. And now, these loves continue to exist in the development stages of any committed or monogamous relationship.

RELATING THE FIVE STEPS OF DATING TO GREEK MYTHOLOGY

Dr. John Gray has written numerous books that explore the depth of certain phases that occur before, during, and after a romantic relationship develops. From gender intelligence to dating, he covers all of the important subjects, and one particular book, *Mars and Venus on a Date*, relates at least five—if not all eight—of the Greek love types in "5 steps for dating."

1. Attraction
2. Uncertainty
3. Exclusivity
4. Intimacy
5. Engagement

Attraction certainly involves a lot of playful and innocent love. It's a phase in which we don't want to be too serious and need time to explore who the other person is in relation to ourselves. While Ludus may be difficult to express when we meet someone new, it asks us to remain lighthearted and open-minded. This type of love is great for keeping attraction alive and deepening intimacy. However, maintaining playfulness within a long-term relationship can be difficult, as other love types can overwrite the genuine and generous inner child.

Uncertainty is a state of mind and an honest reflection of how good, happy, loved, or respected we truly feel when with a new person. In order to understand our own wants and needs in our intimate relationships, we must also seek to understand the other person's wants and needs. Before giving too much love away, a different type of love wants to be acknowledged. Self-love, Philautia, is born when we differentiate between how our parents felt and cared for us and the love we gradually learn to feel through self-care and self-responsibility.

Exclusivity is the decision to make a commitment to yourself and the other person while developing an enduring love, Pragma, for one another. Why is this love type so important during the growth process of a committed relationship? Women require certainty and safety in their connections with suitable men in order to open up sensually and sexually. Men, on the other hand, want to feel that their emotional investment in a connection with a woman they care about is truly acknowledged and received. The increasing polarity between two lovers is the ultimate bond that grows between them.

Physical intimacy opens us up to the passionate love of Eros that most of us so deeply desire. The colorful process of revealing our deepest dreams and fantasies to each other is hugely powerful. In this phase of dating, so much is revealed about the chemistry between both people. The masculine as well as the feminine pole create balance and harmony in the organic exchange of playful and enduring love, Ludus, in and around the bedroom. Additionally, Philia, friendship love, bonds us as two close and trusting friends with an ability to trust and communicate more consciously day by day, week by week.

Engagement is the most fascinating of the five stages of dating, simply because it reveals the other Greek loves we feel for ourselves and the world around us so unpretentiously. Depending on the values we share with our partners and lovers—or not—men and women often bring a great level of Mania, obsessive love, into a new or undeveloped relationship. Many women are dealing with insecurities and codependent tendencies, and this global lack of intimate intelligence doesn't make it easy for love-seeking men to feel trusted and appreciated for the masculine counterparts they truly seek to be. Earlier generations are known for hopeless games of jealousy and covert power, hidden affairs, and wild make-up sex, particularly in the 1960s, 70s, and 80s. Nowadays less and less, mature adults will affirm that they're proud of the upbringing and role modeling they received surrounding married life, and their parents' behavior is reflected in their future intimate relationship conditioning.

Developing a long-lasting, marital friendship, lived and expressed as Philia, takes quality time and healthy routines. You must reshape existing values and adopt new relationship rituals frequently. Many couples, young and old, describe themselves as "best friends," and companionship is often a greater driver than physical intimacy for maintaining a long-term bond.

Storge, the love for family and ancestors, is a core need for many, particularly when children are conceived within a loving relationship. The healing of the ancestral father line as well as the karmic mother line is essential before bringing children into the world. The mother line shapes our ability to authentically create human relationships and is an expression of Venus's connection with the Sun, the energy we are birthed from and born into. In comparison, the father line expresses our values to create a realistic bond with the material world, which brings us back to Mars's and Venus's connection to the planet Saturn, Mars's big brother.

Whether spiritual or religious, Agape, universal love, can be a potent tool for guiding couples through any human development passage into greater expansion and spiritual enlightenment. Divine and heavenly all-ness is an evolution we can cultivate together, and practicing Agape wholeheartedly can be a leading aspect of life, shown to and shared with our own children as a vital part of their emotional and spiritual evolution.

CREATING HEAVEN ON EARTH

Do you love Bali? I do. How many of us cherish the famous biographical trilogy *Eat, Pray, Love* by Liz Gilbert that became so famous after publication in 2006? Liz beautifully portraits the eight types of love in her very authentic personal development story. In each of her *Eat, Pray, Love* encounters, she reflects on the inner growth and awakenings around certain aspects of herself. First, in Italy, she experiences deep friendships and the release from obsessiveness related to her rebound lover as well as the enduring love shared with her first husband in New York. Liz's deep engagement in the feminine healing process has inspired millions of readers.

Then, in India, Liz cultivates self-love and the love to God and the universe in quietness and aloneness, spending months in an ashram practicing meditations and rituals that heal her even more. Ultimately, she arrives in Bali and breathes and lives almost all forms of love while developing deep relationships with saints, healers, men, and women of all ages and from different cultures. Finally, there's Felipe, her future husband, who becomes her beloved and life partner expressed in living Eros after initially being a true and authentic friend and companion. Here, Liz expands in her self-realization process even more.

In Bali, statues and plants embody living spirits, and ocean gods and goddesses live closely together, residing in the hearts, homes, and temples of the Indonesian people.

As guests in Bali, we feel spiritually home on this island paradise, as though we belong.

Being the transformational and awakened love coach I am, I truly adore the feminine essence and magic resonance that Bali constantly infuses us with, enhancing the power of transformation that often occurs.

Since 2014, I've been conducting Bali Love Coach retreats in the North of the island. Coaching and transforming one love life and relationship at a time in holy and sacred space is my true passion and purpose. On each day of my eight-day residential retreats, miracles and manifestations beyond our wildest dreams materialize. Bali, much like ancient Greece, relates its culture and mythology to the powers of gods and goddesses, creating Heaven on Earth for those who know how to create it.

Do you believe in Heaven on Earth? I do. Why? Because we are all and always one with Heaven. A oneness we can only describe when we're willing and courageous enough to practice and cultivate all eight love types. Creating Heaven on Earth requires self-awareness and the consciousness to differentiate parts and expressions within our human nature. In order to develop relationship skills and achieve great results, we need historic, invisible, and spiritual as well as earthly, authentic, and living role models. We need masters in their professional and creative fields to shape and transform our perception and capacity to think and feel beyond our human needs and desires. Dr. John Gray is certainly one of *my* greatest love and relationship mentors, and I'm truly grateful to be a part of his international coaching team.

Both John Gray and Liz Gilbert are phenomenal storytellers. Therefore, I wish to close this chapter with Liz's words, as she is an influencer and global role model for many seekers of love, particularly modern women. In the final chapter of *Eat, Pray, Love*, she speaks these words to Filipe before they sail into the South Bali sunset: "I decided to keep my word. 'Attraversiamo.' It means, let's cross over." And, so it is. Liz embraces Filipe to declare her newfound commitment to crossing over and leaving the past behind, with the vision to co-create an amazing love life together. Aren't these closing words a beautiful metaphor for expressing the intent to create Heaven on Earth together?

Within the quantum field of astrology, individual planets frequently take the lead to "cross over" into vibrational alignments with the next one of the twelve known star signs. Equally, we human beings are destined to shift our state of renewal within the quantum field of our broken and existing intimate relationships into happiness and fulfillment. Therefore, could it be that you will also seek to forgive and complete all of your past love relationships? Even more, could the cosmic power of now compel you to consciously embrace a more expanded Mars Venus paradigm, one that will elevate you to an even higher love and allow you to co-create your very own Heaven on Earth? If yes, what else is possible?

RECOVERING RELATIONSHIPS

— MOHAMMAD AL HUWAIDI —

Mohammad "Mah" Al Huwaidi is a certified Mars Venus coach as well as a licensed therapist and hypnotherapist. Mah specializes in relationship and business coaching. Though his practice is based in Kuwait, he travels throughout the United States, Middle East, and GCC, coaching those in need.

Mah's corporate experiences as an affluent sales manager and senior auditor in Kuwait's banking sector have helped prepare him for his successful career as a coach. During his career, Mah has learned to educate others on how to communicate effectively. This comes from assisting men and women in understanding their differences in how they work, think, react to stress, and communicate. Watching a once-broken relationship become refreshed and brought back to life is why Mah became a Mars Venus coach.

QUESTIONING MY PURPOSE

In 2003, I started a journey of inward reflection. My thoughts often turned to, "Why am I here? What is my purpose? How am I to make my mark on the world and help others?" My pondering led me to learn more about how the human mind works and how I could help others achieve clarity and success. I started to find that there was not a "one size fits all" program. As I learned more, I realized that there were distinct differences between how men and women think and process the world around them. I started to research how to become a better coach to both genders. This is when I picked up *Men Are from Mars, Women Are from Venus* by John Gray.

I read the book three times; each time I learned something new! After that, I tried to implement the tools in my own life for about six months. As I learned more and more about Mars Venus, I felt the desire to become a coach. I spoke with the president of the company who asked me why I wanted to be a coach.

"I like the method of gender intelligence," I replied. "I want people to know about it."

I started coaching with Mars Venus and went through an education process on how to implement these methods to my own clients. After that, I started my coaching program!

A BETTER METHOD

As I learned more about Mars Venus coaching, I realized that the therapy I had studied and implemented earlier in my career was simply not as effective as John Gray's methodologies and philosophy. Therapy systems I had learned about in the past did not address the differences in men and women; it never dawned on me that men and women needed to be coached differently. With Mars Venus, you have to think: What do men need? What do women need? How do women think? How do men think?

A coach friend of mine put it this way: if you're making a commercial to market to people, you have to learn how to market to each gender. One advertisement may mean one thing to a man and something completely different to a woman. Women react more positively to words about feelings; men react more positively when they hear words that are logical.

The Mars Venus method, I learned, improves one's gender intelligence (GI). Through the gender intelligent method, you learn how to create teamwork. For example, if you were a manager, you could implement your gender intelligence by asking different genders to perform different tasks. If you were distributing a task to the team, for example, it would be beneficial to give each man a task and a deadline and *then* they will bring their ideas to the table. Women, however, are different. The women on your team would work more effectively by taking each task, sharing part of it as a group, and then taking it to work on themselves. Men would say, "Do you think that is the right way to solve it?" Whereas women think, "Do you feel this is the only way to solve it?" As a banker, I have implemented this method. Mars Venus shows you how to understand the way people think and help others get what they want out of life.

I am very proud to be a part of the Mars Venus coaching team. The methodologies I have learned and implemented personally, professionally, and educated others on are priceless!

MARIAM'S REQUEST

After I completed my coaching studies, I felt the need to share what I had learned. I began posting on various social networking sites about the differences between women and men and how the Mars Venus method describes what women and men need. I distinctly remember one post in which I wrote, "Women need communication and men need their caves." It was after this went up that I received a call from Mariam.

Mariam, a thirty-five-year-old woman, asked for my coaching expertise. She was frustrated with the way her life was going and felt like she would never be in a successful relationship. Her romantic relationships in the past were filled with anxiety and lacked communication.

After she asked for my help, I agreed to coach her. I told her I would send her the pre-diagnostic test. This was so I could see how she rated the various aspects of her life so I could tailor coaching sessions to meet her needs.

"No," she said. "I have a problem. I want to talk."

I listened carefully. I took notes and soon understood what she needed: to feel valued and heard. After I listened to her, she agreed to fill out the pre-diagnostic sheet and returned it to me.

When I read her responses, I saw that she rated many areas of her life as "very unhappy." When we discussed what specifically made her feel so unhappy, she explained that she was lonely.

"I'm thirty-five," she said. "I don't have close friends, I don't have a significant other . . . I don't want to be alone."

Throughout my coaching courses, I learned that every person has a "love tank." If one feels lonely, misunderstood, or unlovable, their love tank is empty. I discussed this with Mariam, and she concluded that her love tank "for sure was not full," and she needed to fill it back up again. The first step in doing this? Learn to love yourself. She didn't love herself; that was maybe one reason why she couldn't find love on the outside.

We spoke about her goals. One of her goals was to meet someone, fall in love, and eventually get married. After we talked about these things, I asked, "Can you commit to yourself that you will work toward these goals?" Mariam agreed wholeheartedly. She admitted that she felt it was time to make a change and that she was ready and willing to do whatever it took.

First, we talked about her language. She was always saying, "I don't want to be alone, I don't want to be a loser, I don't want this . . ." As we talked, she realized that using negative words (e.g., don't, can't) was actually sabotaging her and making it almost impossible to have a positive outlook on the future.

So, we flipped the language. We changed her "I don't want" to "I *do* want." After that, we discussed her inner peace. I hoped that if she could find inner peace, it would roll over and pour into every facet of her life. I asked her to do ten minutes of meditation a day to meet with herself to work toward peace.

At the end of each session, we set aside a few minutes to discuss the next task. This is the main value of coaching; we give a task to our clients and follow up with it to verify the progress. Each session, we recapped what our goal was last time, and then we talked about the benefits of each exercise and what she gained through them.

When I saw that she was starting to find inner peace, we moved on to focusing her to find happiness in relationships, whether it be with friends or in a romantic setting. Instead of going straight from home to work and back again, she now had to go to the gym and make new friends. Not only did she get exercise, which boosted endorphins and improved oxytocin levels, she was also stepping out of her comfort zone by speaking to new people and forging friendships. Her new target was to do this every week.

At first, she didn't like it. I remember Mariam called me one day and said, "I can't do it." I changed her language and asked her if she was still committed to reaching her goal of finding meaningful relationships.

"Yes," she replied. "I want to have meaningful relationships."

"What do you want to achieve?" I asked her.

"I want to be loved," she told me. "And that will take getting out of the house."

As Mariam worked to meet the goals we had set, she started to feel better about it. The more she tried new things, the more she started to enjoy it. After about a month and a half of going to the gym and talking to people, she called me and said, "You will not believe it! A guy called me and wants to meet my father!"

As our coaching sessions progressed, I could see the life in her coming back. When she first started with me, she always seemed so sad; she looked at her feet; she mumbled; she had no excitement in her voice. The difference from our first meeting to seven months later was amazing! She was so happy, shining, and excited about her life.

SARAH'S STRESSORS

Another client, Sarah, was feeling overwhelmed with the stress in her life. She was thirty years old, married, and a working woman with two kids. After she attended one of my workshops on how to deal with stress, she sent me an email and told me what her problem was. Lately, Sarah had been feeling that her husband did not participate and engage with her as he did in the beginning of their marriage. She loved her husband and her two kids; she just felt that her husband was growing distant.

After I read her email, I took her through the Mars and Venus process. I sent her the pre-diagnostic survey and had her measure all the aspects of her life on a scale of 1–10. When she sent it back, I noticed that more than 80 percent of her ratings were less than one.

It made sense that she felt that her husband was not connecting with her anymore. The point of our coaching session was to find the areas of her life that were causing her stress and work to remedy them.

I asked her each problem she faced and asked a variety of questions: How did she feel when she was lonely? Did she not have time for herself? Did she not take time to spend with friends? She felt that her husband did not participate or connect with her as before, and this made her feel unloved. She felt lonely and thought her husband wanted time away from her and the kids.

We talked about how men and women deal with stress. When a man experiences stress, he retreats to his cave. It doesn't mean he doesn't love his wife anymore; it simply means he needs space. Stress increases a hormone called cortisol. When those levels increase in men, they tend to desire time to themselves to deal with it.

Sarah realized that her husband needed time to decompress. She decided to let him have his time to work through his stress alone and tell him simply, "I'm here for you," and let him be alone. By giving him his space, he would take the time he needed to reconnect with himself and would come back to her with more love and happiness.

When a woman produces cortisol, she feels a lot of pressure to push through it. This can be isolating and develop feelings of loneliness. There are many different ways to decrease cortisol and raise your oxytocin levels. Knowing this, I suggested to Sarah that she start taking time for herself. Whether this meant having dinner with friends, going to the gym, painting, whatever it was, Sarah needed to do it.

We made a schedule for her to take time for herself every day. Every week we had a session and talked about her progress for the week. I'd make sure she did what we had discussed, and then I supported her and asked if she struggled and what she could do to make the process better. After the tenth session, she got used to the changes in her life: taking time for herself, spending time with the kids, knowing how to relate with her husband when she felt disconnected, etc.

Sarah started to see changes in her life. She noticed that when she left her husband alone and simply told him, "I'm here if you need me," he became more loving and more affectionate. She also noticed a difference in her stress levels and enjoyed running and made time for it almost every day. Sarah said her mood improved immensely; she was actually happy.

"If you're happy, your husband will be happy and your kids will be happy as well," I said. "It will be contagious. If your happiness comes from inside, it will shine on those around you."

Sarah's relationship with her husband became much more fulfilling, and her relationship with her children has improved because she's spending more nourishing time with all of them.

AHMAD'S BUSINESS WOES

I received an email from a man named Ahmad. He was interested in learning how to start a business. I replied, "Let's set up a meeting for a pre-diagnostic session." In our first meeting, I asked him what he needed out of coaching and asked him to write it down. We discussed this as well as his pre-diagnostic worksheet for several hours.

During the session, he realized that there were some questions he had not thought of yet. I noticed by the look on his face that he was starting to realize he hadn't thought his plans out. When we wrapped up our session, he was anxious to set up our next meeting.

When our second session began, I asked Ahmad what he wanted. I listened to his response and then helped him reframe his vision to allow him to see it clearly. As soon as his vision was clear, we started a ninety-day plan. He set the first three goals: completing a feasibility study, establishing the company as an official body, and creating a logo for his business.

He established his business and began to achieve his goals. We designed the task of keeping track of his achievements so he could see he was getting closer to his objectives. During this time, I showed him the strategy for each element of the five principles of business—leads, conversion rate, number of transactions, average amount of sales, and margin—and how he can utilize each one to increase his profits. He set his strategy developing the system in addition to testing and measuring in parallel with the Mars Venus methodologies for business. Now, he has a company with fifteen employees and a capital of 50,000 KD (Kuwait dinars, approximately $150,000 USD).

METHODS FOR MARRIAGE AND MEETINGS

Mars and Venus coaching methodologies are able to span a variety of relationships: marriage, parent and child, employee and employer, and one's relationship with oneself. The methods of John Gray can cover gender roles, generational lines, and workplace hierarchies. This is why I enjoy being a Mars Venus coach.

REVIVING MASCULINE AND FEMININE DYNAMICS

— JUSTINE BARUCH —

Justine Baruch is a life and relationship coach who helps men and women better understand themselves and each other to restore the value and beauty of masculine feminine dynamics. One of the biggest shifts that Justine went through in her life was learning to embrace her femininity. For the first half of her life, she was unknowingly living in her masculine, with no awareness of how it was compromising her own physical, emotional, and mental well-being as well as the quality of her intimate relationships. She now helps powerful ambitious women learn to embrace their femininity and bring it into the corporate world as well as their own homes. She also helps men to reclaim their masculine presence in their relationships and learn how to best support their women in getting back into their feminine.

Justine loves supporting couples in creating harmonious, passionate, and thriving relationships. In her online group programs (one for men and one for women), she breaks down how men and women are different to bring more understanding and acceptance to these differences instead of trying to make each other the same.

Justine currently offers high-touch one-to-one and couples' coaching as well as online group programs and transformational retreats. Her full range of services and additional information are available on her website.

LEARNING TO EMBODY THE FEMININE

For the first half of my life, I had no clue about the concept "feminine," let alone what it meant or what it looked like to embody it. I was an athlete, always up for an adventure, loved a challenge, and was a natural leader from a young age. I've always had a lot of energy and have been the kind of woman who takes action and gets stuff done.

I still remember the moment when my journey into the feminine began. I was in a bookstore in India, sipping on my chai and flipping through pages, trying to decide which book I would buy next. I was exploring a book about women, and a passage cut right through everything and landed deep inside me. Up until that moment, I prided myself on being a feminist and a strong, independent, opinionated woman who didn't need a man. The passage in the book spoke about how the women's liberation movement was a farce. Many women were fighting for equality by going into their masculine and acting like men. While women were becoming equal, the feminine essence was becoming oppressed. I realized that I was one of those women who was strong in my masculine and held little regard for my own feminine.

I came to see that there was a huge difference between fighting for equality—equal rights and equal pay—and equally valuing the masculine and feminine. I knew that I didn't want to be the source of my own oppression, and so my journey to embrace my femininity began.

After I read that passage, it was as if it opened a portal into a new dimension, and one lesson after another kept coming my way, helping me to see and grasp this new understanding.

The next week I had a session with an Ayurvedic doctor. Normally when they took my pulse, they would tell me I was pitta vata, but not this one. The first thing he said to me was that I was a very masculine woman. The following week, I had a session with an astrologer, who would normally tell me I was an Aquarian, but again, not this one. He told me I was a very solar woman, aka masculine. Several months later, I met a guy who supposedly read auras. When I sat in front of him, he said I was very yang, aka masculine again.

The next step was to try to figure out what it meant to be a feminine woman. It took several years to digest all of this. I found a mentor to get me started, and to this day she says that I was the most difficult student she'd ever had. Initially, I thought stepping into my feminine meant I had to become softer, quieter, and smaller. I was a strong, ambitious woman, and I didn't want to give that up. Thankfully, I didn't have to. Instead, I learned how to channel my masculine power through my feminine essence, and, as a result, I became more powerful, influential, and impactful than I ever could have been when operating primarily from my masculine.

Embracing my feminine has improved every area of my life, especially my relationship. I was the kind of woman who ran the show at work and at home, taking care of everything and everyone. Because I am quick, it resulted in me taking the lead on most things. Sometimes, it felt like nothing would have gotten done without me.

I had a decent relationship, but it was not without its frustrations. I wanted him to take action, get things done without me having to ask, and create some romance and quality time for us. I generally thought I was a great partner and that he was the one who needed to step up, take initiative, and do his inner work. Wow, has my perspective changed since then! And thankfully it did because that kind of attitude is a downward spiral.

I came to see how being in my masculine in the relationship was pushing my partner into a more passive state. It wasn't that he needed to step up and go faster than me; it was more that I needed to slow down, learn how to make kind requests, stop controlling how and when things should be done, and learn how to receive. I became aware of the many ways that I was unknowingly emasculating my man. I often chose efficiency over connection and gave unsolicited feedback on his ideas, telling him how he could improve, and what he could do better. I thought I was helping and didn't realize it was actually having the opposite effect.

Thanks to the teachings of John Gray and several others, I've learned how to bring my feminine essence to my relationship and support and inspire my man's masculine presence. When I shifted my attention from what he was doing wrong, or not doing, and started to focus on what I could do differently, everything in my relationship changed.

We now share an incredible and fulfilling relationship. I honestly didn't think this kind of connection was possible with this man. I thought he needed to change for us to get here, but when I started to do my work, he met me in each of those new spaces. People are constantly reflecting us back to ourselves. There's so much power when we create change from the inside out instead of trying to change others.

Embodying my feminine has been one of the biggest and best shifts I've made in my life, so, naturally, I was attracted to John Gray's work. I related to his background—a combination of spirituality, psychology, and nutrition—and his alternative approach to life. By the time I became a Mars Venus coach, I had been teaching workshops on sexuality and relationships for almost a decade. I wanted to use some of John's methods in those courses, so I used the "contact me" form on his website to ask if there was a way I could be empowered to teach his material. That's when I learned about Mars Venus coaching.

During my first call with Rich Bernstein, CEO of the organization, he explained that learning how to conduct workshops based on John's material was part of the training coaches received. I signed up immediately. This was exactly what I wanted. Prior to joining the program, I didn't know there was a profession called coaching. I had been conducting workshops, retreats, and supporting people in one-on-one sessions since 2006 but considered myself a teacher or facilitator, though I was doing much more than just teaching. I became elated when I started to read the Mars Venus coaching manual, as it outlined everything that I had been doing. Suddenly, a whole new world opened up to me. I couldn't believe that an entire profession existed that entailed exactly what I had been doing for years.

In my youth, I never would have guessed I'd be coaching men and women around masculine/feminine dynamics and helping women to embrace their femininity. I've witnessed countless couples completely turn their relationships around while going through my three-month online programs, even those who were on the brink of divorce. I also celebrate the growth that I witness in my CEOs, VPs, and business-owner clients as they embrace and embody their femininity and bring it into the corporate world and their homes. The world needs more feminine leadership—not just women leaders.

Knowledge about masculine feminine dynamics is truly life-changing.

MAINTAINING MASCULINE FEMININE DYNAMICS IN RELATIONSHIPS

Learning about how men and women are different has been beyond profound for my personal life and the thousands of people I have helped since 2006. The depth and practicality of John Gray's wisdom never ceases to amaze me. He is one of my biggest mentors.

I've had many women come to me who were just like me in thinking that their partner was the problem. They perceived themselves as having done lots of their own work and extensively studied communication and relationships. It seems that sometimes those who are on the "path" of personal development are sometimes more blind to how we are contributing to the very problems that we complain about. I know I was.

Several women have sought me out for coaching because they were extremely unhappy in their marriages and wanted to leave their husbands. Each one was convinced that the man she'd married wasn't right for her. After taking a good look at themselves and making some positive changes—and watching their husbands change in return—they realized that they actually had a great catch all along. Now, they all have quality relationships that others look up to and admire.

THINKING HE'S THE PROBLEM IN THE RELATIONSHIP

Fanny was one of those women who had done her own work but was caught in the trap of thinking her partner was the problem. She joined my Adored program because she thought she was going to learn how to get her partner to step up and behave better. What she actually got was a deeper and more intimate connection with herself. She joked about how I tricked her and that she probably wouldn't have signed up for Adored if I had told her she was going to be working on herself, but, in the end, it is what delivered her the relationship of her dreams.

Fanny: "We were having lots of communication issues and fighting a lot. I was frustrated with his lack of prioritizing our relationship and quality time together. We were on the verge of breaking up when I found Justine. After the first week of Adored when I learned about all the ways that I was emasculating my man, things already started to shift in my relationship, and hope returned that we could make it work.

Adored far exceeded my expectations. I've done extensive reading and courses on self-development and relationships, but Adored offered very practical information that was easy to apply to my daily life and facilitated an unexpected deep healing journey.

I became aware of how I was unknowingly blaming and criticizing my partner and putting him on the defense, even though I thought I was approaching our conversations in a conscious way. With the skills I learned from Justine, we now have much more harmony in our conversations, including the difficult ones, and we both feel heard. Our relationship has changed drastically, and the biggest shift came from me. I went into thinking I was going to learn about my man, and I ended up learning so much about myself along the way. I realized how my lack of self-worth and not feeling good enough was projecting itself onto my relationship and creating lots of conflicts. Justine said it only takes one person to change the relationship for the better, and she was absolutely right.

Justine helped me to be a better version of myself, which made it possible to have a better relationship. I am calmer now; I take better care of myself; I express my wants and needs in a kind and loving way, and my relationship is better than it has ever been."

MEN AND WOMEN ARE DIFFERENT

Fanny, myself, and many other women had good intentions to improve our relationships but were unknowingly emasculating our men and pushing what we wanted further away. We were blind to the ways we were contributing to the problems and stuck in patterns of complaining, criticizing, and being disappointed. There's so much empowerment and freedom in seeing what we can do differently to create the relationships we are longing for.

I've had the honor of witnessing many women go through this same transformation, and I want to share with you some of the main areas where men's and women's differences collide and how to navigate them in a smoother way.

I hear so many women say they want their man to step up, take initiative, and lead the way, but they don't realize how they are shutting down his masculinity and sabotaging that from happening. Some of the ways women do this are by: withholding (appreciation, admiration, sex, participation, etc.), not trusting him, comparing him unfavorably to someone else, not letting him impress them, assuming he's being insincere, acting impartial to his passions, refusing his help, demeaning his capabilities, blowing off his ideas and suggestions, ignoring him, criticizing him, interrupting him, being impatient with him, taking over something they gave him to do, shutting down his storytelling, demanding that things are done their way—the list could go on. In my online courses, I break each of these down into more detail and highlight all the ways they creep into our daily life interactions.

Men and women are literally wired differently and when I explain the science behind our differences, it helps to bring more understanding and acceptance. All too often there are unrealistic expectations in relationships because women expect men to act like women and vice versa. Some of the biggest areas where I see misunderstandings happening are communication, sexuality, emotions and stress.

My relationship has been one of my best teachers, so I will share from my personal experience. All of what I am about to share are generalizations. I've seen them apply to many of the couples that I've worked with, but not all of them. It's important to take what resonates with you and leave what doesn't.

To start with, I want to speak about how the masculine and feminine have different ways of connecting . . .

CONNECTING

Once, my partner and I had been away from each other for a couple of months. We talked every day on the phone, and when I was traveling to finally meet up with him again, we messaged throughout the day. When I arrived home, he took me in his arms and put me on the bed. To which, I responded: "Can we connect first?" I wanted to talk, and he wanted to make love.

He then said: "This is the most intimate way I know how to connect with you. What is making love for you?"

I loved how this moment highlighted how most women's primary source of connection is communication, and men's is sexual intimacy. While I highly enjoy and value connecting sexually, I first want to connect through talking. Communication opens me up to want to make love. A good conversation literally turns me on, and for my man, it's the other way around. When his sexual desires are met, he's more open to engage in other ways of connecting.

Understanding that men and women connect in different ways has been helpful in several areas. It helps to minimize judgment around the beliefs that women talk too much, and all men want is sex. It brings awareness to how women need time to warm up for sex, and men need time to warm up to heavy conversation. It also brings perspective to how a man might not be in the mood for a conversation, but he is up for sex. There are biological explanations around each of these ideas that have helped my clients to really accept these differences instead of judging them and arguing that things should be different. Prioritizing time for sexual connection and for quality conversations is key to having a thriving relationship.

COMMUNICATION

At the end of the day, I love to share what has happened, whereas my partner often feels tortured if I try to extract the details of his day. He doesn't like having to recall what he deems to be insignificant information, and he for sure doesn't like calling up the problems that he hasn't yet solved. What's de-stressing for me can be stressful for him. So, we have found a harmonious rhythm in him asking and listening about my day, and, in return, I ask him: "Is there anything about your day that you would like to share with me?" If the answer is no, I leave it at that. No judgment or guilt around how things are or how they should be.

Our ability to do tasks and engage in conversation is also vastly different. I can easily coach a friend through a problem while cooking a meal or even while working out. Whereas I was once planning a date with my partner while he was making a sandwich and when I showed up that night ready to go out, he wondered why I was there. While he engaged in the conversation, it didn't actually register. I used to get upset with him, but I have since learned about how our brains are wired differently. Men's brains are not built for multitasking. I now take responsibility for when I choose to speak to him. I not only take into consideration if he's busy doing something, but I also check in to see if his mind is working on a project. This way I set us both up for success.

EMOTIONS

Another understanding that has facilitated a lot of connection and harmony in our relationship is around how each of us deals with our emotions. When I am emotional, I want to talk about what's going on, whereas my partner wants to be alone. I used to think he would feel better if he talked it out, but this was me assuming that what works for me would work for him. This is a mistake I see many women (partners, mothers, and therapists) making with men. Men experience and process their emotions in a different way, and it is crucial that we honor that. I also came to realize that if my partner consistently complains to me about his day, it impacts my attraction. So, for multiple reasons, I have stopped encouraging him to process his challenges with me and instead trust and honor his intuition to support himself in whatever way is best.

We have different emotional processing systems in our brains that explain why men default to problem-solving and women to feeling. When emotions arise, the TPJ (temporoparietal junction) system of a man's brain kicks in and gets him to analyze the emotion and look for a solution. Understanding this has helped to minimize the frustration women feel when men go into "fix-it" mode instead of just listening. With this new understanding, there isn't a right or wrong way; there are just different ways. I encourage women to connect with their man's good intention at that moment and to make a clear and kind request for him to just listen. When I am in a space where I need my partner to just listen, I use a code word that we have set up that signals that I need that type of support.

STRESS

Another big area where our differences appear is in how we experience and handle stress. When women get stressed, we go into overdrive and try to outrun our to-do list. We may be exhausted, but we keep going, thinking that we will feel better if we can just get it all done. We try to rope our men into joining our impossible mission and get upset with them for resting when they are tired at the end of the day.

When women get stressed, we become very aware of others' needs and struggle to take care of our own. Men, on the other hand, become very aware of their own needs and struggle to take care of others when in that state.

Sitting down to rest is more replenishing for men because they can actually turn off. Whereas sitting down doesn't often have the same effect on women because when we sit, our mind is still running. We need oxytocin to start to slow our system down. Two of the best ways my partner supports me in getting the oxytocin pumping is by asking me about my day and just listening, and curling up for a cuddle on the couch. Both of these things help to shift me out of my masculine "do mode" and lower my stress. The to-do list remains unconquered, but it doesn't bother me in the same way when my stress levels are down.

However, when he's stressed, he just wants to be left alone. Initially, he thought this was what I wanted when I was stressed, so he would steer clear and let me be, but I ended up feeling ignored and unsupported. Learning about these differences helps each of us take better care of ourselves and give each other the support that we actually need.

When we learned how to manage my stress better and get me out of "do-more" mode, I was more able to get into my feminine and be available to share sweet intimacy. Otherwise, I was often too exhausted, distracted, or busy to connect in that way.

John Gray's teachings have been fundamental in highlighting the problem areas, patterns, and expectations in my relationship, as well as providing the insights, understandings, and tactics to deal with them.

THE FEMININE IN CORPORATE

Many of my clients are powerful women who hold high corporate positions or run their own businesses. I love helping them soften into their strength, own their feminine value, and achieve greater success.

To give you an idea of what that looks like . . .

Jane was a member of the board and collaborated closely with her CEO. One day, he told her that she was too emotional and she needed to be more business-oriented. She assumed he was referring to how much she prioritized maintaining a good relationship with her employees and how much she took care of them. She was offended and confused by his request. Thankfully, she brought it to our session before addressing it with him.

I explained to Jane the difference between masculine values (power, competency, efficiency, achievement) and feminine values (love, communication, cooperation, relationships) and that these differences were at play. I helped her craft a way she could respond to her boss in an empowered and respectful way. I also encouraged her to ask him for clarification regarding what he'd said, as she was drawing her own conclusions around the meaning of his words. I gave her some questions to support this inquiry:

1. "What do you want me to do practically when you say that I should be more business-oriented?"
2. "How am I too emotional? How does that show up? What consequences do you perceive to be a result of me being too emotional?"

I advised her not to make it a competition and instead to value him so he could more easily value her and their partnership. I told her to show him how they balanced each other out. She expressed something along the lines of: "I see how you work, and I value what you bring to the table. You keep us focused on success, and you've got your eye on the goal. Under your guidance we're efficient, and the company gets results."

Then I encouraged her to speak about her (feminine) contribution and why it was important: "While you stay focused on the money, I'm focused on the people. I build relationships, inspire loyalty, and ensure that people like working here. Studies have shown that when people are happy at work, productivity increases. While I hear that you want me to be more business-oriented, I don't think that's what would serve you or this company best. Because I'm emotional and relationship-oriented, I bring the feminine connection and valuable interpersonal dynamics into this company, and that's what keeps us rolling."

At the end of the discussion, her CEO said: "You're right, and I need you more than you need me. We actually make a great team." Because she embodied, claimed, and stood for the value of her femininity, it now has a stable presence in an otherwise very masculine environment. Her CEO has requested for the two of them to be partners and create a new company together.

Nicole, a member of another corporate board, jumped on a coaching call loaded with resentment. She felt that the company she worked for gave more money to whoever made the most noise. Men demanded bigger salaries, and they usually got what they wanted. She felt that compensation should align with how hard people worked and the responsibilities they had, and she had many more duties than the other men on the board. While she was managing eight areas, the six male executives managed just one area each. Even though she had a lot more people working under her, it was not reflected in her pay.

She approached me with the argument that women are treated differently in the workplace, to which I responded by asking if she'd ever requested a raise. I wasn't surprised when she said she had not. I pointed out that men ask for raises more often than women, and this is one of the reasons why discrepancies in pay occur.

She was making the same typical play that women often do when they have a desire. She expected the man—in this case her boss—to mind-read and realize that she hadn't expressed what she truly wanted. I helped her see that she wasn't owning her worth and was avoiding the vulnerability that comes with asking. She'd hoped that others would recognize her value so she didn't have to step up and state it to them.

Before we spoke, she'd planned on complaining about how she wasn't getting paid as much as the men. Instead, we formulated a much more respectful, self-honoring, and self-empowering approach. She outlined her responsibilities and contributions to the company, explained how she invested herself in her work and the business, and stated that she would like her salary to reflect this.

And do you know what? She ended up getting the best evaluation and, in turn, the biggest raise of anyone on the board.

Very often the problem isn't what we think it is.

ELEMENTS OF PHILOSOPHY AND STYLE

I work with men and women, singles and couples, and all different kinds of temperaments. My clients are from all over the world, with different kinds of professions and backgrounds. Part of what allows me to work with such a diverse clientele is not having a cookie-cutter process. I know that what works for one person may not work for the other. I work with each person and go deep into understanding them, what they really want, and what's blocking them. I customize my coaching to fit my clients.

PHILOSOPHY

My philosophy is one of curiosity, acceptance and accountability. Many problems in life are a result of misunderstandings, making wrong assumptions, placing blame outside of yourself, and trying to change something that is out of your control.

I help people to identify where they are giving their power away, recognize their blind spots, and discover what they can do differently to create the life they want. In every complaint, there is a request to be made or an action to take. Complaining is a way of tricking the ego into thinking that it is doing something about the problem. Blaming results in forfeiting the opportunity to heal, grow, and take action to impact how you are feeling and your present circumstance.

Another core philosophy in my coaching is to place equal value on emotions and thoughts. I often see teachers and therapists place more emphasis on one over the other. In my opinion, both need attention, and they need different kinds of attention. Repressed emotions can produce negative thinking, and negative thinking can produce certain emotions.

It is important to clearly distinguish between an emotion and a thought so you can deal with each in its respective way. Emotions are felt as physical sensations in the body, and thoughts/perceptions/beliefs are questioned. If you fail to attend to one, certain triggers will continue to provoke unfavorable reactions. Working with your emotions and thoughts is fundamental to heal the core wounding that causes many conflicts in relationships.

STYLE

I studied psychology and sociology at university but didn't continue because of the limiting factors I perceived therapy to entail. Instead, I chose to custom design my practice over the next twenty years. I read countless books, took many courses, attended numerous retreats and workshops, and have stayed forever committed to my own healing and awakening. Some of my clients have said that my tool kit is like the Mary Poppins bag for personal development.

My practice is a combination of therapy and coaching. I focus on the present moment and helping my clients to live their ideal lives. Sometimes we need to go back into the past to heal wounds and clear programming to be able to effectively move forward. This combination allows me to be the most effective with my clients. Therapy without coaching calls attention to where the wounding happened, but people are often left confused about what to do with that information. Coaching can be too future-focused, and sometimes clients are not able to actually take the steps forward that they want because there are things stored in their subconscious that are holding them back.

I am known for not letting people get away with their "bullshit." I am firm and gentle at the same time and deliver hard truths when needed with a lot of love, acceptance, and compassion. While I am direct, I also have the ability to bring lightness and laughter to situations that are usually heavy with shame. I help my clients to be brutally honest with themselves, while also not taking themselves too seriously and finding the humor in our human experience. I invite them to question the stories that don't serve them and encourage them to step out of their victimhood into a more conscious and empowered mindset.

We all know that growth happens outside of our comfort zone. Therefore, as I encourage my clients to explore and slowly step outside of their comfort zones, I do the same in my coaching. Part of why I am able to be as effective as I am is because I go to the places that make me uncomfortable: I ask the edgy questions, provide reflections that are difficult to hear, and say the things that most people are too scared to be honest about.

When it comes to couples, I encourage both members to work with the same therapist or coach. Some therapists have a rule against working with both partners, but I find it incredibly helpful to see beyond each individual's lenses, blind spots, and biased perspectives. Often when I take on couples, I coach them individually and also together. For most couples, I've found this combination to be the most effective way to achieve results.

Because of my extensive studies about the differences between men and women, I help them to understand each other, have realistic expectations, call attention to role reversal, and help to restore the beauty of polarity. I am an advocate for men and an advocate for women. I place a huge emphasis on accountability and empathy, and this is imperative when it comes to working with couples.

Navigating couple's therapy can be a tricky line to walk. I've heard from several people how it made matters worse because the therapist would take sides or validate one partner's self-prescribed victimhood. One of my clients shared with me that she was never concerned about what was happening in her husband's session with me because she knew that I always brought it back to the person who was in front of me. As frustrating as that can be at times, it creates a safe container for each person and for the relationship.

MISSION

My mission is to help restore equal value of the masculine and feminine gifts, clear up the confusion that has arisen in modern times, and help couples correct the role reversals that are compromising the quality of their relationships.

I strive to wake women up to the value and beauty of living in their feminine. I see many women thinking and acting like I used to, completely stuck in their masculine, and many are not even aware of it. They are pushing their bodies to function in ways they weren't designed. They suppress their feminine needs and desires and are left exhausted and unfulfilled. I help women to reconnect to their essence, access the power of their softness, and restore the importance of feminine qualities.

While helping women to connect to their femininity, I also support men in reclaiming their masculinity, counteracting the movement in modern society that is feminizing men and demonizing masculinity. I am adamant about bringing attention to how terms like "toxic masculinity" have a negative impact on the masculine psyche and our society at large.

Prior to working with me, many men have shared how they felt ashamed just for being men and believed there was something wrong with them because they didn't function like women. I've had several men thank me for giving them permission to be masculine again, as it was something they had compromised due to the pressures from their partner and society.

My mission is to restore respect for masculine traits, help men better understand themselves, and give them the language to explain to their partners so that she can easily understand, accept, and respect his masculine ways.

WISDOM FROM WITHIN

To complement all that I have shared, here are a few more principles that have been my guiding lights . . .

Be accountable, and you will be victorious. Fall into blame, excuses and denial, and you will be a victim of your circumstances. If you get caught up in blaming and criticizing, you're missing an opportunity to grow, and you are left powerless to create the change you want. Don't try to shift things in your life by trying to change other people without first looking at yourself. When you focus on changing the other person, your efforts are likely to have the opposite effect, and you will push what you want further away. Take responsibility and ownership for the life you are living.

Life is happening for you, not to you. Whatever or whoever comes into your life is there to teach you something. Be open to the lessons. Don't walk away from things, only walk towards something. It's a matter of perspective and mindset. Focus on what you want, not what you don't want. When you walk away, you are likely to walk into the same situation, problem, or type of person further down the road. If you notice negative patterns in the partners, friends, clients, and other people you attract, recognize that you are the common thread. Look within and heal what is attracting these people to you.

The world is reflecting you back at yourself.

Get curious. Instead of seeing that there is a right or wrong way, see that there are just different ways. Instead of judging and making assumptions, seek to understand why someone did what they did. Instead of getting defensive, look within and see where someone's reflection might be true and what disowned part of yourself needs your acceptance. So much opens up when you let go of your "I know" mind and get curious.

When you enter into a difficult conversation, set the intention to **make connection the priority**. This will help you to pass through the urge to want to be right, to be heard instead of to hear. It connects you to the person in front of you instead of your story, expectation, and agenda.

John Gray's teachings have been fundamental in shaping my ability to understand and communicate the complex dynamics of the masculine/feminine dance. His wealth of knowledge and wisdom is astounding, and his playful and practical way is insightful and grounding.

SEX AND DATING

— LESLEY EDWARDS —

Lesley Edwards has been a Mars Venus trainer and coach since 2011. She has been drawn to the science of love, relationships, and psychology for over twenty years. She started in a different science, as a registered dietitian with a Master of Science in nutrition. Her problematic obsession with love, as well as her own quest for true love, has led her to immerse herself in the study of communication, human behavior, ontology, and developmental trainings about relationships. When she found John Gray and Mars Venus Coaching, she was finally home.

ROMANCE REVELATION

One afternoon, I was driving home after a serendipitous afternoon with a guy I had been casually dating in another city. I fantasized about him calling to say he missed me already and that he just had to have me in his life; no matter how different our schedules, we would make it work! By the time I got home, however, my hopes were crushed. No call, no change of heart on his end. Why had I once again given myself to a man who had told me that while he loved spending time with me, he wasn't ready for the committed relationship I was looking for?

Seriously, what was wrong with me?! I kept dating and seeing other men, playing it cool being the "no pressure" girl. When they weren't ready for a relationship, that was fine; I'd wait. As common sense would predict, none of these relationships progressed. I would receive the occasional text or phone call—for which I'd been anxiously waiting—and kept telling myself that it was all about timing.

I didn't want to see it, but the reality of my dating life was clear: no ideal men looking for long-term relationships were showing up. Why was this happening? And more importantly, why did it *keep* happening? It was time to take a good, hard look at myself and my dating habits.

GETTING MY OWN COACHES

There was one common denominator in my failed dating life: me. Once I acknowledged this, I knew I needed an outside perspective to work through it. I found not one, but two excellent coaches. One of the first things I realized through my work with these coaches was that I was dating guys for "right now." I knew none of them were ideal partner material, but I told myself it was fine for now. I also told myself I was ready for a committed, long-term relationship, but I wasn't! In reality, what I was doing was "putting off a great relationship for later" and "playing it safe," not putting my heart on the line. So, instead of following my heart to a committed relationship, I focused on my business and keeping around the unavailable men that would never require me to actually put my heart on the line.

As a result, I sold out on what I wanted because I was afraid, on some level, I wouldn't get it. After all, I had a ton of failed relationships and heartbreaks already, and the thought of risking that kind of hurt again seemed both terrifying and stupid. I always thought I deserved it, but I didn't realize until that moment what the impact of saying, "Not now, I'm fine with these so-called relationships" was really having on my love life. It hit me like a truck. As long as I had the great relationship scheduled for later, it was never going to be *now*. Also, no one ever fell in love playing it safe and keeping their heart to themselves. I was the one standing in the way of the love of my life.

That wasn't all. I was also allowing myself to become intimate with men much too quickly and for the wrong reasons. I was looking for commitment and love through sex. Then I'd begin the cycle of pursuit, which would inevitably leave me feeling awful. The cycle of my pursuit looked like this:

1. I'd have sex for all the wrong reasons, even in a relationship (to get him to commit, prove to him I really wanted to be with him or that I could be the right one for him, give him what he wanted so he'd like me more, or out of obligation—thinking he'd expect it).
2. Then I'd expect more from him now that we've been intimate, assuming it meant some new level of commitment.
3. Then I would start following up and checking in with him.
4. He'd become more distant or disappear.
5. I'd wind up hurt, frustrated, and hating the whole dating process.

THE MARS AND VENUS AHA MOMENT

Then, I read *Mars and Venus on a Date* by John Gray, and things finally began to click for me! In the book, John talks about two major principles that I was violating. The first being: don't pursue a man more than he pursues you. The second principle was that commitment *has* to come before sex. To be honest I thought, "I'm not pursuing! I just want to make sure things move along," especially after I had been intimate with a man. And, "Being in a committed relationship *before* choosing to have sex is asking too much in this day and age! What man would wait?" Definitely not the ones in my life . . . or so I thought.

THE SCIENCE OF LOVE

In On a Date, John Gray explains that what builds attraction for men is *pursuing* and *providing* for a woman and *experiencing* being successful with his efforts. Therefore, anticipating that he can do what it takes to make her happy gives him the motivation to go for it and pursue her. At the same time, what builds attraction for women is *anticipating* that said man can make her happy. Perfect! So where was the problem? The problem lies in *not* following John's second principle: commitment before sex. After a woman has been intimate with a man, she releases the hormone oxytocin (the bonding hormone) and becomes more attached, therefore, more likely to pursue. Without a commitment in place, women become assertive and pursue, and men become passive and often lose interest. The bottom line? Sex without commitment throws everything off, because what works is the balance and complement of him is in his masculine (providing and being successful) and her in her feminine (receptive and responsive).

Now, what do I mean by "commitment before sex?" It was clear to me that having sex only in a committed relationship would save women from needing to pursue; however, in my case, I was thinking of relationships and commitment too narrowly. What I came to realize is that all a relationship is is a set of mutual commitments; in other words, for a relationship to work, both parties must be committed to—or value—the same things.

To explain this further, let's compare two very different relationships: a one-night stand versus newlyweds. The one-night stand is a short relationship, and the mutual commitment may be safety, respect, exploration, and fun. With the newlyweds, the relationship is long-term—till death part them—and the mutual commitment may be exclusivity, love, support, and family. The commonality between the two examples is this: before you have sex with someone, both of you must be on the same page about what you are committed to. As I said above, I was committed to an exclusive, long-term, loving relationship; however, the men I was dating were committed to "having fun," "seeing how things go," and not jumping into "anything too serious." Not exactly aligned—no wonder I got hurt!

How did I know they weren't committed? They told me! They would say those exact phrases, yet I ignored them and decided I would win them over by not pressuring them and saying all I wanted was to have fun and see how things go too. Lies! I wanted the whole relationship package but denied it for years to avoid being disappointed and hurt. The irony, I ended up disappointed, hurt, and unfulfilled anyway.

GETTING CLEAR

When I finally got clear about what was really going on in my love life and what I truly wanted, I got power. The power to attract a man who wanted the same things and create the relationship I always wanted.

When you are crystal clear about what you want, it is a lot easier to see it when it shows up.

Are you having trouble getting clear? Ask yourself these questions:

- What results do you have in your love life right now? How's it going?
- What do you really want? (The relationship that, if it were truly possible, would light up your life?)
- What are you looking for in a partner? (Be specific! Physically, mentally, emotionally, sexually, spiritually, etc.)
- How do you know when you are loved?
- How do you know when you are supported?
- Why do you want this ideal relationship? What is the difference it would make in your life?

Answering these questions gives you the coordinates of both where you are right now and where you want to go, with landmarks along the way. Without them, you are like a hitchhiker in your own life, ending up wherever you get dropped off. It will also give you a sense of what you are committed to creating in your love life, so you don't settle for less.

MOVING FORWARD

Once I got clear about what I wanted, asked for what I wanted, and/ or ended it with the wrong guys, I opened my heart, and within six weeks the love of my life showed up. Neither of us have ever been this happy or in love. I feel like he was made for me, and he insists he created me in his dreams. I know, a nauseatingly happy ever after story, but you can't make this stuff up! My clients, of course, learn all my secrets and are meeting and marrying the partners of their dreams as well.

Sandy was a successful career woman with limited time for dating when she finally realized she longed for deep connection and a supportive, loving man. She had spent years settling for scraps with the men in her life, never feeling like a top priority. Once Sandy told the truth to herself about not treating relationships or herself as a priority, her whole life shifted. After the Unleash Your Inner Goddess Weekend, she decided to take time away from work and met the love of her life five weeks later, and they are both happier than they've ever been.

Rob was a busy business executive who was great on a first date, but after three or four dates the women he was interested in didn't feel the same, or he would sleep with them before committing and lose interest. Once Rob saw where he was playing it safe and holding back instead of taking a risk, putting his feelings on the line, and being clear about his interest, he found his love. They got on the same page, before having sex, about what they were each looking for and committed to in a relationship, and he proposed six months later on Valentine's Day.

LEARN AND GROW

The most valuable lesson I've learned from John Gray is "commitment before sex." Before you are intimate with someone you are dating, be clear about what you are committed to: what each of you want, value, and think is important in a relationship. Be open and upfront about these with your partner and make sure you are aligned in mutual commitment, whether you are boyfriend/girlfriend, husband/wife, or you just met. Learn from my mistakes: selling out on what your heart truly desires leaves you unfulfilled, and settling—don't do it! You deserve better.

My intention is for you to wake up from any romantic encounter satisfied, empowered, expressed, and in control. If your negative dating experiences persist (disappointment, guilt, frustration, regret, upset), get perspective from an expert who can see what you can't. You are worth it!

PAIN VERSUS SUFFERING

— CLAY SMITH —

Clay Smith is a Mars Venus life coach who has been interested in John Gray's work since childhood. While his two sisters were borrowing books about fairy tales from the library, he was checking out John Gray's teachings. Clay attended a seminar put on by John Gray and was inspired to help others.

Clay also attended Nazarene Bible College, studying counseling and psychology. Soon after starting college, he attended another seminar, met a Mars Venus life coach, and began his own journey toward becoming a Mars Venus coach. He has been coaching for over a year and specializes in physical health and teaches the importance of keeping a healthy body and reducing stress.

SHARON'S BIG DECISION

Often people come to me and complain or want advice. From what I learned from John, you should almost never give advice, but rather ask questions. Get people to think about what they are saying and play out all possible situations.

John calls it letting people come to their own conclusions.

One day, Sharon and I were having a conversation about her current marriage of twenty-three years. When I say we had a conversation, I mean she talked and I listened—a great example of a "Venus talk."

She shared with me the problems in her marriage, the abuse and relentless bullying from her husband. She recognized she was in a very unhealthy relationship but felt an extreme amount of guilt at just the thought of getting a divorce or leaving her husband. Our talk took a critical turn when she asked me what she thought she should do. Rather than give advice, I asked her a series of questions that made her think. Finally, we came to two options: stay with him and the abuse, or leave and get help.

Instead of telling her which option to take, we drilled down deeper and discussed the pros and cons of both choices. By the end of our hour-long session, she came to the conclusion that she should leave her twenty-three-year marriage and get help. Since then, she has moved on and is very happy.

She thinks I helped her by telling her what she should do. All I did was follow John's philosophy by asking questions and letting my client come to their own conclusion. I used John's questioning skills and asked her what decisions she thought she should make, what her options were, and what the consequences of those options would be. I was able to listen to her and at the end of our talk, I wanted Sharon to feel her needs had been met.

John mentions that women predominately need to feel heard and understood. As a coach, I show empathy and support my clients to expose themselves to nourishing experiences. While having these coaching interactions, I keep in mind the brain differences of men and women and what each gender needs. In this way, I can meet those needs while also helping my clients find clarity around their issues. I truly felt as though I was able to make the difference with that conversation.

DIANE'S GLIMPSE OF HOPE

One of my clients, Diane, came to me pretty discouraged by life. She had started a small business making craft purses and women's accessories, but with the economy at a low, her great business idea didn't come to fruition. Along with the failure of her startup business, she was unhappy at work and dissatisfied with the way things were handled at her current occupation. During our first session, she shared all the areas of her life in which she was dissatisfied. Oftentimes, when I see people unhappy with their jobs or marriage, there are underlying reasons as to why this is. I utilized John Gray's listening techniques. I listened to her and learned all I could about what she tried, what worked, what didn't work, and what she was planning on doing. Then, using the coaching strategy of SMART planning, we took her proposed goals and asked specific questions. Were her goals specific, measurable, attainable, realistic, and timely? We found they weren't. I took this client from focusing on what wasn't SMART to focusing on what she really wanted. Through our talk she gained clarity on what wasn't going to work, what wasn't SMART, and we were able to put a business plan together that she was excited about and could follow through. She was filled with hope, and it was rewarding to see her goals and plan work out in her favor. She got her business up and running and it is successful!

As a coach, it is my job to take someone from their disappointments and shift the conversation to focusing on what they want and how they can achieve it. As we continued our conversation, we imagined the possibilities of things going right in her world. Instead of focusing on the things that could go wrong and what she did not want, we dreamed a little bit and imagined how it would feel to have things unfold in her life to the specifications her heart desired. With each suggestion she shared, I asked more questions, prompting her to spell it out and clarify certain things she wanted to have happen in her life. After our first session, she was excited to work toward the goals we set and had the hope needed to keep pressing through.

A LOOK AT MY OWN LIFE

I grew up in a home where father figures seemed to come and go through a revolving door. My childhood was centered on family drama and several divorces. Life was filled with times of sadness, grief, loss, and fear. Throughout all the pain, I found a way to come through it. John Gray's "Healing the Heart Technique" has helped me recover from those hurts and become a better person.

John's healing technique involves evaluating your own feelings, expressing those emotions, and reconciling hurt. John's instructions are to write a letter to someone who has hurt you, articulating your anger, sadness, fear, or regrets. Then, using visualization, you imagine the person responding to your letter in a way that is loving, supportive, and receptive to what you have written.

As a teenager, I committed to writing a feeling letter as often as once a week. I wrote one to my dad, my mom, my siblings, and even to God. Those years that I went through the healing process were so valuable to my relationships. Instead of harboring resentment toward my dad, I can love and forgive him. Instead of holding it against my mom for getting a divorce, I let that go and have a healthy relationship with her.

PAIN AND SUFFERING: THERE'S A DIFFERENCE

John talks about the difference between pain and suffering. He says that pain can come into our life, but suffering is optional. Pain is the thing in life that we don't like, such as divorce, the death of a loved one, or anything that causes heartache. When these things happen, we can move through the pain, find restoration for our heart and soul as well as closure, and grow stronger through the difficult times. Suffering is when we have negative beliefs about what is happening to us. Suffering is holding on to the pain and not letting go. As a student of John Gray's for sixteen years, one of the most valuable things I have implemented in my life is, when I have moments that cause pain, I have two options: I can use that hurt and learn to find healing and closure, or I can keep that pain and suffer through, holding on to a grudge or believing negative thoughts associated with the pain we experience. This is how we reconcile our grief. This is how we grow and become the best we can be. This is how we are able to "Make the Difference" as John has encouraged me to do.

HAPPINESS IS A LIFESTYLE

— SAMAR SHOWAIL —

Samar Showail came to Mars Venus Coaching after a professional journey that began in 2001. She primarily worked in the banking industry between retail, investment, corporate banking and throughput management. Samar holds a master's degree in fraud and risk management, a degree in computer and network programming, certifications in MCP, MSCE, MCSA, MCDBA, MCDST, PFS, CBM, KPI, performance management, and Mars Venus business, executive and life coaching.

Those who know Samar call her the fixer, the problem solver, the enhancer, the "what if we take it to the next level" person. Her job is to help people maintain prosperity and security with a dash of happiness. She has helped develop and inspire people to be the best at what they do—or what they want to do in the future—and has gotten many to the next level of excellence personally, professionally and financially.

Samar believes that if you keep your eyes open and your feet moving forward, you'll find what you need and learn who you are, where you are, and what your true calling is. Happiness isn't a destination; it's going through the journey of fulfillment and reaching your goals.

By the way, Samar was born on Venus but, curiously, was raised on Mars before moving to planet earth. Although she currently resides in the Kingdom of Saudi Arabia, she has lived abroad and been exposed to many different societies and cultures. Her experiences in the wider world give her the ability to embrace and cherish diversity as a beautiful part of life, one that fills the world with amazing color.

HOW TO REACH HAPPINESS

Happiness is a lifestyle. How many times do people confuse enjoyment with happiness? Many of us say, "I'd love a cup of coffee." The act of drinking the coffee may be pleasurable, but it's not happiness. Happiness comes from the journey. The process starts with thinking about the coffee, then going to the machine, grinding the beans, smelling the aroma, and creating an atmosphere where you can sit and enjoy what you've made. Drinking the coffee leads to enjoyment, which is fine, but in the process itself is where happiness lies. So many people confuse emotions such as love and joy with being happy, but they're not the same. These are of course positive feelings, but they're not the one we're looking for. Happiness is something more.

Even unfortunate people can live happy lives. Those who've experienced terrible accidents, diseases or intense pain can still enjoy life. The key is to embrace the smaller details and avoid overcomplicating things. For example, if you're sick, you can embrace the bed rest and try to make the most of the downtime. With the right mindset, almost any unfortunate moment can become a positive experience.

Many books discuss how to be happy, and they offer a lot of creative ideas on the subject, but few mention how to maintain the sought-after state once you reach it. Achieving happiness is just the first step. Choosing to remain in happy mode throughout your life journey comes next. I believe that every human being deserves happiness, regardless of their ethics, education, background, or finances. When you treat happiness as a lifestyle, you can be content under any circumstances. Mary Poppins had the right idea when she sang, "a spoonful of sugar helps the medicine go down."

But once you reach happiness, how do you stay there? Achieving a happy state comes from gaining clarity around your purpose, which then cascades into all areas of your life, allowing you to be present and live in the moment. Purpose is important, and I always send my clients a specific Mars Venus questionnaire to help them gain clarity in this area. Sometimes, after reading their answers, I know their purpose immediately, but I never reveal it. Who am I to spoil it for them? Instead, we discuss their answers, and I ask question after question until they unearth the treasure themselves. When they discover their own purpose rather than have it handed to them, they appreciate it much more. And once they have a clear picture of why they're here, they can begin to plan the next part of their journey.

Reflecting on different memories when structuring future strategies is important.

Positive moments, we can mimic and repeat; difficult experiences, we can learn from. Even painful memories grant us something very useful: the opportunity to heal beautifully and powerfully. When we build a solid foundation of happiness, magic begins to happen, and the world becomes a different place.

Happy people have a higher tolerance for injustice. Their mental immune systems work better. They can think about issues painlessly, talk about them, and create the mindset needed to do something about them. When you're happy, even someone lying to your face makes you laugh. You'll simply ask yourself, "Are they so afraid of me that they're lying?" You see everything from a different perspective, and few things in life can change that. When you exist only in happy mode, no one can ruin your day. No one can drag you down. No one can take your happiness away.

HOLDING ON TO HAPPINESS

Once you reach happiness, staying at that positive place takes conscious effort. Some days, everything will seem perfect. On others, you'll wake up on the wrong side of the bed, and holding on to happiness becomes more difficult. However, two simple concepts can help you remain at that happy place that you worked so hard to reach.

1. **Know who you are**

   Gaining clarity around yourself, your vision, and your purpose is crucial to remaining happy. If you're struggling with these things, a coach can certainly help. The key is to love what you do and who you are. You shouldn't be rigid, but you also shouldn't let people toss you around like a ball. Being kind to people and smiling is good—but only on your own terms. When you have a clear image and understanding of yourself, you can season life to your taste and maintain a happy mindset. While we should always seek to grow, we should never change for someone else. When you truly know yourself, nurturing your true self and maintaining happiness becomes that much easier.

2. **Be friends with what you see**

   When you accept and love yourself, no one can bring you down. We aren't static beings, and we do evolve over time, but we should always seek to enhance rather than change. There's no need to tear it all down and start anew when we can build on what we've already got. When we seek acceptance from others, we often try to change ourselves to win them over. But this avenue doesn't lead to enduring happiness. Instead, we should seek to accept ourselves and value who we are. Once you reach that level of acceptance, you'll wake up every morning, look in the mirror, and say, "Hello, gorgeous. Isn't it a good day?" If you meet each morning this way, your happy tune will carry on throughout the day. Try it—it really does work like magic. With this simple trick, you can start your day on a high note and create happiness that endures throughout.

WASTE NO OPPORTUNITY

In the year 2000, I went to Spain with my husband (now ex) for a holiday. We were only meant to stay for one week, but life had different plans. After arriving in the evening, we dined at Puerto Banús in Nueva Andalucía, which was a great way to start our holiday.

The next day, we rented a jet ski and took it out on the water. I'm a very sporty person, and I thrive on physical activity. Unfortunately, the ocean was rough that day, and I got into a serious accident. After being rescued, an ambulance rushed me to hospital and when I arrived, the doctors were very concerned. They said they'd do their best to ensure that I wouldn't be paralyzed, but I'd need a lot of scans and multiple surgeries before they could be sure of the outcome. I looked at them, smiled, and said they could do whatever they wanted because this was God's will.

When you have a solid foundation of happiness, everything else becomes small and inconsequential. You're a piece of art in the making. If you deal with negative energy when it arises, you can learn from it, grow from it, and become a better version of yourself.

Once the medical staff had a clearer picture of my condition, one of the doctors explained the situation: "You broke two vertebrae in your back, but I want to congratulate you. It's a miracle that you're not paralyzed. If the damage had been one millimeter closer to your spinal cord, I'd be delivering very different news right now." Due to the severity of my injury, I had to stay in the hospital, laying on my back, until I recovered, which would take at least three months.

In the first week, I wasn't allowed to move anything at all, and a neck brace kept my head firmly in place. In the second week, I was allowed to start moving my hands and feet a bit. In the third week, the doctors removed the neck brace, and I was allowed to move my head from side to side. At around the two-month mark, my country sent a medical airplane to retrieve me from Spain so I could recover in Saudi Arabia. Before I left, the doctors said that walking would always be difficult, and I'd never wear high heels, dance, or do sports again. They said never; I said, "We'll see."

Once I returned to my country, I spent another month and a half in hospital, laying on my back, and eating through a straw. Even so, I was always in a happy mood. But I was also heavily medicated. During my recovery, I had to relearn how to walk. Whenever I stood up, I'd feel so much pain. Eventually, I returned home to complete my recovery, but I was only allowed to walk two times a day. I'd go from my bed, to the toilet, to the living room, and spend the entire day there. Then, when the time came to return, I'd repeat the journey in reverse.

The whole experience showed me how blessed we are. Sometimes, we forget to appreciate the small things and when they're taken away, we feel miserable. But I didn't let the situation bring me down. Instead, I took the opportunity to finish something I'd been putting off for far too long. While I was stuck at home recovering and barely able to walk, I completed my college degree.

As my recovery progressed, I started wearing high heels, dancing, and doing sports again. The doctors didn't believe I'd ever do these things again, but that didn't matter because I believed in myself. Sometimes a little self-belief is all you need to succeed. Courage is also important: the courage to try and fail. Every time I don't succeed, I assess why and try a different approach. The journey of life is filled with learning moments, but, in order to progress, we must be open to receiving them. If it weren't for my accident, I wouldn't have completed my education, joined the banking industry, and become the successful person I am today. As difficult as the experience was, I wouldn't change a thing.

AN UNEXPECTED GIFT

In 2016, I lost my mother to leukemia. She was the one who introduced me to the world of books when I was very young. My mom had a massive library and would read about any topic. When I was little, she would take me to the book fair. The deal was always the same: I could choose two books, and she would choose one for me. Everything she chose was filled with big words and heavy content. She never let me off with an easy read. However, on the last page of each book, I'd always find ten dollars as a reward.

Over the years, I read a lot of John Gray's work. His books fascinated me. The way he uses metaphors to illustrate the big picture is helpful and works with all ages, genders, and backgrounds. I tend to take the same approach with my clients, using metaphors to help them gain clarity and pay attention to details.

After I lost my mom, I started asking God what my purpose in life was. I was sure it wasn't to be a workaholic trying to get ahead in the banking industry. With no idea about what to do with my life, I asked God to show me a path.

In early 2017, John Gray came to Saudi Arabia for the first time, and I immediately enrolled in two of his workshops. I figured that if I missed something in the first, I would pick it up in the second. The opportunity was too good to waste. On the day of the initial workshop, I was the first attendee to arrive, and I became John's guinea pig for the event. At the second workshop, I was his guinea pig again. After the event, as he sat behind a table signing my copy of *Beyond Mars and Venus*, I asked him a question: "Can women come from Mars?"

He stood, looked me in the eye, and said, "Very rarely, Samar. Very rarely."

"Thank you so much for writing that book," I said. "Once I read it, I started knowing who I am, seeing myself, recognizing my worth, and having a relationship with myself. I'm not a freak. I'm just different. Because of your book, I know this now."

Then he said something I didn't expect. "Can I offer you a free coaching session?"

I was almost jumping up and down on the spot. "Sure, yes!" I said and gave him my business card.

On the plane trip home, I realized that there were more than 600 people at that workshop. If he took business cards from half of those in attendance, that's still 300 people. How many of those would he actually contact? Likely, my card would get mixed up with all the others, lost in the crowd, and I'd never receive that call. But I'd had a great experience, and I accepted the fact that the coaching session wouldn't go ahead.

After my mom passed, I threw myself into work and education. I'd leave the house at 8am and not return until midnight. At that time, the Saudi 2030 vision had just been introduced, and I'd been selected as a leader in the campaign. One day, while working at my banking job, I was trying to decide what to give myself for my birthday. I always buy myself a birthday gift, but this year I didn't know what to get. As I considered the options, I asked myself, "What am I doing here behind these four walls?" Suddenly, I realized that I didn't belong there. I belonged outside where the vision was happening. I wanted to be a critical brick in the new Saudi Arabia that we were building.

Without thinking, I opened my computer, wrote a resignation letter, and sent it to HR. After hitting send, I immediately freaked out. My colleagues asked me what was wrong, and I told them I'd sent in my resignation. They couldn't believe it—and neither could I.

Eventually, I calmed down and told myself that everything happens for a reason. Saudi 2030 relies a lot on key performance indicators (KPIs) and when I did my research, I discovered that only a handful of people in the entire kingdom were qualified in this area. I decided that I would become the KPI guru. On the same day that I resigned from my banking job, I received an email from Mars Venus Coaching CEO Rich Bernstein, and we arranged to meet for my free session.

I always thought of coaching as a kind of therapy that would involve lying on a coach, talking, and crying. But it wasn't like that at all. At the beginning of the session, Rich asked me to tell him about myself. So, I started talking. Then I continued to talk. And then I talked some more. After about seven or eight minutes, Rich asked me to stop, but I didn't listen. I just kept talking. He had to ask several times, quite firmly, before I finally got the idea and fell silent.

"Now I know," he said.

"Know what?" I asked

"Why John hasn't stopped asking if I'd talked to Samar yet." "Oh." I didn't know if what he'd said was good or bad.

"Let me ask you a question," Rich said. "Do you want to become a coach?"

I burst out laughing like a baby. "I'm a Martian," I said. "I don't deal with people or feelings. I'm a banker. I deal with numbers."

"John saw something in you, and I saw the same thing within ten minutes."

As a banker, I never say no to an offer. I always say yes. So, I said to Rich, "As a banker, I'll accept your offer, but I can't say that I'm ever going to work as a coach."

When I finished my KPI and Mars Venus courses, I wanted more, so I completed businesses and executive coaching certifications as well. After that, Rich told me to fly, and I did what I do best: I connected people and created communities. Using WhatsApp, I formed a worldwide Mars Venus Coaching community. I also initiated annual meetings that take place in a different capital city each year, to which all of our coaches are invited to attend. The first event took place in Dubai and the second in Cairo. I never thought I'd be a coach, but now the path seems clear. I love people. I connect them with each other. I build communities. Finally, I've found my life's purpose, and happiness stays with me every step of the journey.

Going back to the basics and embracing common sense are essential to achieving the quality of life you desire. Everything is connected, which means you must consider all factors. Ideally, you should start with a clear vision of your purpose in life, your core values, and your beliefs. But don't hesitate to question these ideas regularly. You must give yourself the power to change and amend all throughout your life journey. When you remain in happy mode, you live in the best way possible. You embark on an upward journey of fulfillment to meet your goals and achieve great things. Once you reach that summit of success, you can guide others to join you at the top.

A WORD ABOUT COACHING

Because life coaching and business coaching are relatively new professions, and many people haven't had any direct experience working with a coach, the question of "How does coaching work?" is something we frequently hear.

One of the biggest misconceptions is that coaching is about giving advice.

Coaching, whether you work with a life coach or a business coach, asserts that all of the answers we seek are inside of ourselves. A good coach will not tell you what to do. The reason to work with a coach is to empower yourself, to listen to your own inner voice, and to investigate the full spectrum of possible solutions to the barriers holding you or your business back. Seeking outside help can help you gain the clarity and focus necessary to succeed.

Life and business coaching are about permanent and fundamental shifts in your view of yourself and your business. Coaching is about helping an individual or organization see a way to achieve a goal, remove a roadblock to achieving a goal, or a combination of the two.

According to Einstein, "We can't solve problems by using the same kind of thinking we used when we created them." A coach can help you shift your thinking into that new perspective. A coach's tools are great, probing, enlightening questions. And a great coach has enough experience to ask the right questions at the right time to help you make that shift quickly.

To read more about coaching visit:
marsvenuscoaching.com/join-our-team

MARS VENUS
C O A C H I N G

ABOUT THE AUTHORS

We are truly grateful for the awesome coaches who have shared their wisdom, stories, and journey within coaching to make this book possible.

Please feel free to contact them directly on the details below if you would like more information, or visit **marsvenuscoaching.com/find-a-coach** to find a coach near you.

Adriane Hartigan-von Strauch

book@lovecoach.co.nz
www.lovecoach.co.nz
www.marsvenuslovecoach.com
www.quantumlovecoach.com
www.quantumintimacymovie.com

Asma Shaheen

asma@marsvenuscoaching.com
www.marsvenuscoachasma.com

Caterina Tornani

caterinatornani@me.com
Phone: 33 31882740

Chahira Taymour

chahirataymour@marsvenuscoaching.com
www.facebook.com/chahirataymourlifecoach

Christian Braga

christian.braga@bragagroup.it
Calendar: https://calendly.com/christian-braga/30min
www.coaching.bragagroup.it

Clay Smith

sitainsa@gmail.com
Phone: 719-510-1626
www.calendly.com/mars-venus-coaching/complimentary-coaching-call

Emily MacLeod

emily@marsvenuscoaching.com

www.marsvenuscoachemily.com

Eric Lanthier

coach@ericlanthier.net

www.ericlanthier.net

Gabriella de Leeuw

gabrielladeleeuw1@gmail.com

www.gabrielladeleeuw.com

www.yourpower2love.com

Hilary DeCesare

hilary@therelaunchco.com

www.therelaunchco.com

Justine Baruch

justine@justinebaruch.com

www.justinebaruch.com

Karen Leckie

karenleckie@gmail.com

www.karenleckie.com

Lena JO

lenajo61@yahoo.com

www.linktr.ee/Lenajo

Lesley Edwards

ledwards@marsvenuscoaching.com

Phone: (416) 855 1116

www.marsvenuscoachlesleyedwards.com

www.linkedin.com/in/edwardslesley

www.instagram.com/lovebylesley

Liza Davis

liza.davis@coachingandtraining.com

www.coachingandtraining.com

Mahmoud Khater

mskhater@gmail.com

Phone: +1-647-878-3918

www.mahmoudkhater.com

Michele G Festa

michele.festa@me.com

Phone: +39 335 30 62 82

MK Mueller

mk@8togreat.com

www.8togreat.com

Mohammad Al Huwaidi MAH

mah@marsvenuscoaching.com

info@mohammadalhuwaidi.com

Phone: +96555040084

www.marsvenuscoachmah.com

Monique Sarup

monique@moniquerene.com.au

www.moniquerene.com.au

Neelofar Qasmi

niloofarqasemi@hotmail.com

www.marsvenuscoachneelofar.com

Nissara Chitwarakorn

nissaracoaching@gmail.com

www.nissaracoaching.com

Oksana Irwin

oksana.irwin@gmail.com

www.the-art-of-femme-dating.mailchimpsites.com/coaching-mentoring

Dr. Rani Thanacoody

thanacoodyr98@gmail.com

www.marsvenuscoachrani.com

Reem Suwayd

rsuwayd@yahoo.com

www.marsvenuscoachreem.com

Rich Bernstein

richbernstein@marsvenuscoaching.com

Phone: (702) 835-9295

www.marsvenuscoaching.com

www.coachrichbernstein.com

www.marsvenuscoachrich.com

Richard Wann

rwann@comcast.net

Samar Showail

samar.showail@marsvenuscoaching.com

marsvenuscoachsshowail.com

Sophie Tan Li Koon

tidalwavesepic@gmail.com

www.marvenuscoachingsophietan.com

www.calendly.com/sophietmm

Susan Dean

susan@deanpublishing.com

www.deanpublishing.com

Tanweer Ahmad Khan

takhan786@gmail.com

www.xpocoaching.com

JOIN OUR TEAM

Mars Venus Success Coaching, one of the world's fastest-growing licensing and certification systems, evolved from one of the world's strongest brand identities and the high-profile international speaker, media identity, and international best-selling author, John Gray, Ph.D.

Dr. Gray's book *Men Are from Mars, Women Are from Venus* became the highest-selling commercial book of the 1990s after the Bible. This created a true megabrand that has been supported by constant media attention across the world. Additionally, with $50 million spent internationally on brand development, a demand for the Mars Venus brand was established that is second to none.

Simultaneously, the coaching industry continues to be one of the fastest growing industries in the world. Coaching has become a much sought-after and necessary part of both professional and personal life development across the globe; and the Mars Venus brand is synonymous with coaching successes.

To find out more about becoming a **Mars Venus Coach** visit:
marsvenuscoaching.com/join-our-team

"Coaching is a calling. If you're wrestling with the decision to become one, then it's probably not for you."
John Gray Ph.D.

ENDNOTES

Hilary DeCesare

1   Williams, Alan. "Why Values Driven Organizations Improve Your Bottom Line." CEOWORLD Magazine. July 9, 2021. https://ceoworld.biz/2021/07/09/why-values-driven-organizations-improve-your-bottom-line/

Christian Braga

1   Dyer, Wayne. "5 Lessons to Live by - Dr. Wayne Dyer (Truly Inspiring)." Fearless Soul. March 15, 2018. YouTube video, 11:39. https://youtu.be/dOkNkcZ_THA.

Michele Festa

1   Mars and Venus—it's not the only way, but it is very direct, efficient, result oriented, and it can be practiced by coaches who do not feel it is appropriate, for some clients, to put them through a long psychotherapy.

2   Booth, Alan and James M. Dabbs Jr. 1993. "Testosterone and Men's Marriages." Social Forces 72, no. 2 (December): 463-477.

www.ingramcontent.com/pod-product-compliance
Lightning Source LLC
Chambersburg PA
CBHW060221030426
42335CB00015B/1802